Property Development

By the same authors

The Valuation of Property Investments (N. Enever, D. Isaac and M. Daley)
Property Companies: Share Price and Net Asset Value (D. Isaac and N. Woodroffe)

Property Development

Appraisal and Finance

2nd Edition

David Isaac

Professor of Real Estate Management, School of Architecture and Construction, University of Greenwich

John O'Leary

Senior Lecturer, School of Architecture and Construction, University of Greenwich

Mark Daley

Senior Lecturer, School of Architecture and Construction, University of Greenwich

palgrave
macmillan

First published 2010 by
PALGRAVE MACMILLAN

Palgrave Macmillan in the UK is an imprint of Macmillan Publishers Limited, registered in England, company number 785998, of Houndmills, Basingstoke, Hampshire RG21 6XS.

Palgrave Macmillan in the US is a division of St. Martin's Press LLC, 175 Fifth Avenue, New York, NY 10010.

Palgrave Macmillan is the global academic imprint of the above companies and has companies and representatives throughout the world.

Palgrave® and Macmillan® are registered trademarks in the United States, the United Kingdom, Europe and other countries

ISBN 978–0–230–20178–1 paperback

This book is printed on paper suitable for recycling and made from fully managed and sustained forest sources. Logging, pulping and manufacturing processes are expected to conform to the environmental regulations of the country of origin.

A catalogue record for this book is available from the British Library.

A catalog record for this book is available from the Library of Congress.

10   9   8   7   6   5   4   3   2   1
19   18   17   16   15   14   13   12   11   10

Printed and bound in Great Britain by
CPI Antony Rowe, Chippenham and Eastbourne

To our students past and present.

Contents

Preface to the First Edition

This book is intended to reveal the property development process from conception (almost) to completion and to look at the process as the development passes through the various stages. It is intended to give an overview but also, more realistically, to concentrate on the 'core' areas of the process. I have taken these core areas as financial appraisal and finance of the project but as part of the process of development I have also looked at other areas whilst recognising these may be in the domain of other professionals. The approach taken is to look at the property development process as a project manager, providing a sufficient overview for the role of project management without falling into the trap of dealing with specialist areas too lightly. That is the intention, an overview of the process comprising an introduction, a specification of the role of the project manager, details of the appraisal process, the financial appraisal, project and corporate finance, design and construction and finally the process of marketing and disposal. The core areas are contained in chapters 4–6 for the financial appraisal and chapters 7–10 for property development finance.

The book will be useful for both students and practitioners. For students it will provide a text at intermediate level (2nd–3rd year undergraduates) in estate management, property, surveying, planning, design and construction disciplines. Those in adjacent areas of study such as housing and economics will find this a useful introduction to the area of commercial property development. Practitioners involved with property development, and this includes a wide area of professionals, including surveyors, builders, construction managers, architects, engineers, estate managers and agents will find this a useful overview, perhaps enlightening them to the range of activities involved in the development process and updating them on some basic techniques in the process. Professional advisers such as bankers, financial advisers, accountants, investors, analysts and lawyers should also find this text useful as an aid to their dealings in the property development sector.

Where possible I have obtained data and statistics to place the property development process appropriately in the wider economic context of the property and construction sectors. I have aimed to reference the material as well as possible but apologise for any omissions. There are relatively few texts in the area of property compared to most other investment sectors and I have tried to reference existing ones as fully as possible to provide additional views and perspectives for the reader in a very complex and potentially riskful area of activity. The art of property development in the decades following the Second World War was relatively sure-fire but three property slumps later we should be much wiser, or are we? Perhaps property development requires individuals to throw caution to the wind and strike out imaginatively in the way many entrepreneurs have successfully completed complex and enormously expensive schemes with confidence and alacrity in difficult circumstances? Anyway that is the content of another book!

Finally, I would like to thank those who have assisted me in writing this book, Professor Ivor Seeley, the series editor who has provided ongoing advice for my writing and encouraged many authors in the property and construction area and Malcolm Stewart, my publisher who is ever patient and supportive. I would also like to thank Mike Riley and Chesterton International for practical support in my researches. Many colleagues and external organisations have provided me with information and assistance and these are listed in the acknowledgements below. I would also like to thank Terry Steley, John O'Leary and Simon Birchall of the University of Greenwich and Keith McKinnell from the University of Hong Kong for their help and observations on the book. Finally, as ever, I am reliant on the continued support of Professor David Wills, Lewis Anderson and the staff of the School of Land and Construction Management at the University of Greenwich to develop my research and studies and I am grateful for their help.

David Isaac
University of Greenwich
School of Land and Construction Management
1995

Preface to the Second Edition

In this second edition, two additional authors have helped to update the work by introducing new concepts and case studies. Each chapter has been substantially revised with the addition of new material and references which has repositioned the text in three distinct ways:

- Property development and appraisal is put in a wider economic environment and the appraisal process is treated in a more holistic manner.
- More case studies and examples are included, and each chapter is framed with clear objectives, key terms and summaries.
- To examine in more detail the property development and appraisal process in relation to sustainability and other key issues such as climate change, the changing financial environment, planning, design and global influences.

Finally, we would like to thank those who have assisted us in completing the book especially Helen Bugler, our publisher, for her patience and continued support. We would also like to thank Mike Greenslade for reviewing Chapter 9 and Sue Collins for her help in revising some of the graphical material. As ever, we are reliant on the continued support of Professor Richard Hayward and the School of Architecture and Construction at the University of Greenwich to develop our research and studies and we are grateful for this help.

Caveats

This book should not be relied upon as a basis for entering into transactions without seeking specific, qualified, professional advice. The authors cannot take any responsibility for any damage or loss suffered as a result of any inadvertent inaccuracy within this text.

David Isaac, John O'Leary and Mark Daley
University of Greenwich
School of Architecture and Construction
2010

Acknowledgements

The authors and publishers wish to thank the following for the use of copyright material in this second edition: Bank of England; British Property Foundation; Fletcher King.

Every effort has been made to trace all the copyright holders, but if any have been inadvertently overlooked, the publishers will be pleased to make the necessary arrangements at the first opportunity.

Abbreviations

AOD	above ordinance datum
ASF	annual sinking fund
BCIS	Building Cost Information Service
BREEAM	Building Research Establishment Environmental Assessment Method
CABE	Commission for Architecture and the Built Environment
CBD	central business district
CGI	computer-generated imagery
CHP	combined heat and power
CIL	Community Infrastructure Levy
CSO	Central Statistical Office
DCF	discounted cash flow
EIA	Environmental Impact Assessment
EPC	Energy Performance Certificate
ES	Environmental Statement
EUV	existing use value
FRA	flood risk assessment
FRI	full repairing and insuring [lease]
GDV	gross development value
HBF	Home Builders Federation
HCA	Homes and Communities Agency
hrh	habitable rooms per hectare
IRR	internal rate of return
JCT	Joint Contract Tribunal
JV	joint venture
KPI	key performance indicator
LDF	Local Development Framework
LEED	Leadership in Energy and Environmental Design
LIBOR	London Inter Bank Offered Rate
LPA	local planning authority
LTC	loan to cost ratios
LTV	loan to value ratio
MC	marginal cost
MMC	modern methods of construction
MOF	multi-option facility
MR	marginal revenue
NIMBY	'not in my back yard'
NPV	net present value
OISD	Oxford Institute for Sustainable Development
pa	per annum
PFI	private finance initiative
PPP	public private partnership
PPS	Planning Policy Statement

PTAL	Public Transport Accessibility Level
RADR	risk-adjusted discount rate
REIT	Real Estate Investment Trust
RFR	risk-free rate
RIBA	Royal Institute of British Architects
RICS	Royal Institution of Chartered Surveyors
RPI	retail price index
RSS	Regional Spatial Strategy
SBC	Standard Building Contract
SEEDA	South East England Development Agency
SEGRO	Slough Estates Group
TC	total costs
VAT	Value Added Tax
YP	years' purchase

Statutes, regulations and cases

1

The property development process

Aims

This chapter introduces the basic definitions of terms used in property development and it puts the development process in an economic and sustainable development context. The chapter provides an overview of the development process and considers the roles played by stakeholders in that process.

Key terms

>> **Property development** – the process of erecting buildings for occupation, sale or investment.
>> **Sustainable development** – development which supports a better quality of life now and in the future. The concept embraces economic, social and environmental criteria.
>> **Development value** – where land or buildings can increase in value by the application of capital.
>> **Residual valuation** – the valuation of a site which has development potential. This is calculated by deducting the costs of building plus a profit from the development value leaving a residual sum which represents the land value.

1.1 Introduction

Property development is the process by which buildings are erected for occupation or for sale. Properties may be developed for owner occupation, for example a major retailer may erect a supermarket for corporate use. Alternatively, a property developer might construct a similar building for lease or sale. The process may be the same although some aspects of the financial appraisal may be different. A building produced for sale or investment is driven by a profit motive, while a building developed for owner occupation may be related to the profitability of the enterprise which will use the building and thus the profit motivation is indirect.

Property development may also be initiated by not-for-profit organisations such as when a public body procures a building which goes some way towards meeting social or cultural policy objectives rather than profit aspirations. The social enterprise or third sector in the UK also comes within the not-for-profit category. Organisations here include charities and voluntary organisations such as housing associations (also referred to as *registered providers*) where the objective is to meet specific needs while not to making a loss. Thus the motive for development is not to make a profit but to meet social objectives without compromising the financial viability of the whole organisation.

Property development also takes place in the context of partnerships between organisations from the public, private and voluntary sectors. In recent years these partnerships have taken a variety of forms in the UK and they include those brokered under the private finance initiative (PFI). The latter takes a number of forms but for example might see a primary healthcare trust procure a new hospital under a PFI contract which secures private sector development expertise and funding. The healthcare trust then operates the new hospital and gradually pays off the PFI contractor over a fixed number of years at a specified rate of interest to reflect the risks involved. There are conflicting views on whether PFI contracts represent good value for money for public sector organisations and whether the risk involved to the private partners really justifies the rates of return that they receive. However, the model is increasingly used to procure large bespoke properties for public sector organisations.

In the UK a number of joint ventures (JVs) sometimes referred to as special purpose vehicles, have been formed in recent years between landowning local authorities, private developers and housing associations under which large public sector housing estates are redeveloped to meet modern standards. One model for these JVs which has emerged is the Local Housing Company promoted by the Homes and Communities Agency (2009) in England.

Figure 1.1 below attempts to capture some of the main types of organisations who commonly initiate development, although the chart could easily be extended to include financial institutions such as pension funds, universities, government departments and even community land trusts. Property development is therefore undertaken directly or procured by a wide variety of organisations to meet a wide variety of objectives.

It is not possible or necessary in this book to categorise all types of developer, nor map out all of the contexts in which development may take place. Readers who are particularly interested in learning more about the various permutations could examine Havard (2008: 1–28) or Millington (2000: 25–38). In this book the emphasis will be upon commercial development in the private sector. However there will also be occasional references to development activity in the public and voluntary sectors and to development undertaken in partnership between organisations from each sector.

Type of developer	Commercial property developer or housebuilder.	Local authority or government agency.	Voluntary, charitable or not-for-profit organisations.	Partnerships, joint ventures and special purpose vehicles.
Sector	Private.	Public.	Third sector.	Combined.
Examples	Volume housebuilders such as Bellway Homes and commercial property developers such as Hammerson and Land Securities.	The Homes and Communities Agency (England), regional development agencies and urban development corporations.	A housing association, also known as *registered providers* in England and Wales.	A local regeneration partnership comprising a private developer a landowning local authority and a housing association.
Primary motive for engaging in property development	Profit.	To meet social and economic policy objectives.	To meet specific charitable purposes.	Partners will have different individual motivations as reflected in the columns to the left.
Typical type of scheme	Retail, office, industrial, warehousing, leisure and housing development.	Developments with insufficient return for private developers but are valuable in terms of job creation or affordable housing provision.	Provision of affordable housing for those in need.	Redevelopment of a specific site or housing estate in the interests of regeneration.
The importance of property development for these organisations	Property development is the *raison d'être* for these organisations.	Property development is a means to an end and may only represent a modest part of the organisations overall activities.	Property development may play a role in adding incrementally to the stock of buildings managed by the organisation to meet its wider objectives.	Property development is a means to an end for those involved in the joint venture.

Figure 1.1 Some organisations which initiate property development

1.2 An overview of the development process

Property development is much like any other economic activity in that it seeks to satisfy demands arising in a market through the application of scarce resources. The word 'demand' is used here in a broad sense to encompass 'needs' as the latter is not strictly something which can be expressed in a market sense. In the case of property development, the demand is for space to work in, to operate businesses from, to live in and to provide space for leisure and recreational activities.

The process by which buildings are erected employs the factors of production: *land* for the site, *capital* for purchase of the land and materials, *labour* to erect a building and manage the process. The entrepreneurial talent of the property developer is needed to initiate the process and combine these factors successfully in a project.

A simplified approach to property development envisages a timeline from inception to completion involving a number of stages and this is sometimes referred to as an 'event sequence model' as follows:

- choosing a location;
- identifying a site and carrying out a detailed site survey;
- providing an outline scheme and appraisal;
- negotiating for site acquisition;
- design;
- planning consent;
- finance;
- site acquisition;
- detailed plans;
- tender documents for construction;
- construction;
- marketing for sale or letting with potential ongoing asset management.

The process is not as strictly linear as suggested above and activities may take place in parallel or be reordered to suit project realities. For example marketing may begin very early in the process and it may continue throughout if the developer has an aspiration to achieve advanced sales off plan or to achieve pre-lets.

For the process to be initiated there would have to be demand and this would stem directly from a client seeking a building for owner-occupation or the demand will be detected by the developer through interpretation of market conditions. As in any commodity market where demand outstrips supply the price rises and in commercial property the main indicator is that the rental value of floor space will tend to move upwards.

Regardless of whether a developer has a client or is responding to market signals a prudent developer would establish whether the completed sales value of a scheme exceeds the costs of producing the development. The profit margin arising from the development would need to reflect the efforts and risks to the developer. If market research carried out for a proposed development reveals sufficient demand, then the developer can produce sketch plans to ascertain the development capacity of a site. The sketches will also be used as a basis for early discussions with the planning authority.

In the UK, as in most countries, development of land is subject to planning controls and this is one of the first hurdles in the development process. A planning consultant will be invaluable at this stage for advising on the type and scale of development which may be acceptable to the local authority. The consultant will also be able to negotiate any planning agreements which in the UK will typically arise on a development of any magnitude. Depending on the scheme, planning obligations may range from the provision of onsite affordable housing to payments for the provision of infrastructure or both. These obligations may have a significant effect on the developer's budget and this might threaten the financial viability of a scheme, particularly during a credit crunch when completed development values will tend to fall but costs may remain fairly constant.

In parallel to working up a development concept which would win the support of the local authority, initial development appraisals are also undertaken. On the basis of the scale and type of development envisaged, a value can be assessed and rough costs calculated and this will indicate whether there is any profit in a scheme and whether it is worth continuing further. From a developer's perspective therefore a scheme can only be viable if two preconditions are met: (a) that a planning consent either exists or there is a realistic prospect of achieving consent; and (b) there is market demand for the development which would produce a development value in excess of all the costs involved. Initial schemes will evolve considerably at the drawing board stage so that these preconditions can be met more fully.

The costs of construction are usually assessed by comparison at this stage and there are online databases and source books which distil costs arising from recent building contracts for different types of building. In the UK the Building Cost Information Service (BCIS) is one such source which is available to subscribers at: www.bcis.co.uk. There are other similar sources such as the Spons building price guides produced by cost consultants Davis Langdon. A construction cost per square metre can thus be identified and applied to the gross internal floor area (measured between the internal faces of external walls) of the building envisaged.

Discussions with the planning authority will lead to a planning application which may be in outline form seeking consent on the general principles of a scheme and subsequently for detailed permission. When the characteristics of the scheme are confirmed, then a detailed financial appraisal can be undertaken. The architect would also be instructed to produce detailed construction drawings and in a traditional approach to development the drawings would be used by a quantity surveyor to produce a bill of quantities. Funds will be sourced to purchase the site if it is not already owned and a loan facility will be arranged to cover the costs of the construction contract plus ancillary costs.

Where a building is being developed on a speculative basis and there is no client or particular end user in mind, a valuer or agent would normally provide advice on a marketing strategy as well as actively seeking possible purchasers or occupiers. The ambition is that once the building is completed there will be a minimal period when the property is empty and not providing a return. The return will be a rental income if the property is let and retained as an investment or a capital sum if the building is to be sold. If the building is procured by a corporate owner-occupier, then a notional rent can be assumed to be passing.

1.3 Development value

Development value exists where land or buildings can increase in value through the application of capital. This can arise from a change of use of the land or existing buildings, but the property development process usually involves the creation of new buildings. The developer normally evaluates development value in a residual appraisal and while this topic is covered in more detail in chapter 2 some preliminary points can be made here on this process.

The residual valuation is one of the established methods of property appraisal which assesses the profitability of development proposals. The method calculates the increased capital value of the land due to the proposed development and then deducts the costs of works and the original value of the land and buildings. Costs in the equation should include a profit which reflects the risk and commitment of the developer. However, given the timeline over which development takes place, there are a range of possible outcomes regarding the developer's profit if a site has been purchased at the commencement of a development. If development values increase significantly over the development timeline, then the developer may make an abnormal profit.

When development values realised at the end of the development correspond to the appraisal undertaken at the time when the land was purchased several years earlier, then a developer will make the profit anticipated at the outset.

During a recession or when credit becomes difficult to obtain as between 2008 and 2009 then development values will tend to fall, sometimes quite dramatically. In that scenario a developer who has not commenced development will tend to 'sit on the land' and will wait until the market becomes more favourable. In the UK, planning consent lasts for three years and so a developer could begin construction at any point over that term with a view to completing a development in a rising market. Of course this is where market intelligence and forecasting come into play, although even armed with the most sophisticated analysis the future is still uncertain and the risks for a developer never entirely dissipate.

Where a significant start has already been made on construction a developer may well be facing significantly reduced profits or the scheme may go into receivership as costs escalate against falling values. These are the risks attached particularly to speculative property development. While developers can take some mitigating action to control development costs they have very little control over falling market values unless they have already achieved pre-sales or pre-lets.

The residual valuation essentially begins by looking at the completed gross development value (GDV) of a scheme which in the simple example in Figure 1.2 below is £20 million. The costs, which include the developer's profit, are then deducted to identify the land value. In the example below the total costs are £15 million and this is deducted from the GDV to identify a residual sum of £5 million for the land. The development appears viable as both sides of the equation balance and the developer looks to have made a prudent decision by purchasing the site for £5 million. It will be assumed in this example that the development will take two years to complete and sell.

Let us now imagine that over the two-year development period there is inflation in development values due to buoyant demand in the property market for

	Developer's profit @ 15 per cent of GDV = £3 million.
Gross development value (GDV) estimated to be £20 million at the beginning of a two-year development timeline.	**All development costs** including professional fees, construction costs, ancillaries, contingencies, finance charges, marketing, letting and disposal fees = £12 million.
	Land value inclusive of purchase costs, interest payments and land tax = £5 million.

Figure 1.2 Development value where GDV is £20m.

the type of development being produced. When the development is therefore sold it achieves £22 million rather than the £20 million envisaged two years earlier. The result would be that the developer earns a windfall additional profit as shown in Figure 1.3 below where a 10 per cent increase in the GDV has generated a 66 per cent increase in the developer's profit.

However, given an alternative scenario where a speculative development was embarked upon and reached the market two years later when development values had fallen 15 per cent, the developer's profit would have been entirely wiped out and in all probability the scheme would be in receivership. This is exactly what has happened to some developers during the global credit crunch in 2008 and 2009.

	Developer's additional windfall profit = £2 million
Gross development value (GDV) actually realised at the end of a two-year development process = £22 million, i.e. 10 per cent more than expected.	Developer's profit @ 15 per cent of original GDV = £3 million.
	All development costs including professional fees, construction costs, ancillaries, contingencies, finance charges, marketing, letting and disposal fees = £12 million.
	Land value inclusive of purchase costs, interest payments and land tax = £5 million.

Figure 1.3 Development value where GDV is £22m.

Gross development value (GDV) of £17 million actually realised at the end of the two-year development timeline during which the economy has gone into a recession.	**All development costs** including professional fees, construction costs, ancillaries, contingencies, finance charges, marketing, letting and disposal fees = £12 million.
	Land value inclusive of purchase costs, interest payments and land tax = £5 million.

Figure 1.4 Development value where GDV is £17m. (post-recession)

It should also be noted that the site value in Figure 1.4 above of £5 million would need to be higher than the land value in its current use, otherwise there will be no incentive for the land to come onto the market as a development opportunity. Thus valuers will also look at the existing use value (EUV) of a site relative to its value in a development scheme. Thus a simple example might be that a 1 hectare field used for agriculture might have an existing use value of £100,000. Given the realistic prospect of planning consent for housing on the land, its development value might be £1.5 million and thus the gap between the existing use value and the development value is so significant that the site will almost certainly come forward for development.

Differences in value will not always be so clear-cut in an urban context where the value of a site in existing use might not always be significantly increased by a planning consent for a new development combined with market demand for that development.

The basic formula for the residual valuation therefore reflects the fact that the land is normally the unknown residual element as follows:

GDV − (building costs + profit margin) = land value

If, however, the land value is already known because it has been agreed as a purchase price then the residual equation can be transposed to identify the profit margin as follows:

GDV − (building costs + land value) = profit margin

The need to use a residual valuation approach arises because of the uniqueness of land and property as an asset class and this is reinforced by the uniqueness of development proposals for each site. If equal-sized plots of land were being sold in the same location and those plots were earmarked for the same density and type of development, then a form of comparative analysis could be applied, such as a price per hectare. In these cases adjustments would still need to be made to reflect the minor differences between each site. Thus the value of a 0.5 hectare site benefiting from sea views in a coastal town, unencumbered by legal constraints and with planning consent for twenty houses might be £1 million.

However the value of a 0.5 hectare site also with planning consent for twenty houses at the back of the same town but close to an industrial estate and crossed by an overhead power line will be significantly less than £1 million. The judgements required to distinguish the value of the second site in monetary terms using the comparative method could easily stretch the credibility of the valuation. What could safely be said is that the value of the first site does provide an upper benchmark for the value of the second site.

While the comparative method might be a little simplistic for complex situations, the residual method has also been criticised by the Lands Tribunal which is the highest court for dealing with property valuation and compensation issues in the UK. The Tribunal felt that the method could generate unreliable values because of the number of variables in the calculation and the degree to which the calibration of those variables depends on a series of assumptions. The Tribunal prefers a comparative approach to be taken where that is possible. However, despite the misgivings of the Tribunal, practitioners continue to use the residual method in circumstances where there is development potential because of the limitations in the comparative method noted above. The strengths of the residual method are that it is explicit about the components of development value and costs and it reflects the fact that the type and scale of development will be unique from site to site.

The residual valuation is therefore used in development situations but it in turn relies on other valuation methods. In fact there is agreement that there are five main methods of property valuation which are:

• the investment method;
• the comparative method;
• the contractor's test (a cost-based method);
• the profits method; and
• the residual method.

The residual method may rely upon the investment method to determine the gross development value of a proposed commercial development. It may use the comparative method to compare capital or rental values from the market. The costs calculated for building works are a form of the contractor's test. Depending on the type of property, the profits method may also be used to determine the gross development value. However, the residual method has become an accepted and important development appraisal tool and the logic that it employs regarding the interplay of variables is also used in more sophisticated cash flow approaches which will be explored later in this book. For now it is worth noting that the main variables in the residual calculation are as set out in the following sections.

Value of the proposed development

This depends upon the market demand for the envisaged use in the particular location, the quantity of units or floorspace permitted under a planning consent, the quality of the building design and layout and the proximity of services and infrastructure. The value can be affected significantly by the presence of negative or positive externalities. Negative influences on value could be proximity to noisy and pollution-generating roads, landfill sites and whether a locality has a high crime rate. Positive factors might be scenic views, proximity to good schools and services and accessibility to efficient public transport.

Cost of construction

As for value above, the costs of construction result from the interplay of a number of factors including the size, design, type of building, quality of materials and the extent of landscaping envisaged. Costs may also arise where the developer has to part fund infrastructure or where site access needs to be improved. Where there is ground contamination or a threat of flooding there may be significant additional costs referred to as 'abnormals' in order to overcome these constraints.

Increasingly the regulatory regime in which developers work is becoming more stringent in the interests of fostering sustainable development and this is likely to add some costs to projects. For example costs may arise from increasing the standard of insulation and build quality and/or in terms of incorporating renewable energy technology or low-energy services in buildings. This equipment will normally attract a higher capital cost at the point of development although users of the building during its lifetime should experience lower operating costs.

Value of the site

As explored in the simple examples above, the site value will normally be a residual amount reflecting the difference between the GDV and the costs to produce a scheme. However, site values may also be affected by legal encumbrances, topography and adverse ground conditions.

The extent of the variation in these factors and how they combine for each scheme means that each residual appraisal will be unique. Syms (2002: 147–60) for example shows how the residual appraisal can reflect significant abnormal costs associated with ground remediation where a site has been contaminated. In some circumstances where costs like this arise, sites may have negative values and development in those circumstances will only take place where there is gap funding such as a public sector grant.

Perhaps a final point to make on the uniqueness of the calibration of variables in each residual valuation is that the value of land is determined by its use and intensity of use. Land may have development potential but it will require planning permission for any form of development (except for some minor works and some changes of use). In England the Town and Country Planning Act 1990 determines that planning consent is required for anything defined as 'development' which the Act defines as:

> the carrying out of building, engineering, mining or other operations in, on, over or under land or the making of any material change in the use of any building or other land.

A planning consent therefore confirms development potential and on this point some *trader developers* specialise in purchasing sites with hope value but no planning consent. They then invest time and effort in achieving a planning consent which confirms a site's maximum development value. At that point the site is sold onto another developer who actually builds the scheme. The trader developer is therefore making a profit from purchasing a risky site at a nominal value and selling it perhaps one or two years later at a considerably higher value reflecting the certainty provided by the planning consent. Developers sometimes refer to land purchased with consent as 'oven ready' in that very little needs to be done before starting construction.

Property appraisal

There is sometimes an understandable degree of confusion surrounding the use of the similar terms 'property valuation' and 'property appraisal'. The distinction between the two terms in the UK first arose in the 1980s when there were criticisms of traditional approaches to property valuation. This led to demands that a more extensive property analysis be provided for clients. What emerged from that period was a more precise terminology around property valuation work. Thus as Baum and Crosby (2008: 3–5) confirm, *property appraisal* should contain two distinct aspects: property valuation for purchase (that is the valuation for market price or exchange value); and the subsequent analysis of performance. The first aspect is valuation and the second aspect is analysis and the combination of the two is property appraisal.

1.4 Stakeholders in the development process

No development is exactly the same as another and the combination of stakeholders and the roles that they play will be different each time. For example in one scheme a developer will be both landowner (having already purchased a site) and developer whereas in another scheme the landowner retains a separate identity as a site freehold owner in partnership with a developer. Even the lines of communication, which are simplified diagrammatically below to represent the developer at the fulcrum of the process, are not always that straightforward. For example the developer will often work through the professional team which screens and filter contacts with some of the other stakeholders. In particular the developer's project manager might be given considerable delegated power to deal with the main contractor and other third parties. Thus it is not wise to overgeneralise on the organisational combinations and interactions which can arise in development. However, there are some general patterns of stakeholder involvement which are worth considering as follows.

The developer

As discussed at the beginning of this chapter there are numerous types of developer straddling public, private and voluntary sectors and so for simplicity here it assumed that the developer is a private sector commercial property developer. This broad category would include trader developers who tend to develop speculatively in order to sell completed schemes before moving onto the next development opportunity and investor developers who tend to retain completed schemes for rental income and capital growth.

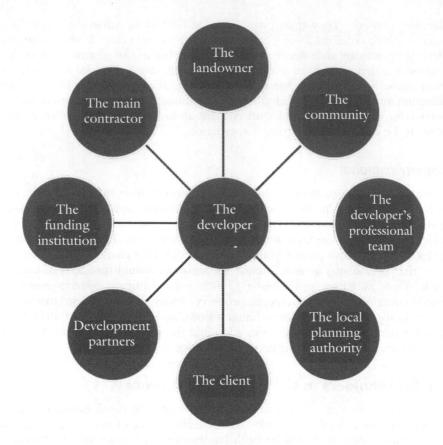

Figure 1.5 Stakeholders in the development process

Marriott (1962) provides an interesting historical perspective on how a number of the leading development companies in the UK began as very modest organisations which exploited opportunities in the property 'boom' of the late 1940s and early 1950s. The early growth of these companies was financed almost entirely by borrowing in a context where there was rental growth, low building costs and low-interest rates. From those humble beginnings there is now in the UK a premier league of property companies who since 2007 have converted to Real Estate Investment Trust (REIT) status in order to benefit from the tax advantages that this vehicle offers.

Typically these companies will be active developing major office schemes in prime locations, large city centre retail malls and edge of city business and retail parks. The largest UK REITs include British Land, Land Securities, Derwent London, Hammerson and the Slough Estates Group (SEGRO) and together they have a market capitalisation in excess of £20 billion. Readers who are interested in finding out more about the value and activities of these companies could examine the information portal: www.reita.org which provides links to company accounts and annual reports. It is this type of developer that will interpret wider economic conditions before engaging in major property developments.

The developer's professional team

Depending on the type of development, the professional team can be quite extensive, although the following would normally feature as the core professional team in a large commercial or residential development: a project manager, an architect, quantity surveyor, valuer, planning consultant, construction manager, structural engineer, services engineer, landscape architect and possibly a highways consultant.

The local planning authority

The local planning authority (LPA) would normally have policies set out in a local development plan and it will use these policies to negotiate with developers so that the resulting scheme is policy compliant. This is termed the *plan-led system*, in that a local authority will refuse development proposals which do not go far enough in meeting the policy ambitions in the development plan. As well as enforcing policies, in the UK it is increasingly common for LPAs to negotiate planning agreements with developers in order to create 'planning obligations'. The latter require the developer to contribute to the provision of infrastructure, impact mitigation or affordable housing.

The LPA also occupies an important pivotal position for the developer as one of its roles is to evaluate public representations regarding the developer's scheme. The LPA is not duty bound to reject a development just because there is local opposition. However the LPA does have a legal duty to evaluate objections and to explain the weight given to objections in the decision-making process.

Where there are significant highways issues the LPA will work with the highways authority to ensure that these issues are factored into the final planning consent.

The client

If the development is speculative, the developer will be working to fulfil general market demand by selling or letting a building. Thus the concept of a client or specific end user becomes notional, and in that context the developer will probably produce a building which has the widest possible market appeal. That is one which is visually appealing, adaptable and in a popular location. Where there is a client, who may be a landowner, a public body, a business seeking new premises or a funding institution building up its property investment portfolio the developer will be working to a more specific brief.

Development partners

Sometimes the scale of a development requires a joint approach in order that a developer is not singularly overexposed to the risks involved. In other circumstances where the development is particularly challenging there may be a need for specialist partners to become involved. This is common where large brownfield sites (previously developed land) are being redeveloped and where the inputs from regeneration agencies such as urban development corporations may be needed to bring sites up to a developable condition. In other circumstances the landowner may wish to play a role as a development partner and by sharing the risks will be looking to participate in the rewards from the completed development.

Specialist organisations such as housing associations might also be involved where there is a substantial housing element in a scheme. Development in partnerships has the potential to bring synergies to a development, spread the risks between parties and enables participants to exert some control over the outcome. Those readers who are particularly interested in this specialised area of development are directed to Dubben and Williams (2009).

Funding institutions

As Wilkinson and Reed (2008: 125) point out there is traditionally a distinction drawn between institutions which fund property development in the short term covering the construction period (typically banks) and those with longer-term interests in the investment performance of property (typically financial institutions). The latter includes pension funds and insurance companies who vary in their degree of enthusiasm for acquiring property as part of their overall investment portfolios.

During periods when these institutions are actively investing in commercial property they may forward fund developments which are pre-let to business tenants or they may agree to forward-purchase a development conditional upon a tenant being found within a specified timescale. Alternatively a fund might employ a developer as a project manager in order to carry out a development on a site which it has acquired. In these circumstances a financial institution will exert considerable control over a developer who may have to accept a lower profit margin for the certainty provided by the involvement of an institution.

The role of a bank is normally to provide development funding usually geared to a proportion of the value or costs of the development. A bank will evaluate a developer's loan application and will take a view on the degree of risk faced when setting the interest rate which the developer will pay. Thus a bank would normally evaluate a developer's credit rating and track record for delivering developments on time. A bank would also consider its own exit strategy in a worst-case scenario where it had to take possession of a site because a developer had defaulted on a loan. The credit crunch during 2008 to 2009 exposed some toxic loans in the property sector and Phillips (2009) reported that only two UK banks were subsequently interested in making new property loans exceeding £25 million. In 2009 two leading UK banks, Lloyds TSB and HBOS, had between them over £97 billion of loans extended against building and property and both banks were seeking to reduce this exposure. To put this into some perspective, Lloyds TSB's exposure to building and property amounted to £23.2 billion in 2009 which represents approximately 15 per cent of its overall lending portfolio.

The main contractor

The contractor is employed on the construction of the building and may in turn employ specialist subcontractors. For large projects there may be twenty to thirty subcontractors whose specialist contributions to the project are coordinated by the main contractor or project manager. The procurement route used and the type of building contract will determine the relationship of the main contractor with the developer, and some of the main options are discussed in chapter 9 of this book. However at this juncture one of the options which a developer might explore is to try to pass on a lot of the risk involved in the construction stage of the project by negotiating a fixed-price contract with the contractor which may also include penalty clauses for project overruns.

The landowner

As mentioned above the developer may have acquired the freehold of a site and will thus be the landowner. However, particularly on town centre retail schemes, the landowner may be the local authority and there may be a lease and leaseback arrangement whereby the developer has the opportunity to undertake the development and may then share in the rental income from the completed scheme along with the local authority. The division of the returns will act as an incentive for the developer to become involved so that there is a relationship between risk and reward.

Landowners may also have agreed to enter into option agreements and conditional sales agreements with developers under which a developer agrees to undertake the work involved in obtaining planning consent. If consent is subsequently agreed, the developer may exercise the option or fulfil the terms of the conditional contract by purchasing the site at an agreed market valuation. This is a useful arrangement for a developer in that while they might have to pay a value for a site reflecting its full development potential (less their costs of obtaining consent) they will not have to acquire a site upon which it was not possible to obtain planning consent after having made all reasonable endeavours.

The community

Local residents, businesses and organisations will tend to form opinions on development proposals of any significance and they will make known their views to the local authority during the planning consultation period. In the UK a pejorative term, NIMBY (not in my back yard), is often used to describe any group or individual who opposes development. Local objections to eco-town proposals, wind farms and airport extensions show that local protest is very much alive. While local objections will not always result in a scheme being refused by the local authority, local pressure can result in developers having to rethink or concede on aspects of a scheme. Some would say that local objectors have too much power to veto development while others would say that this is the sign of a healthy democracy.

1.5 The economic context for property development

The development process has so far been discussed in terms of the stages and organisations involved and how development viability may be assessed using the residual method. The development process also has a wider economic context in which the contribution of the developer may be seen as revitalising local economies and utilising assets in a production process which generates economic growth.

Keynesian economists would advocate that during recessionary periods governments should invest in major infrastructure and construction projects in order to create an economic multiplier. Assuming this perspective, governments would be expected to invest in or incentivise major construction projects such as high-capacity fast rail links or airport expansions. Governments which bid to host the Olympic games are also demonstrating their awareness of the potential that these events have in terms of job creation and upskilling the workforce as venues are prepared and infrastructure is upgraded. The upfront costs may be significant but the potential multiplier effects felt throughout the economy may more than justify the investment.

Property development is an important element on the supply side of a country's economy as businesses require land and premises in the same way that they require labour, machinery and financial capital. The demand for property is therefore ultimately *derived demand* in that it stems from the activity of busi-nesses and firms. When the economy is contracting and firms are downsizing, then the knock-on effect will be reduced demand for business space. Conversely when an economy is expanding and there are new business start-ups and busi-ness expansions the demand for premises increases and this is usually reflected in rental growth. The challenge for property developers is to deliver the build-ings that businesses need at the required criteria of cost, quality and time. The growth of an economy could be badly affected by shortcomings in the quantity and quality of property supplied.

Economic theory and property development

However, developers tend to approach property from a different perspective to that of economists. D'Arcy and Keogh (2002: 19) confirm that developers are more likely to focus on a narrow band of the property market and they will be more concerned with the marketability and profitability of potential develop-ments. The concentration is more on new space and speculative schemes, rather than on the larger stock of older occupied properties.

Economists are more interested in the influence of property on economic growth and efficiency and the effect of location on firms and jobs. Economic theory tends to ignore the supply of land and property and sometimes assumes that there is an automatic adjustment of supply to meet demand. Economics may have failed to incorporate land and property into its analysis in a satisfac-tory manner. Neo-classical economics suggests that the price adjustments of rent and land values will regulate the demand for and the supply of physical space. But in a mixed economy the workings of the price mechanism are condi-tioned and controlled by public policy to the extent that the forces of the free market and intervention become interdependent. Thus the pattern of land values is a reflection of both market forces and land use planning policy.

Another major shortcoming of economic theory is that it cannot accommo-date the physical nature of property. Once a factory has been built, it cannot be moved, even if its original user deserts it. Ideally the supply of property would adjust quickly and smoothly to meet the needs of firms, but in reality there are time lags in the supply of property and this may exert a negative influence on the performance of firms and the national economy. Buildings vary in age, layout, size and design so it is difficult to find close substitutes. The property market is also dominated by the price of second-hand stock, because the volume of new property coming onto the market is small compared to the existing stock of buildings.

Determining the scale of development

Development is essentially a conversion process by change of use and the construction of buildings. If it is assumed that developers and property owners seek to maximise profits, then the property developer is faced with a range of decisions on each project to enable a profit maximisation position to be achieved. The principle of discounted returns which underlies such decisions has been considered by Balchin *et al.* (2000: 320–2). In theory a developer will neither strive to minimise total cost nor maximise the value of the completed property but to maximise the (discounted) difference between them. This principle will also dictate whether a developer should refurbish or redevelop. In conceptual form the optimal size of a building to erect on a cleared urban site is illustrated below in Figure 1.6.

The optimal size of the building is shown by X units of accommodation, because Y is the profit maximisation point where marginal cost (MC) = marginal revenue (MR), at this point the site value is V. Marginal revenue is the extra revenue to be earned from the addition of each successive unit (or floor) of accommodation to a site. However there comes a point where the addition of extra floors or units of accommodation is not worthwhile as demand decays. This phenomenon can be seen in multilevel retail malls where it is often difficult or impossible to let retail units profitably on the higher floors. Increasing inaccessibility means that the unit value begins to fall and the economic expression for this is diminishing marginal returns.

In many countries the developer does not have to confront this phenomenon as planning controls or zoning ordinances will limit building heights and densities on sites. In those contexts a developer will probably build up to the limits if market research suggests that there will be demand for the units or floorspace provided. However in countries such as the Gulf States where policy

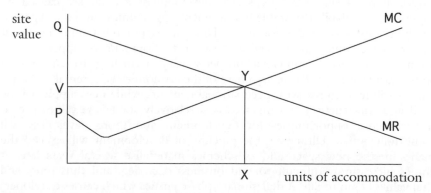

Figure 1.6 Optimal size of a building

is deliberately relaxed with the intention of creating a development boom, the developer is faced with the dilemma of how high to build. The lack of policy controls may create overspeculation and oversupply, exposing developers and their funders to considerable risk if the market were to turn.

Marginal cost (in the diagram above) represents the additional costs of adding each additional unit of accommodation to a building. Initially marginal cost falls, for example when a second storey is built, but then it increases as additional storeys will necessitate more powerful lifts, deeper and more expensive foundations and the project period is extended. The latter increases finance costs.

In the conceptual depiction of the interplay of marginal cost and marginal revenue above the area represented by PQY should equal the profit the developer would make, which is the difference between the total revenue and cost. Of course this is a simplified conceptual representation and in reality the developer's professional advisers would model different development scenarios armed with up-to-date market intelligence while factoring in constraints affecting a site.

Some of the constraints typically encountered by developers in this type of exercise are heritage related involving conservation areas, listed buildings and even protected views which limit the height to which buildings can be developed.

In the commercial property sector there are policy constraints on developing out-of-town retail centres and business parks. However there are also opportunities identified at strategic employment locations in cities where transport infrastructure is being upgraded and where high buildings proposals are encouraged. The Canary Wharf cluster in London's former docklands is one such centre which benefits from the intersection of underground, light railway extensions and the city airport and where additional investment is being made in the Crossrail scheme. Successful developers will therefore be those who stay attuned to policy so that they are able to take options on sites in locations where development is encouraged while avoiding locations where policy constrains development.

Cyclical development activity

Changes in the level of private sector development activity are caused by changes in the availability of viable development opportunities and the expected profitability and risk of development. Thus the opportunity and the profit motive for development both need to exist for development to happen.

Rental values for commercial property vary according to changes in economic activity. In a reflationary phase of the economic cycle, rental and capital values will tend to rise with occupational demand, while new supply will be limited and construction and finance costs relatively stable. As values rise so there are more opportunities for development and more developers will become fully active. Ultimately the pipeline of development will exceed the demand for the new space and as schemes materialise several years later it becomes increasingly difficult to find business occupiers and thus rents and capital values begin to fall. A deflationary phase ensues which causes developers to scale down their operations in the face of reduced demand.

Although the term 'property cycle' is sometimes used to reflect these periodic variations in development activity, research by the Investment Property Databank and the University of Aberdeen (1994) found that over a 30-year period the depth and duration of these fluctuations was not regular, predictable nor subject to any formula.

Thus while it is important to consider the broader economic context in which property developers operate and to accept that there will be fluctuations in development activity, it is also important to recognise that economic theory has yet to provide an adequate explanation of the activities and contributions made by developers.

1.6 Sustainable development

The discussion above reveals that a number of practices have evolved concerning property development and that the focus has perhaps understandably been on economic viability. However in recent years the threats posed by climate change have become apparent in extreme weather events and this has raised the level of concern regarding the environment. The consequences for property development are that the concept of sustainable development is being taken more seriously than it once was.

Of course environmental regulation has impacted upon the built environment for many years and for example in most countries major developments must undergo environmental impact assessment. In Europe this requirement dates back to a 1985 directive. However, the sustainable development agenda entails more than just the environmental screening of projects, laudable though that might be. As Ratcliffe *et al.* (2009) point out, discussions on sustainable development tend to begin with the report of the World Commission on Environment and Development (1987) *Our Common Future* (more commonly known as the Brundtland report) which contained the following user-friendly definition of sustainability:

> Development that meets the needs of the present without compromising the ability of future generations to meet their own needs. (Brundtland cited in Ratcliffe *et al.* 2009: 4)

The Brundtland definition has subsequently influenced thinking and policy affecting all sectors of industry in most countries and the UK is no exception. The environmental theme is evident in that interpretation, but as established in Agenda 21 at the Rio Earth Summit in 1992, there are three interlinked aspects of sustainability as shown below in Figure 1.7.

Most readers would correctly make the connection between sustainable development and environmental concerns such as climate change. The environmental strands of sustainable development are of course important, but the *economic* and *social* facets, which receive less attention, are also important considerations.

While some progress has been made on establishing the link between sustainability and property development by authors such as Keeping and Shiers (2002) the agenda is developing fast and is still largely unexplored. For the purposes of this discussion therefore a sustainable building which attempted to address all

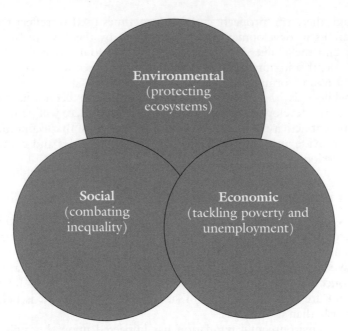

Figure 1.7 Three interlinked aspects of sustainability

three sustainability facets might achieve some of the criteria as set out in Figure 1.8.

Of course not all of those issues can be addressed in all commercial developments. It must also be accepted that some of the measurable 'quick wins' on the sustainability agenda are more easily achieved on the environmental dimension while some of the more subtle social and economic ambitions are not as readily achievable. Perhaps it is for these reasons that the environmental aspect of sustainability has achieved greater prominence in relation to property development.

Sustainable development: policy and regulation

Given that a tipping point has been reached in the collective consciousness on climate change most individuals and national governments now recognise the need to take measures to tackle the problem. The political manifestation is that nations have signed up to meeting carbon reduction targets, a process which first came to global prominence under the Kyoto protocol in 1997.

There was understandably some scepticism by developing countries that pressure to sign up to carbon reduction targets was a covert way of preventing them from reaching levels of development already enjoyed by developed countries. However as Lord Stern (2006: viii) has pointed out:

> The world does not need to choose between averting climate change and promoting growth and development. Changes in energy technologies and in the structure of economies have created opportunities to decouple growth from greenhouse gas emissions. Indeed, ignoring climate change will eventually damage economic growth.

	Use of sustainable building materials such as softwood.
	Use of renewable energy sources such as onsite micro-generation.
	Energy efficient building services and reduced reliance on air conditioning plant.
Environmental dimension	Use of brownfield sites and avoidance of building on floodplains.
	Higher-density development located close to public transport nodes in order to reduce reliance on the car. Adoption of green travel plans.
	Ensure building components are lifecycle costed, so that they require less maintenance and repair.
	Ensure that heating and other equipment can easily convert to cheaper energy sources.
Economic dimension	Adoption of high insulation standards to reduce heat loss.
	Ensuring internal space is adaptable to meet a variety of user needs.
	In housing development providing a dwelling mix to meet the needs and demand arising from different-sized households.
Social dimension	Ensure development is close to social infrastructure, so that building users/residents have convenient access to schools, healthcare facilities, shops, leisure and recreational opportunities.
	Improved security by incorporating crime reduction advice from the police force at the design stage.

Figure 1.8 Some sustainable development criteria applied to property development

Like any other industry, property development has to accept its share of responsibility on this agenda, particularly as it is estimated that 18 per cent of the UK's carbon emissions are produced by non-domestic buildings and the additional emissions from housing more than doubles this figure. Reducing carbon emissions from development can of course be achieved on a voluntary basis or through regulation or by introducing incentives such as grants or tax breaks or a combination of all of these approaches.

From a regulatory perspective, governmental ambitions to foster sustainable development will result in gradually more exacting standards which will present some new challenges to property developers. For example at a macro level, the UK government has put in place a Code for Sustainable Homes which will ultimately require that all new housing produced after 2016 to be zero carbon.

At a micro level Energy Performance Certificates (EPCs) were made mandatory in the UK in 2009 for all domestic and non-domestic buildings. While EPCs do not specify minimum levels of energy performance they do increase the degree of transparency and information regarding a building's energy efficiency.

There is also considerable interest in how renewable energy technologies might contribute to reducing carbon emissions. In this context the London Borough of Merton in the UK came to prominence because it embedded a policy in its Unitary Development Plan which stated that:

All new industrial, warehousing, office and live/work units outside conservation areas and above a threshold of 1,000 square metres will be expected to incorporate renewable energy production equipment to provide at least 10 per cent of predicted energy requirements. (London Borough of Merton 2003: 86)

The 10 per cent renewable energy contribution was to be provided on-site and the policy became known as the 'Merton Rule'. Other local authorities subsequently adopted similar policies which required new developments to incorporate some renewable energy technology.

Although the Merton Rule began by targeting large commercial developments, the policy had obvious implications for housebuilding, given that the government has set a target that all new housing should be zero carbon by 2016. The volume housebuilding industry is not known for its innovative approaches to producing low-energy housing and authorities such as Merton have argued that they need controls to force developers to produce more sustainable housing.

Hewitt (2007) a supporter of the Merton Rule, argues that the additional cost of adding renewable energy equipment, such as micro-generation equipment, to an average new home is around £2,000. Even if this is passed onto the end user, Hewitt argues that the reduction in energy bills will soon make inroads into the initial capital investment. The resale value of the dwelling could also be expected to reflect an energy efficiency advantage over standard housing.

A number of volume housebuilders in the UK and the industry's representative body, the Home Builders Federation (HBF) has argued against an application of the Merton Rule to housing. The HBF and other objectors claim that while the costs are easy to calculate, renewable energy technologies are relatively untried and some of the methods are not particularly attractive in terms of payback rates on initial capital investment.

Scott (2008) for example reports on trials conducted by housebuilder Barratt at their eco-village at Chorley in Lancashire. Barratt support the move to zero carbon housing and are testing various renewable energy technologies on standard house types. Photovoltaics and heat pumps have performed well in terms of energy generation, but their payback times, when measured as a ratio of cost savings against capital outlay were reported to be 'prohibitive'. Given current technology, photovoltaics would take more than 37 years to pay back and heat pumps 15 years. Micro wind turbines were found by Barratt to perform disappointingly in terms of energy generation and therefore pay-back times, while combined heat and power units performed well. Trials are continuing on a range of renewable and low-carbon energy technology, but it is clear that the housebuilding industry is still very much on a learning curve regarding the identification of the technologies which will be cost-effective energy generators.

Objectors to the Merton Rule have also suggested that a blanket percentage target for renewable energy for all developments would be arbitrary and unjustified because while the target might be achievable on some sites, it might be difficult on others due to aspect, topography or cost.

The HBF are also concerned that there is an overemphasis on new-build when it only represents a small fraction of existing housing stock. The HBF feel that there should be more focus on ways to bring existing dwellings in private, public and social ownership up to near zero carbon standards. As Whitaker, a spokesperson for the HBF, states:

> Modern day homes may account for 25% of UK emissions, but this needs to be seen in context. New homes also account for barely 1% of housing stock each year, so while the need for greener homes is obvious, without an emphasis on existing homes any drive for lower emissions is doomed to futility. (Whitaker 2007: 335)

Having considered these arguments, the government in England (Communities and Local Government 2007) issued a Planning Policy Statement (PPS) on climate change which endorses local action consistent with the Merton Rule. The policy emphasises how important tackling climate change has become in the political arena:

> The Government believes that climate change is the greatest long-term challenge facing the world today. Addressing climate change is therefore the Government's principle concern for sustainable development. (Communities and Local Government 2007: 8)

Among other things the policy requires local authorities to encourage renewable and low-carbon energy generation but with some important qualifying criteria. Local authorities should have an evidence-based understanding of the feasibility and potential for renewable and low-carbon technologies, including micro-generation, to supply new development in their area. The policy endorses the principle of setting a target percentage for the energy expected from renewable sources but that this should not prescribe particular technologies and should be flexible in how carbon savings from local energy supplies are to be secured. The policy requires local authorities to set out the type and size of development to which the target will be applied in consultation with developers.

The policy ambition to include renewable energy in new development is therefore one of the positive ways that carbon emissions from buildings can be reduced. However it is also important to consider the property market response to the sustainability agenda.

Sustainable development and the property market

Market forces can work in harmony with many sustainable development objectives. For example at the micro level house purchasers might well be interested in energy efficient appliances in their homes and while such appliances might have a marginally higher initial capital cost, they will pay for themselves over a lifetime of use. However, market forces may not always be conducive to fostering sustainable development. For example, social and economic problems in an area may have arisen precisely because the market has failed to invest there and in such areas intervention may be required to stimulate development in the interests of regeneration.

To foster sustainable development an ideal framework would contain a combination of regulation and incentives for developers. Thus far the focus has been on regulation and so the discussion now considers whether there are any financial incentives in the market for a developer to provide more sustainable buildings. This is not a discussion about whether there are or should be grants to subsidise the provision of sustainable buildings but whether there is evidence of any market demand for such buildings. If the concept of sustainable property development is to become established, it must be self-sustaining in a market sense.

The Oxford Institute for Sustainable Development (OISD) research on landlord and tenant attitudes towards sustainable offices, identified a 'circle of blame' (OISD 2009: 12) in which developers claim that they are not requested to produce sustainable buildings by end users or investors, so there is no incentive for them to produce buildings which exceed the statutory minima in the building regulations. The end users (business tenants) claim that they are not offered sustainable buildings and so sustainability is removed from their search criteria. Property investors claim that they would invest in sustainable buildings if more were produced by developers to create an investment market for such properties.

The OISD research therefore investigated whether there was any truth in the assertion that the end users of commercial property (businesses from all sectors of industry) were simply not requesting sustainable buildings. The OISD research focused upon commercial tenants search priorities when they were looking to lease office space. The study concluded that (2009: 12):

> This research has shown that although there is evidence of an emerging and increasing demand for sustainable offices, other factors such as location, availability of stock and building quality remain more important in determining occupiers' final choice of office.

However, the OISD team detected that companies which had a *corporate social responsibility* policy were leading the way in specifying sustainability in their search criteria for office space. One of the survey respondents summed up this position in that companies needed to be seen by their clients to 'walk the talk' on sustainability and it was this type of company that took space in BREEAM-rated office buildings.

Research funded partly by the RICS on the office market in the United States and carried out by Eichholtz *et al.* (2009) explored whether office tenants were willing to pay a rental premium to lease energy efficient buildings. In the USA the terminology used is 'green building' which are certified under one of two recognised green rating systems which are the LEED system (Leadership in Energy and Environmental Design) and the Energy Star label.

In a similar vein to the OISD research in the UK Eichholtz *at al.* (2009) noted that the occupier market in the USA contains an increasing proportion of companies which have a corporate social responsibility policy which extends to taking practical measures to tackle climate change. This, the team felt, was conducive to the cultivation of a more discerning market for commercial buildings and it is likely that sustainability will begin to feature more highly in occupiers' expectations when searching for premises.

Having considered a wide sample of office buildings in American cities, Eichholtz *et al.* (2009) detected a 6 per cent rental premium for buildings certified under the Energy Star system. While the team did not find a premium for LEED-rated buildings they concluded that in aggregate there was a 3 per cent rental premium achievable for green buildings. The research also examined the capital values achieved on the sales of office buildings. After controlling for location and quality the team found that those buildings which were accredited with green status attracted a 16 per cent higher capital value than standard buildings.

While the research suggests incentives for developers, the cost side of the equation also has to be considered as the incentive of a 3 per cent rental premium could be eradicated if the costs to put a building in that category are an additional 6 per cent.

There is a widely held perception that the additional costs incurred in producing a sustainable building will either be exorbitant or that those costs will not be recovered by the developer through added value at the point of sale. This assertion was investigated in research by construction and property consultancy Cyril Sweett (2005) which examined the cost implications of achieving enhanced environmental performance for four typical building types which were: a four bedroom house, a naturally ventilated office building, an air-conditioned office building and a healthcare centre.

The Cyril Sweett research team adopted compliance with the UK building regulations as the baseline for each development from which to assess the cost of improvements necessary to raise each project progressively to 'good', 'very good' and 'excellent' under the BREEAM (Building Research Establishment Environmental Assessment Method) ratings.

BREEAM is the recognised industry standard in the UK for measuring the sustainability of a building and it awards credit points for enhanced environmental performance through management, design and specification. It is the sum of the credit points which attracts the rating categories mentioned above. For example a building which attracted a score of between 40 to 55 credit points would attract a 'good' rating under BREEAM.

Table 1.1 Developing sustainable buildings (BREEAM ratings)

Building type	Additional capital cost required to raise the project to BREEAM 'good'	Additional capital cost required to raise the project to BREEAM 'very good'	Additional capital cost required to raise the project to BREEAM 'excellent'
Four-bedroom house (115m² gross floor area)	0.3 per cent to 0.9 per cent	1.3 per cent to 3.1 per cent	4.2 per cent to 6.9 per cent
Naturally ventilated office building (493m² gross floor area)	–0.3 per cent to –0.4 per cent (i.e. cost savings)	–0.4 per cent to 2 per cent	2.5 per cent to 3.4 per cent
Air-conditioned office building (10,098m² gross floor area)	0 to 0.2 per cent	0.1 per cent to 5.7 per cent	3.3 per cent to 5.7 per cent
Healthcare centre (6,400m² gross floor area)	Baseline	0 per cent	0.6 per cent to 1.9 per cent

It is not necessary here to unpack the intricacies of BREEAM and the research methodology adopted by the Cyril Sweett team, but the findings summarised above in Table 1.1 provide some evidence that cost may not be an insurmountable issue when trying to develop sustainable buildings.

The range achievable in each category above in Table 1.1represents choices about the site location. Thus the reuse of a brownfield site which is close to public transport will bring the development to the lower end of the cost range in each case. Conversely the use of a greenfield site which is inaccessible by public transport will mean that more must be spent on achieving the necessary credits to raise the scheme to a higher BREEAM category. Site location is thus a key issue in determining the degree of environmental sustainability achieved by new buildings.

BedZED: a sustainable property development

In the UK the most well-known pioneering sustainable development was designed by a team led by architect Bill Dunster and completed in 2002. The scheme occupies a 1.4 hectare site at Beddington in the outskirts of London and is known as BedZED.

The 'ZED' in the scheme's name stands for *zero (fossil) energy development* as the heat and power for the scheme sought to rely entirely on renewable energy. Approximately 10 per cent of the renewable energy is provided by roof and façade-mounted photovoltaic panels which also provide energy for electric car charging points. The remaining 90 per cent of the scheme's energy requirement is provided by a combined heat and power (CHP) unit fuelled by wood pellets produced from forestry waste. The latter is one of a number of biomass sources of energy.

The client for the development was the Peabody Trust, a large and well-established housing association which had acquired the brownfield site at below market value from the local authority: the London Borough of Sutton.

The award-winning scheme is a high-density mixed-use development containing 82 flats and maisonettes, 1,600m^2 of business space available for letting in 23 separate units and social and recreational facilities. The mixed tenure housing element comprises 34 open market units, 23 shared ownership units, 10 key worker rented units and 15 social rented units. There is a sports pitch, café, shop, a healthy living centre and nursery.

As Towers (2005: 251–6) points out, the development uses the site very efficiently and for example the net density of the residential element is 128 units per hectare. This is a very sustainable use of land and significantly exceeds densities achieved on contemporary flatted developments in outer London.

Key BedZED features are its green travel plan and a car pooling system for the residents. Some of the larger residential units are live-work units which enable flexible lifestyles and reduce the need for residents to commute. There is water recycling and rain-water harvesting and the scheme's roof gardens can be used for food production.

The development maximised the use of recycled building materials such as steel and brick and in the sourcing of all building materials suppliers within a 35-mile radius of the scheme were prioritised. All building materials are non-toxic and from sustainable sources.

The detailed construction specification at BedZED achieves very high standards of insulation, so that energy is not wasted. The buildings' thermal mass has been designed to smooth the profile between periods of heat gain and dissipation. The potential of solar gain is maximised by the form of the buildings and their orientation along an east–west axis upon which the residential units face south and the employment units face north.

Heat exchangers operate in roof spaces in conjunction with the roof-mounted wind cowls which are a distinctive feature of this development. This arrangement is known as passive heat recovery ventilation, as wind passing across the cowls creates a natural vacuum which draws stale air out of the building which in turn creates a vacuum which draws in fresh air. The result is dramatically reduced fuel consumption during the winter months when there is no need for conventional central heating and in the summer months there is no need for air conditioning.

In terms of the market response to BedZED all of the open market and shared ownership residential units sold on completion of the development and their resale values are estimated at 20 per cent above the sales values for comparable units in the area. All of the business space was let and there have been no difficulties in reletting the space at competitive market rents.

However, as with any pioneering scheme, there will inevitably be some setbacks, which is part of the learning curve on developing sustainable buildings. There have been periods when the CHP plant has not worked properly and this necessitated the installation of conventional boilers (powered from the national network) in the apartments to provide hot water. The waste treatment system has also been out of service because of the difficulties in sourcing a reliable operator.

Because BedZED is an innovative scheme involving a lot of non-standard techniques combined with a range of ambitious project goals the construction costs went 30 per cent over budget. This of course does not suggest that every sustainable building would experience a 30 per cent cost overrun, as economies of scale and standardisation of construction techniques tend to iron out initial cost discrepancies. Because the land was obtained at less than market value and that the client was a not-for-profit organisation there was no pressing need for the scheme to show a clear profit so long as it did not at the same time make a loss. Given that the business units in the scheme let and the properties sold quickly the scheme was not in the end a loss maker for the client.

BedZED is one of a number of exemplar sustainable developments in the UK which have informed a ZED toolkit produced by Dunster *et al.* (2008) which illustrates practical ways that the ZED principles can be applied to different building types and scales.

1.7 Summary

This chapter began by considering the property development process from a conventional perspective and it was found that there are a number of economic principles and appraisal techniques which have evolved and continue to serve a purpose. The profit motivation in this risk-prone process continues to drive the major private sector developers and that scenario is unlikely to change significantly. However property development has become a very diversified business and now includes a sizeable not-for-profit sector which includes government agencies and the voluntary sector.

Property development takes place within a dynamic context in which the direction of travel of government policy is increasingly towards the production of sustainable buildings. These changes may add additional costs to projects but there is some research evidence to suggest that these costs need not pose an insurmountable problem for developers. The likelihood is that the additional project costs will be: (a) marginal; (b) will gradually reduce due to standardisation and technological innovation; and (c) may in any event be recoverable in added project value as building users and owners begin to recognise and adopt sustainability as one of their selection criteria.

There are also sustainability toolkits and exemplary sustainable property developments, although for developers to fully buy into the concept of sustainability there will need to be a combination of regulation and market incentives. There are still a number of unexplored research agendas regarding sustainable development, although there are tentative signs that indulging in sustainable property development may not be inconsistent with a developer's profit motive.

References

Balchin, P., Isaac, D. and Chen, J. (2000) *Urban Economics: A Global Perspective* (London: Palgrave).

Baum, A. and Crosby, N. (2008) *Property Investment Appraisal*, 3rd edition (London: Blackwell).

Communities and Local Government (2007) *Planning Policy Statement: Planning and Climate Change: Supplement to Planning Policy Statement 1* (London: The Stationery

Office). Available in e-format at: www.communities.gov.uk/documents/planningandbuilding/pdf/ppsclimatechange.pdf

Cyril Sweett (2005) *Putting a Price on Sustainability*, Building Research Establishment Trust. Readers may also be interested in Cyril Sweett (2009) *Costing Energy Efficiency Improvements in Existing Commercial Buildings*, Investment Property Forum. Available in e-format at: www.cyrilsweett.com/pdfs/IPF_low_energy_improvements_summary_report.pdf

D'Arcy, E. and Keogh, G. 'The market context of property development activity', in Guy, S. and Henneberry, J. (eds) (2002) *Development and Developers: Perspectives on Property* (Oxford: Blackwell).

Dubben, N. and Williams, B. (2009) *Partnerships in Property Development* (London: Wiley-Blackwell).

Dunster, B., Gilbert, G. and Simmons, C. (2008) *The Zed Book* (Abingdon: Taylor & Francis).

Eichholtz, P., Kok, N. and Quigley, J. (2009) *Doing Well by Doing Good? An Analysis of the Financial Performance of Green Buildings in the USA* (London: RICS Research Report). Available in e-format at: www.rics.org/NR/rdonlyres/44F67595-7989-45C7-B489 7E2B84F9DA76/0/DoingWellbyDoingGood.pdf

Havard, T. (2008) *Contemporary Property Development*, 2nd edition (London: RIBA Publishing).

Hewitt, A. (2007) 'Realities of the Merton rule', 76 (10) *Town and Country Planning*, 332–4.

Homes and Communities Agency (2009) notes on Local Housing Companies can be found at: www.homesandcommunities.co.uk/local_housing_companies

Investment Property Databank and the University of Aberdeen (1994) *Understanding the Property Cycle* (London: RICS).

Keeping, M. and Shiers, D. (2002) *Sustainable Property Development* (Oxford: Blackwell Science).

London Borough of Merton (2003) *Unitary Development Plan*, London Borough of Merton. Available in e-format at: www.merton.gov.uk/living/planning/planning-policy/udp.htm

Marriott, O. (1962) *The Property Boom* (London: Hamish Hamilton).

Millington, A. (2000) *Property Development* (London: Estates Gazette).

Oxford Institute for Sustainable Development (2009) *Demand for Sustainable Offices in the UK*, Investment Property Forum. Available in e-format at: http://members.ipf.org.uk/membersarealive/downloads/listings1.asp?pid=292

Phillips, M. (2009) 'The rush for the exit', Estates Gazette, 14 March, 47–9.

Ratcliffe, J., Stubbs, M. and Keeping, M. (2009) *Urban Planning and Real Estate Development*, 3rd edition (Abingdon: Routledge).

Scott, M. (2008) 'The heat is on', RICS Business, April, 14–17.

Stern Review, the (2006) *The Economics of Climate Change* (London: HM Treasury). Available in e-format at: www.hm-treasury.gov.uk/sternreview_index.htm

Syms, P. (2002) *Land, Development and Design* (Oxford: Blackwell).

Towers, G. (2005) *At Home in the City: An Introduction to Urban Housing Design* (London: Architectural Press).

Whitaker, A. (2007) 'Wanted – a national framework', 76 (10) *Town and County Planning*.

Wilkinson, S. and Reed, R. (2008) *Property Development*, 5th edition (Abingdon: Routledge).

World Commission on Environment and Development (Brundtland Report) (1987) *Our Common Future* (Oxford: Oxford University Press).

2

Development appraisal

Aims

This chapter considers some of the key opportunities and constraints which developers will typically face when initiating a development project. The chapter will therefore look at location, the physical, legal and planning characteristics of sites. The chapter will also examine the role that market research can play in assessing project viability.

Key terms

>> **Opportunities and constraints** – the legal, policy, physical and financial factors which present challenges and opportunities for a developer. The combination of factors will be different for each site and will require applied research and interpretation.

>> **Land bank** – a collection of sites owned or held under option agreements by a developer which can be brought forward for development in order to provide continuity of production.

>> **Development appraisal toolkit** – a software package usually based upon Excel spreadsheets, which enables developers to input the anticipated costs and values of a development proposal to identify whether full policy compliance is also financially viable.

>> **Community infrastructure levy** – an optional approach for local authorities to attach a levy to specific sites which developers are required to pay to meet the cost of infrastructure.

>> **Sequential test** – used by local authorities to steer development to sites which have the least flood risk. A sequential test can also be used to steer retail development to the most appropriate sites in order to prevent retail impact on town centres.

>> **Overage agreement** – also known as claw-back and which forms part of a land transaction enabling the vendor to share in the future profits when value is ultimately realised from the development of a site.

2.1 Introduction

At the inception of a project a developer will need to undertake some applied research in order to understand and interpret the opportunities and constraints suggested by a site. Much of the research work will be carried out and reported upon by the developer's professional team but it is the developer's ultimate responsibility to evaluate and act upon the recommendations arising from the team. During this survey and evaluation stage of the project the developer's team may well be temporarily expanded to include specialists instructed to advise on the variety of issues which arise. For example there may need to be inputs from an archaeological consultant as well as civil engineers with highways, geotechnical and possibly hydrological expertise. Specialist lawyers and surveyors may need to be instructed to advise on legal encumbrances such as easements, restrictive covenants, rights to light, party wall or boundary issues.

This fact-finding and interpretation stage can be expensive for the developer in terms of professional fees but the investment made has the effect of gradually reducing project risks. The developer's team will normally be identifying and reporting upon the significance of the constraints in terms of the developer's ambitions and providing the developer with realistic solutions to the constraints identified. Professionals in the developer's team should therefore be adding value to a project by thinking creatively so that constraints can be turned into opportunities or at least accommodated into a scheme in a satisfactory manner. However before that stage is reached a strategic decision will have to be made by the developer regarding the site to focus upon.

2.2 Committing to a site

As Wilkinson and Reed (2008: 32) point out:

> Site selection is vital to success as it affects the nature of a project. If the site has a poor location or there is a lack of demand for the accommodation irrespective of location, no amount of good design or promotion can overcome this disadvantage to the project.

Sometimes the decision to commit to a site has already been made as it might be one of a number held in a developer's land bank. Volume housebuilders operate in this way by undertaking a strategic search of potential sites within a region and then focusing upon the firmer prospects where both ownership and planning consent might be achieved. As sites are developed, they deplete the land bank and so new sites need to be found and brought into the land bank to replenish the supply. Thus an important role within housebuilding companies is the strategic land buyer.

Some commercial property developers have established search patterns so that they will only investigate sites in a particular region or city with which they have familiarity and confidence that their type of development will have a market in that location. Within the strategy more specific criteria might be specified such as the minimum size of site and context. For example a developer may only be interested in prime sites capable of accommodating $X,000$ m^2 of floorspace within the central business district (CBD) or within Y miles of a motorway junction or Z miles of an airport. Large retail developers have specialised search criteria for sites which involve modelling population catchments within drive time isochrones and which factor in the existing quantitative and qualitative supply of retail floorspace.

Where a client comes forward with a site which is already part of their estate the commitment decision has already been made, although even here a developer might suggest a land swap or part disposal and purchase of neighbouring land if that would better suit the client's needs.

Sites may also be identified through policy steering whereby the government is providing a clear indication on where development will be encouraged and where it will be constrained. Thus in England the government's *Sustainable Communities Plan* (ODPM 2003) identified four growth areas in the South East: Ashford, the Thames Gateway, Milton Keynes and the M11 corridor. In these areas the government pledged additional public spending on infrastructure and a positive planning framework as inducements to private developers to source and develop sites in those localities.

Site finding

The developer's skill and knowledge is important in identifying areas where market forces will provide demand for accommodation which will exceed supply by the time a development project is completed. While recognising the risks, a successful developer will tend to seek opportunities to be ahead of the market.

The proactive developer would also be examining trends in rental and capital values and investigating whether there will be any infrastructure improvements in an area which would stimulate demand. Developers will also commission market research which will seek to identify the current and projected levels of supply and demand of various types of accommodation in a particular area.

As Wilkinson and Reed (2008: 40) point out some of the larger developers will have in-house site finding teams which include a land agent and planning consultant whose roles are to follow up leads within the corporate land acquisition strategy. Site finding requires research into planning policies and the ability to identify sites which may be brought forward through the development plan process. This can be a lengthy process involving the submission of representations on draft local plans and the giving of evidence at local plan inquiries. The search process can be quite systematic and may involve the compilation of databases containing site descriptions, summaries of the planning history and details of ownership.

Developers may also employ agents to find sites in a particular area and the agent's fee is paid if a site recommended is subsequently acquired by the developer. The fee is normally one per cent of the land price but could be subject to negotiation. Agents tend to have good local knowledge and local contacts and they may be able to negotiate the purchase of sites before they go on the open market. A developer may also search an area to try to identify possible opportunities. When sites are identified, it is necessary to ascertain their ownership by examining the planning register, asking local agents or occupiers or consulting the Land Registry.

Other obvious means of acquiring sites include obtaining particulars of sites when they are advertised for sale by agents. Advertisements can also be placed in journals such as *Estates Gazette* indicating that sites are sought in a particular area and that a fee will be paid for introductions leading to site acquisitions. Sites are also purchased through company takeover and merger. For example larger housebuilders will sometimes purchase smaller housebuilders simply to replenish land banks.

Sites also become available on a wind-fall basis due to wider policy or economic changes. Thus the closure of a car plant due to the loss of international markets might create a local property development opportunity. The restructuring of large government departments like the Ministry of Defence may also result in large sites coming forward. Large transport operators like Network Rail also use property transactions to cross-subsidise their core business and this can create property development opportunities below and above main railway stations and parts of the track as well as under viaducts and on land elsewhere which is surplus to operational requirements. Primary health care trusts and universities are also active in the land market in terms of disposals, land swaps and sometimes promoting partnership development opportunities in order to optimise the use of their estates to support core activities.

Methods of site disposal

Formal and informal tenders

Site disposals may take place through informal tender and invitations to offer or formal tenders, competitions and auctions. Informal tenders or invitations to offer, require interested parties to submit their best bids by a deadline. The important point from the developer's perspective is that the bid is made subject to conditions, so that after a bid has been accepted by the landowner, the developer will have the ability to renegotiate the price before exchange of contracts. In the case of formal tenders, the formal tender binds both the parties to the terms and conditions set out in the tender documentation, this is subject only to contract. It is for these reasons that developers prefer informal tenders as there is more flexibility and the opportunity to reduce risk.

Competitions

Competitions are sometimes used when financial considerations are not the only criteria for the disposal of a site. They may be used for instance by local authorities or other public bodies in choosing a developer to implement a major scheme. In these cases a shortlist of developers may be invited to express their interest and they are normally asked to submit details of their financial status and track record and how they would approach the particular development.

An example of the competitive approach to site disposal was used in 2008 by Medway Council to select a developer to carry out phase one of the Rochester Riverside scheme in Kent. The Council had previously acquired this brownfield site through negotiation and compulsory purchase in order to regenerate what was a rundown waterfront area. Assistance on land acquisition and site clearance work was given by the South East England Development Agency (SEEDA).

Following the production of a development brief for the site (Medway

- quality of design proposals
- environmental sustainability of the proposals
- sales and marketing approach
- community participation
- employment and training proposals
- programme and delivery proposals
- land use
- costs
- sales values
- transport initiatives
- affordable housing: delivery, provider and management
- quality of full team
- management proposals
- added value

Figure 2.1 Summary of Medway Council's criteria for selecting a developer for Phase 1 of the Rochester Riverside Development

Council 2004a) the Council granted an outline planning consent for a mixed-use development in conformity with a master plan that had been prepared by consultants for the 34-hectare site (see Figure 2.1). The Council working with SEEDA had done everything to create a 'market-ready' site and was now inviting developers to make bids for phase one, which is 7 hectares in extent. The outline planning consent had earmarked phase one of the scheme for 550 housing units of which 25 per cent were to be affordable. Four major housebuilders were shortlisted to make bids to acquire phase one on a 999-year lease against the Council criteria set out in the tender package (summarised below). The four housebuilders were: Countryside Properties, Crest Nicholson, Bellway Homes with London and Quadrant Group and Urban Splash with Affinity Sutton Group. The latter two bidders were in fact joint bids between private developers and housing associations, although in the end the winner was Crest Nicholson, a developer with a good track record for delivering high-quality waterside residential development. Crest has also established an agreement with a large registered provider: Hyde Housing that in the event of success, Hyde would take on and manage the affordable housing element in the scheme.

Councils in England have a legal duty under the Town and Country Planning Act 1990, s. 233 to obtain best financial consideration when disposing of their land, but a council can approach the Secretary of State to explain why a lower initial capital receipt might be acceptable. Acceptable circumstances might be where the initial capital receipt for the land is supplemented by a profit-sharing or overage clause so that a council will ultimately receive best consideration when the developer has begun to dispose of the completed development several years later. In essence a council could be seen to be backing a quality developer with a quality scheme although accepting a lower initial capital receipt.

A council may also wish to attract a quality developer to the early stages of a much larger scheme so that the presence of that reputable developer will provide confidence and act as a catalyst which will ultimately realise higher values on subsequent phases. In summary therefore a council must not ignore the financial offer from a developer but it is not the only factor in their decision-making process, particularly in regeneration projects where other qualitative issues are important.

Because there is time and cost involved in mounting competition bids in response to tenders like the one above, developers find competitions the least attractive method of acquiring development sites. Although pragmatically they might work to an internal success ratio which offsets losses in competitions against those won.

Auctions

During the 2008–9 credit crunch, sites containing half-completed developments or upon which only a negligible start had been made were commonly appearing at property auctions. Traditionally auction lots tend to include unusual sites and those which may be difficult to sell by conventional means and so there is some degree of risk attached to these sites simply because the mainstream market has passed them by.

At auction, the highest bid secures the site, provided that the reserve price has been reached. The vendor will instruct the auctioneer on the reserve price, which is effectively the lowest price acceptable. If the reserve price is not reached during bidding, then the lot is withdrawn. Auctions may present an opportunity for developers looking beyond an economic downturn to land bank in readiness for an upturn. This contra-cyclical practice has given rise to the rather cruel expression: 'vulture capitalism' but in reality this is simply a reflection of the peaks and troughs of property market adjustment and which all markets are subject to.

Once the site has been identified the issues which will need investigation normally fall into three broad categories:

- Issues which have a legal or policy basis and which potentially limit development potential.
- Issues related to the physical characteristics and context of a site.
- Issues which are to do with the economics of supply and demand and which will affect the financial viability of what is proposed.

These issues will now be considered in turn.

2.3 Legal and policy constraints

Legal encumbrances

Legal encumbrances may include restrictive covenants, issues relating to party walls, rights to light, easements and rights of way. These encumbrances may involve costly legal proceedings and payment of sums to remove the particular encumbrance.

For example where properties are erected against common walls, work to those walls may require permission under the Party Wall etc. Act 1996. In these situations, surveyors for the adjoining owners will inspect proposals for works before agreement for the development of a site. Schedules of condition may need to be agreed and there may be the possibility of party wall awards to the adjoining owner. There may thus be costs which will affect the financial appraisal of the site and which may not have been immediately apparent. Specialist legal advice will also be needed where excavations are envisaged within 3 metres of adjacent structures, where new buildings are proposed at or astride the boundary between structures or where there may be rights to support where demolition is involved.

Rights to light will normally have been acquired by prescription where windows have received uninterrupted light for 20 years or more. The erection of tall structures close to windows in neighbouring properties may result in an injury in civil law attracting damages. As RICS (2009a: 31) advise the presence of a planning consent does not negate a neighbour's right to light and so where this might be an issue the advice of a rights to light surveyor should be sought.

Depending on the circumstances of the case and subject to appropriate legal advice, restrictive covenants can be removed or modified under the provisions of the Law of Property Act 1925, s. 84.

The boundaries are an important element in the demarcation of the land and the title to the land will need to be properly investigated. The boundaries of a site should be clearly indicated from the deeds but these can often be misleading because of the way plans are drawn and thus disagreements can easily arise if issues are not clarified at the outset.

Problems may exist in obtaining vacant possession in order to develop a site as there may be existing tenants or licence holders with rights to use a site or there may be other legal encumbrances. Where redevelopment is envisaged, business tenants may be served a notice in order that the developer may gain vacant possession under the provisions of the Landlord and Tenant Act 1954, Part II. However the tenants may be entitled to compensation depending on the terms and conditions of their business tenancy and any unexpired term on their lease.

Access is important from a legal point of view as it must be determined whether access is provided from a site to a public right of way such as a road or highway adopted by the local authority. If an access road has not been adopted, then research into the deeds to discover the extent of rights over access roads will need to be carried out.

Trees may be protected by tree preservation orders, made under the Town and Country Planning Act 1990. Protected trees may not be cut or lopped and if anyone is convicted of doing so they may be liable to a fine or imprisonment. The law only protects specimens in good condition and an application to fell or lop such a tree would need to be made to the local planning authority.

Regarding hedgerows, there are some controls under the Hedgerow Regulations 1997 although these are highly conditional so that most hedgerows do not benefit from any protection. For example, to warrant protection, a hedgerow needs to be at least 20 metres long, it must meet another hedgerow at either end, it must be growing on or adjacent to common land, protected land or land used for agriculture. Where the regulations are wilfully breached, the local authority has powers to require a hedge to be restored and may issue injunctions to stop unauthorised work.

Ideally a developer will be looking for a site with clean title but in reality there is likely to be a legal constraint of one kind or another which has to be accommodated in the scheme and possibly insured against.

Planning

As RICS confirms (2008a: 4) in the context of devolved government the planning regime differs between England, Wales, Scotland and Northern Ireland and thus it is not possible here to explore variations in all four systems. For practical purposes the emphasis here is upon the system in England and readers will need to check the relevant websites for variations across jurisdictions.

Planning is a broad topic and thus only some of the key aspects which are likely to impact upon the development of a large site are covered here. Those seeking a more comprehensive coverage of the subject could consult Cullingworth and Nadin (2006) or Ratcliffe *et al.* (2009).

The implementation of planning policies by local planning authorities will affect the development potential and hence value of sites in a number of different ways. To begin with, national planning policies in England are set out in a series of Planning Policy Statements published by the Department for Communities and Local Government and those policies cascade downwards

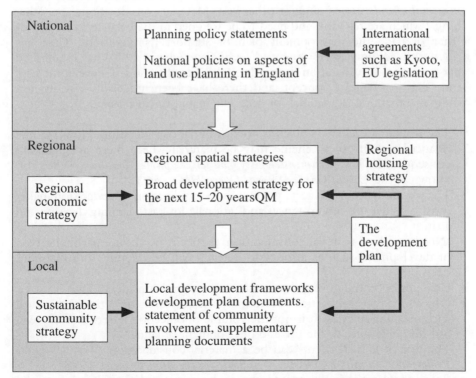

Figure 2.2 Concept of the development plan

to be implemented at local government level. In England under the Planning and Compulsory Purchase Act 2004 national policies are shaped at the regional level in Regional Spatial Strategies (RSSs) before being given precise geographical identity at local level in Local Development Frameworks (LDFs).

The LDF is really a folder of documents containing the local authority's core planning policies as well as supplementary planning documents covering such things as urban design, development briefs for specific sites and conservation area policies. The LDF must also set out how the authority is going to approach public consultation on planning and there must be a sustainability appraisal to show that the policies adopted by the local authority are the most sustainable options available.

As Figure 2.2 above suggests the concept of the development plan is a combination of relevant policies drawn from the RSS and LDF as applicable to a particular planning application. Local authorities have a duty to operate a 'plan-led system' when they make development control decisions under the Planning and Compulsory Purchase 2004 Act, s. 38 of which states that:

> where the development plan contains relevant policies, applications for planning permission should be determined in line with the plan, unless material considerations indicate otherwise.

Local authorities should therefore follow their own planning policies unless '*material considerations*' suggest otherwise. Material considerations are 'other things' which are relevant, and need to be weighed in the balance to see if they either override the development plan or support its provisions. Case law (*Stringer* v. *Minister of Housing and Local Government*, 1970) has established that a material consideration is one that relates to the use and development of land. This is a delicate concept, and there have been numerous cases to test whether something is 'material' or not. The main principles are:

- The size of a developer's profit is not a material consideration. However, the financial viability of a scheme may be material where there are planning consequences (*R* v. *Westminster City Council, ex parte Monahan*, 1988; also known as the *Covent Garden, Royal Opera House* case).
- The planning history of a site is a material consideration. The decision maker must consider the circumstances and rationale for past planning decisions on a site.
- 'Need' can be a material consideration. A special need for a particular type of development such as affordable housing will be relevant to a planning decision.
- Changes in central government policy are material considerations.
- Objections by third parties can be material. However, objections must deal with planning matters. It is not the volume of objection letters that matters, but their relevance to the use and development of land.
- The fear of local residents can be a material consideration (*West Midlands Probation Committee* v. *Secretary of State for the Environment*, 1998).
- Creating an undesirable precedent can be a material consideration (*Collis Radio Ltd* v. *Secretary of State for the Environment*, 1975).

If a site did not possess a planning consent, then a developer would need to take advice from a planning consultant on what the balance of development plan policies and material considerations might mean for a particular site. The same would be true at appeal where there has been a refusal of planning consent as planning inspectors are under the same duty as local authorities to apply the plan-led system. Readers who are interested in exploring some of the intricacies of case law in this field could examine Smith (2006).

Planning obligations and affordable housing

From a developer's perspective one of the key documents in an authority's LDF folder is that setting out the authority's policy on planning obligations, sometimes referred to as a tariff. This document may contain formulas which are used to calculate in monetary terms planning obligations which will be sought from developers.

For example Westminster City Council's (2008) *Supplementary Planning Guidance on Planning Obligations* sets out how the Council will seek contributions from commercial and housing developers to contribute to CCTV instillation, public realm improvements, open space, social, community and cultural projects, education contributions, parking provision and monitoring costs. Of course not all developments would qualify to contribute under all of these headings although increasingly larger developments will end up making payments under several different headings and this can amount to significant project costs. For example in Westminster's document the formula for calculating developer contributions for improving the public realm is set at £150 per m^2 of office floorspace in schemes of 200m^2 or more. Thus where an 800m^2 office building is redeveloped to provide 1,800m^2 of new space the Council will seek a contribution of 1,000 $m^2 \times$ £150 per m^2 = £150,000.

As well as tariff-based policies in LDFs, there are normally policy expectations on affordable housing provision and these must also be factored into a developer's residual valuation, as the effect of these policies can have considerable effect on site values. For example in the London Borough of Camden (2006) one of the planning policies bearing upon affordable housing requires that where the floorspace yield from a redevelopment will be at least 200m^2 greater than the existing floorspace then 50 per cent of that increase should normally be devoted to housing i.e. at least 100m^2. Of the housing element created, the policy requires that 50 per cent be affordable housing.

For example, on a 0.25 hectare site there might exist a redundant four-storey office block covering 65 per cent of the site and whose gross floorspace was therefore 6,500m^2. A developer wishing to redevelop the site to achieve 75 per cent site coverage with a six-storey building would be achieving around 11,250m^2 of floorspace which is an increase on the original building of around 4,750m^2. The Council would therefore begin negotiations with the developer on the basis that 50 per cent of 4,750m^2, i.e. 2,375m^2 would be residential and that might yield 36 flats after allowing for deductions for common areas. However it would further be the Council's expectation that 18 of the 36 flats would be affordable with the ownership of these units normally transferring to a registered provider such as a housing association. Of the 18 flats Camden's policy requires that 70 per cent be social rented (say 13 flats) and the remainder

(5 flats) be intermediate tenure such as shared ownership. The valuation of such a development would therefore be entirely different to the valuation of an 11,250m^2 office scheme.

Of course the precise outcome of policies like the Camden example above is subject to negotiation between the developer and the local authority. The percentage quotas are in fact policy targets and it may not be financially possible to achieve 50 per cent housing and then 50 per cent affordable housing in every development. However it is also unrealistic for a developer to claim that policy targets cannot be met without providing some evidence to support the assertion. This is where development appraisal toolkits and open-book accounting come into play.

In the context of the Camden example, the 3 Dragons development appraisal toolkit promoted by the Greater London Authority is often used to provide evidence that a certain percentage of affordable housing can be achieved. A similar model is used to identify whether the inclusion of affordable housing may justify grant support from the Homes and Communities Agency (HCA). That model is called the Economic Appraisal Tool and it can be downloaded from the HCA web site at: www.homesandcommunities.co.uk.

Appraisal toolkits are sophisticated Excel versions of the residual valuation and they require developers to input scheme data into the model and submit this to a council as part of the planning application process. A council will then normally ask an independent valuer to look at the figures and the outcome might (for example) be that only 40 per cent affordable housing can be achieved in a scheme because it has other infrastructure costs to bear such as payments for school places (also required by the council). When the council is satisfied with the figures planning consent is granted subject to an agreement under the Town and County Planning Act 1990, s. 106 which binds the developer and secures payments for other items of infrastructure as required in the particular scheme.

During the credit crunch some councils have shown sympathy with arguments from developers that schemes simply cannot support the volume of demands made upon them in terms of affordable housing plus infrastructure payments. Some councils have thus not pressed a hard policy bargain while others have agreed to revisit s. 106 agreements where work has not started on sites or has stalled in the financial climate.

The Community Infrastructure Levy (CIL) under the Planning Act 2008 will take a lot of the negotiation out of the equation as it will attach a fixed charge to a site based upon costed infrastructure. This upfront cost will be listed in an authority's charging schedule. Thus any developer interested in a site can inspect the charging schedule to establish if there is going to be an infrastructure cost which will need to be factored into the residual valuation and subsequent land bid.

At the time of writing, further detailed secondary legislation and regulation are required before the CIL can become fully operational. The statutory position at present is that the CIL is a voluntary option which local authorities may choose to adopt or they may choose to continue with a tariff-based system. However, given the greater transparency promised by the introduction of a CIL system, it is likely that it will ultimately become mandatory and will replace negotiated planning agreements. Given that this is an area of law which is in state of flux but which is very likely to have implications for development costs RICS (2009c) has published an information paper on the implementation of provisions in the 2008 Act which it will update as the secondary regulations become finalised.

Development density

There are also density standards in LDFs which govern the number of housing units which may be developed in proportion to site size. For example in Westminster (2007) there are four density zones reflecting the character of different parts of the council's jurisdiction.

Zone 1: 400–850 habitable rooms per hectare (hrh)
Zone 2: 250–500 hrh
Zone 3: 200–350 hrh
Zone 4: 120–350 hrh

A habitable room in this context includes living rooms, bedrooms and kitchens if they are over $12.5m^2$. Bathrooms, toilets, landings and lobbies are excluded from the calculation. The site area for density calculations is measured to the centre of surrounding roads to a maximum of 6 metres. The point of these policies is to try to prevent over-development sometimes referred to as town-cramming, although the City Council acknowledges that the parameters are one factor to consider among others and this is not simply planning by numbers.

Environmental Impact Assessment (EIA)

In England the Town and Country Planning (Environmental Impact Assessment) Regulations 1999 (and 2008 amendments) require that EIA be undertaken to evaluate the environmental effects of a development before it is allowed to be built. The objective is to identify any 'significant effects on the environment' that a project would have and then to see whether those effects could be mitigated satisfactorily. If they cannot, then the project should be refused planning consent.

The regulations identify 'Schedule 1 developments' for which EIA is mandatory and these include crude oil refineries, nuclear power stations and waste disposal incinerators.

For so called 'Schedule 2 developments' EIA may be required, depending on the 'screening opinion' given by the local authority (or Secretary of State on appeal) when the project is assessed against threshold criteria in the regulations. Examples of Schedule 2 developments include large urban development projects, peat extraction, marinas, holiday villages, wind farms, motorway service areas and coastal defence works.

The outcome of various EIA cases is that the courts have taken the regulations to have 'wide scope and broad purpose'. This means that if a project is likely to have a significant effect on the environment, then it will require EIA. In practice this means that most major developments proposed by either the public or private sectors will qualify for EIA.

Where EIA is required, it is the developer's responsibility to employ a team of specialists to carry out the EIA. The 'scope' of the EIA is agreed between the developer and the local planning authority and this determines which aspects of the environment will be assessed in order to predict the 'impact' of the proposed development.

The consultants' assessments are written-up in a document called the Environmental Statement (ES). The ES, which is submitted with the planning application, must contain:

- a description of the proposed development;
- a description and data on the likely effects on flora, fauna, people, landscape and heritage;
- mitigation measures to remedy the identified effects;
- a non-technical summary.

The local authority may employ consultants to check parts (or all) of the ES and they may request further information if a topic has not been covered adequately. The local planning authority and other public bodies must cooperate with the developer's team during the EIA by allowing access to relevant documents and data. Copies of ESs must be made available for sale and as public consultation documents during the 16 weeks allowed for the determination by the LPA. Authors, such as Glasson *et al.* (2005), have explored the EIA process in some depth but what is clear it that developers of sites of any significance will be facing this process. This will inevitably add upfront professional fees to an already demanding and expensive planning stage of a project when local authorities also require transport impact studies, green travel plans and design and access statements.

Third-party service providers

In addition to discussion with the local planning authority, it will usually be necessary to consult service providers to ensure the availability of gas, water, sewerage, surface drainage, electricity, telephones and transport infrastructure including road connections. Given the congestion on most roads today the latter can be a costly and problematic issue for developers where larger sites such as housing estates, business or retail parks are being developed. Thus a key member of the developer's team will be the highways consultant who will undertake traffic modelling exercises with the highways authority and from that an agreement under the Highways Act 1980, s.278 may surface. The latter would normally involve some form of trigger mechanism whereby highways capacity improvements are geared to the progress made on the development site. Alternative arrangements can occur under what are termed Grampian conditions, where a development cannot be commenced in advance of the completion of highways works by the highways authority or other offsite agent.

2.4 Site appraisal

A thorough physical survey of the site is essential and as RICS (2008a: 3) points out this may include assessing the extent of the site, its shape and topography, evaluating the condition of existing buildings (if any), assessment of flood risk, recording the nature and scale of surrounding buildings, identifying whether party wall, boundary or rights to light might be issues, assessing geotechnical conditions, identifying landscape features, verifying access, the presence of services, archaeological remains and establishing if there is ground contamination.

It is not proposed to unpack all of those issues in this chapter but rather to focus upon some of the key issues which are most likely to present challenges in the context of the development of a large site.

Access

Access can be for vehicles or pedestrians or both. For non-residential development access is required for service vehicles and in some situations this needs to be separated from the access provided to customers and staff. Vehicle access could be difficult where for example there are strict traffic management systems in older densely developed heritage town centres. Conventional vehicle access may not be possible and so there might be a need for deliveries to be made out of normal shopping hours. In situations where there is pedestrian access only, there may need to be some form of offsite collection point for heavy goods.

The highways authority will need to be consulted where a new crossover is required into a site from a road and there must be adequate visibility splays for traffic entering and leaving a site before highways officers will support a planning application.

Ground conditions

The ground conditions of a site will vary due to geology and whether the site is greenfield or has been previously developed and is therefore a brownfield site. An assessment of the subsoil to identify its load-bearing capacity will be necessary to determine the type of foundations required. It may be necessary to pile foundations if a firmer base is required. A ground condition survey will include the digging of trial pits and the sinking of boreholes in key positions. Some examples of difficult ground conditions are:

- The erection of two-storey housing on clay subsoil, particularly in the vicinity of tree growth. In this situation more expensive foundations and/or protection against tree root damage and removal or lopping of the trees, may be necessary to restrict movement to the foundation caused by the shrinkage of the clay or heave (expansion due to excess moisture in the clay).
- There could be underground cavities where land has been filled but not compacted properly. There may also be underground voids caused by mining or caverns in the rock formation.
- There could be landslip in areas of coastal erosion or on steep embankments where surface water may accentuate the problem.
- There could be underground structures, particularly in industrial areas, such as storage tanks, foundations or wells. These problems may link to those of contamination mentioned later.

Landscape features

The nature of tree growth and landscaping on the site may determine the surface water run-off and drainage, as well as providing an attractive setting for the development. In the case of science and business parks the quality of the landscape will be one of the determining factors in securing lettings and sales.

Services

The services running over the land are usually electricity or telephone cables while those running below the ground may be cables, drain runs, water or gas mains.

Drains underground include both foul and surface water. A foul water sewer crossing a site will normally have a width of 3 metres to each side in which building is prohibited to ensure access to the sewer. Local authorities should have details of where surface water and foul water sewers are running. For the other services it would be necessary to contact the relevant service provider.

Overhead cables, although unsightly, may provide less restraint on development. There is, apparently, no reason why buildings cannot be erected underneath providing an appropriate gap is provided. However, property owners do not generally like this prospect and there are lingering although unproven concerns regarding possible health hazards to people living close to electricity pylons. From a marketing perspective it is difficult to sell or let property under or close to pylons. Major pylons carry 132kv or 400kv lines and the cost of grounding or diverting these cables is prohibitively expensive in all but rare examples. However it may be economical to move or ground smaller power lines such as those carrying 11kv or 33kv.

Surface water drainage

The development of a site will affect the water table and drainage. The run-off for surface water can be provided in the development in a number of different ways depending on the ground conditions and the extent of the water run-off involved. It could, for instance, run off to soakaways or into a drainage system connected to surface ditches, watercourses or drains. There are cost implications depending on the choice.

An example of the need to provide surface water drainage was in the development of land at Beckton, north of the Royal Docks in London. The area was left as surplus to the original dock development, although it was envisaged that it would be developed for docks at a later time. However, the need never arose because the docks moved to the mouth of the Thames due to the increased size of ships and containerisation. Because of the nature of the surface water run-off and the low-lying topography at Beckton, the land drained into ditches which connected to drainage outlets which discharged into the River Thames.

In the 1980s Beckton attracted a considerable volume of housing and commercial development necessitating the installation of surface water drainage driven by a pumping station to achieve the outflow into the Thames. The provision of this type of drainage work is very expensive and beyond the scope of individual developers to provide and it is in these circumstances where the infrastructure may be provided by a specialist regeneration agency, as in that case the London Docklands Development Corporation.

Flooding

Because of climate change, flooding has become more of a concern for property owners. The updated flood risk maps produced by the Environment Agency in 2009 reveal that around 5.2 million residential and commercial properties in England are at some risk from river, coastal or surface flooding although the degree of risk varies.

It might be supposed that these property owners have some recourse to government to protect their property from flooding but as RICS (2009b: 11) point out there is no general legal right to the provision of flood defences. Public authorities have permissive powers to construct and maintain flood defences but there is no obligation upon them to do so. In essence public authorities do what they can within the budgets available to them. However if they should decide to alter their priorities perhaps by sacrificing one area in order to bolster flood defences elsewhere there is no right of compensation to owners who are subsequently flooded. Not surprisingly therefore, the market simply devalues properties that are prone to flooding.

Given that there are increased risks of flooding which will affect some sites this is an issue which a prudent developer would investigate before committing to a site. This is particularly so given that the Environment Agency's position is that developers should pay for the management of any increased flood risk which they create. Payment can embrace the capital costs of flood defences and attenuation schemes and the ongoing maintenance costs. To forgive the pun, flood risk is an issue which can literally sink a developer's scheme.

An inspection of the Environment Agency's Flood Map (2009) is an obvious first step and if that reveals a risk of any significance then a developer would need to discuss the flood risk implications with the local authority. Local authorities in England have an obligation arising in *Planning Policy Statement 25 (PPS 25): Development and Flood Risk* (Communities and Local Government, 2006) to include flood risk as a material consideration in the planning process, having taken the advice of the Environment Agency.

The policy requires authorities to take a risk-based approach by applying a sequential test so that new development is steered to areas of land with the lowest probability of flooding. That land is zoned in accordance with the Environment Agency's Flood Map. Where it is not possible to locate development in Zone 1, then authorities may consider locating development in Zone 2, where there is a medium risk of flooding, subject to a flood risk assessment. The flood risk assessment will recommend actions required to reduce the flood risk to acceptable levels. This might involve placing planning obligations on developers to improve flood defences or apply sustainable drainage techniques on sites.

A similar principle applies in Zone 3a although the policy limits the uses which should be considered for this zone given that it has a higher probability of flooding. Zone 3b is the floodplain and development should obviously be avoided if at all possible here although where floodplain capacity is not lost there may be scope to accommodate water-compatible development such as docks, marinas, wharves and pumping stations.

The brief summary in Table 2.1 below is included to illustrate the principle of the sequential test and is not a definitive guide to the policy. It is not possible to summarise all of the detail and conditional circumstances explored in the 50-page policy document and the accompanying 156-page practice guide (Communities and Local Government, 2008) which sets out how the policy should be implemented in any particular setting.

Readers who are particularly interested in this topic should obviously explore its contents, available at: www.communities.gov.uk. There are comparable policies produced by the respective administrations in Wales, Scotland and Northern Ireland.

The Rochester Riverside site mentioned earlier in this chapter has a long frontage onto the River Medway and due to the site's low elevation and the poor condition of the existing river wall there was a high risk of flooding. In terms of *PPS25* the site required a flood risk assessment (FRA) before any planning application could be considered. The FRA confirmed the flood risk and

Table 2.1 A brief summary of the *PPS 25* risk-based sequential test for flooding

Environment Agency Flood Zone	Probability of flooding	Statistical probability of flooding	Appropriate uses
1	Low	Less than a 1 in 1,000 years or less than 0.1 per cent	All uses of land.
2	Medium	Between 1 in 100 and 1 in 1,000 years or between 0.1 per cent and 1 per cent.	Water-compatible uses such as shipbuilding and repair, commercial developments such as shops, offices and factories, hospitals and housing.
3a	High	Greater than 1 in 100 years or more than a 1 per cent chance.	Water-compatible uses such as shipbuilding and repair, commercial developments such as shops, offices and factories.
3b	Very high – the floodplain	Greater than 1 in 20 years or more than a 5 per cent chance of flooding.	Only water-compatible uses such as shipbuilding and repair and essential infrastructure which can be designed to operate safely in times of flood while not impeding flood waters.

suggested that without improved flood defences the site would not be suitable for housing development. Given that the Council sought a mixed-use development including 2,000 housing units, the flood risk was a serious deterrent to the regeneration which the Council wished to see take place on the site.

Given the extent of the river frontage, the scale of the engineering works to repair and replace sections of the riverside wall and to raise its overall height would be significant. The flood risk assessment also recommended that the level of the land needed to be raised to 5.8 metres above ordinance datum (AOD) by surcharging so that ground floors of buildings could be constructed 300mm above that to achieve 6.1 metres AOD. This level would achieve a flood probability of 1 in 200 years which is an acceptable flood risk for the mixed-use development envisage by the Council.

Given the scale of the works required at Rochester Riverside, there was little chance that a private developer would take on this degree of risk in this particular location. In order to create some development momentum the South East England Development Agency (SEEDA) became involved in the project as partner to the Council as would be expected of a regional development agency whose remit is to tackle problems such as this.

SEEDA entered into an s.106 agreement with Medway Council (2004b) in order to assist on the flood defence works along with other preparatory works including decontamination, some compulsory purchase of small pockets of land and some off site highways improvements. The work was coordinated in a master plan prepared for the site by consultants acting for the Council and SEEDA. The partnership was able to attract a central government grant of £38 million under the Thames Gateway programme which illustrates the scale of investment required on these large problematic sites.

This type of public investment in regeneration projects, sometimes referred to as 'pump priming', is ultimately evaluated by the Audit Commission to assess its effectiveness in attracting subsequent private investment. Other expressions used in this context are 'leverage ratio' in that for every £1 of public money invested in a site there might subsequently be £5 invested by the private sector. These ratios will vary from site to site depending on the scale of preparatory works required, the location of the site, the scale of development permitted by the local authority and the degree of risk perceived by the private sector. What could be said is that without this pump-priming activity on sites such as the Rochester Riverside it is unlikely that they would ever attract the quality of developers required to invest in such sites.

Contamination

In the interests of fostering sustainable development government policy steers commercial and residential development towards previously developed land known as brownfield sites, so that those sites can be recycled. Because a site has previously been developed it does not necessarily mean that it is contaminated and in fact only a minority of brownfield sites will be contaminated. However in some circumstances contamination can present a challenge and in very serious cases the cost of decontamination and remediation can render land valueless. Potentially contaminated sites will be those where there has been a history of industrial activity such as those used for chemical processing, petroleum and oil processing and storage, gasworks, manufacturing, metal treatment and sites where there has been landfill activity.

Under provisions in the Environmental Protection Act 1990 and the Environment Act 1995 local authorities in conjunction with the Environment Agency have a duty to identify and enforce the remediation of contaminated sites and this obligation will normally fall upon the owner of such sites. Where a developer therefore suspects that a site may be contaminated due to its previous use, it is prudent to commission an environmental risk assessment from suitably qualified consultants.

Consultants will normally begin by looking at historical maps to ascertain the extent of industrial activity before taking soil samples for laboratory analysis and assessing whether contaminants may have migrated into neighbouring land or water courses. In the vast majority of cases there are known remediation techniques which may simply involve containment by clay slurry trenching and capping. There are of course more elaborate techniques as described by experts such as Syms (2004) and they may be recommended depending on the uses envisaged for the site and the extent of the contamination. Armed with this information a developer can factor the costs into a residual valuation so that the additional development costs are reflected in the land value.

However for some large sites where the problems are serious the effect may be to prevent the land coming forward for development and its presence may therefore have a blighting effect on a locality. For example the Woolwich Arsenal site in south-east London was one such site where there had been several centuries of heavy industrial activity linked to armaments manufacture. When production finally ceased the site had negative values from a property development perspective simply because of the scale of the clean-up required. In that situation English Partnerships (now the Homes and Communities Agency) and latterly the London Development Agency stepped in to remediate the site before it could become a property development opportunity which Berkeley Homes have subsequently exploited.

In these situations there can therefore be heavy upfront expenditure by public sector agencies and in order to recover at least some of those costs, disposal of a remediated site to a private developer would normally include an overage or claw-back clause in the exchange contract. These clauses ensure that when development value is realised by a developer in future years, the public agency will receive a share of the returns in order to offset some of the early costs incurred.

2.5 Economic and market analysis

Property developers operate in a demand-led market where because of the time taken to acquire a site, obtain planning consent and build a scheme there is always a time lag between supply responding to demand. To use economic jargon there is an inelastic supply response. Given this time delay it is quite easy for market conditions to deteriorate just after a commitment has been made by a developer to a scheme. This became increasingly evident as the credit crunch took effect in 2008–9. Given the scale of investment involved in property development and the potential scale of the losses there is a requirement for market research and some economic analysis to try to help developers harmonise the supply of their projects with market cycles.

Particularly with regards to speculative development a developer will have to form a judgement about what the market actually needs and whether that demand will sustain over what might be a lengthy development period. To begin with RICS (2008a: 6) has provided a helpful checklist to stimulate thinking around what factors are likely to influence the degree of market demand for a project. These factors include owner-occupier and investor's specific requirements, the location, access and the availability of transport routes, car parking facilities, amenities attractive to tenants and/or purchasers, the scale of the development in terms of sale or lettable packages, the form of the development and market supply, including actual or proposed competing developments.

It is not easy to assimilate all of these factors in an objective manner especially when a developer is facing multiple challenges on different fronts. This is why developers and those institutions lending to developers might wish to take some arm's length advice on whether there is sufficient demand for an envisaged project. Given that some property loans made before the onset of the credit crunch have left some funding institutions facing significant losses, it is likely that when the pace of development quickens after the credit crunch that there will be renewed interest in property forecasting and market research.

Market research

Aspects of this topic are explored in chapter 10 on marketing and disposal and so this section provides an overview of the salient points bearing upon the development appraisal stage of a project.

RICS (2009a) places significance on the role of market research at the initial stage of what it terms the development management process. During this phase the developer is working up an initial concept and as part of that process would ideally commission market research to identify if there is sufficient demand for what is being proposed. The rational advice from RICS is clear:

> Abandon the concept of development if the market research indicates that the development is unlikely to succeed. (RICS 2009a: 4)

Given that market research plays a potentially key role, authors such as Barkham (2002) have tried to set out how the market research process should be undertaken in a property context if it is to add any value.

Barkham suggests that at the outset market research in this field should take an overview of national economic trends so that a view can be formed on whether a development is likely to be launched in a strengthening or weakening economic climate. Thus obvious sources become forecasts produced by the Bank of England and those produced by RICS (2008b) in which a specific property focus is taken. However even here economic indicators such as rising GDP for example might signify rising productivity of the workforce rather than company expansions which might convert into increased demand for business space. Awareness also needs to be given to social and technological change which is not apparent in historical time series data. Thus a shift towards Internet shopping might translate into a further decline in the traditional high street but a greater demand for large distribution warehouses well connected to the national motorway network.

Large firms of chartered surveyors such as CBRE and Cushman and Wakefield have research departments which provide periodic updates on property market data in specific markets so that movements in yields and rents can be monitored. These firms as well as specialist consultancies such as Investment Property Databank can also be commissioned to undertake bespoke market research.

As Barkham (2002: 61–72) explains, analysts such as the above who are operating on a specific market research commission would then be expected to look locally at the interplay between demand and supply. For example the availability of sites and the pipeline of planning consents for similar types of development would form part of the supply side analysis. On the demand side market research might explore business expansions, in-moves and churn (movement from properties at lease expiration) in a locality.

As well as focusing upon the quantitative dimension it might be expected that market research considers qualitative issues in a property sub-market. For example an analyst considering the supply and demand for offices in a particular locality might be able to comment on whether there is demand for high-quality BREEAM excellent-rated sustainable office buildings which is not currently satisfied in a locality.

In the aftermath of the banking crisis in the UK it became clear that there was a culture in financial and property circles that tended to ignore those who

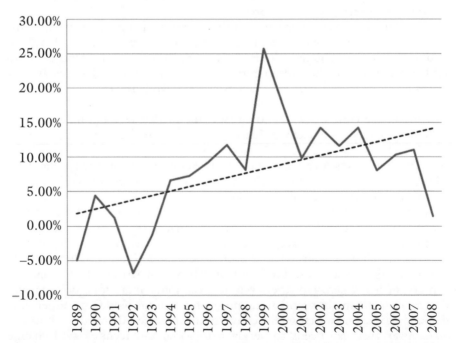

Figure 2.3 Annual percentage change in sales values of purpose-built flats in London over 20 years

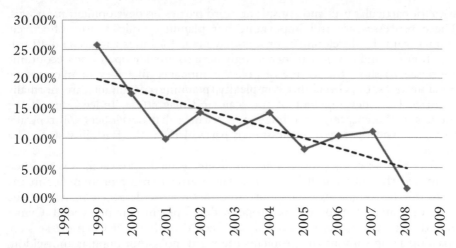

Figure 2.4 Annual percentage change in sales values of purpose-built flats in London over 10 years

suggested caution or presented negative forecasts. This is obviously a cultural difficulty which forecasters often face especially since sceptics would argue that the extrapolation of historic trends is seldom reliable. For example Figure 2.3 above is based upon data published by the Department for Communities and Local Government (2009) showing the change in annual sales values of purpose-built flats across Greater London over a 20-year period. The trend line if extrapolated into the future would predict ever increasing annual values of flats and this might be read as a very encouraging sign by residential developers. However if only the last ten years of the data were selected as being more representative (also presented above in Figure 2.4) then the trend line changes significantly and the extrapolation of that line would suggest ever falling flat values in future.

2.6 Summary

This chapter began by looking at the various ways that exploitable sites may be identified and it was found that this varies considerably between types of developer. Volume housebuilders typically require a land bank to keep front-end production supplied with developable sites while speculative commercial developers might operate on an entirely different basis working from what business tenants or property investors might be perceived to need.

It was found that sites become available in a variety of ways, the more problematic and risk prone might surface at property auctions while others may be identified by land agents. Large regeneration-related sites might come to fruition after considerable site preparation work by public bodies to remove or minimise risks such as contamination and flooding.

Given the legitimate ambitions to foster sustainable development and the reuse of brownfield sites, the planning system is tasking developers much harder than it once did. The planning agenda now goes well beyond zoning sites for particular uses and consulting third parties on development proposals. These processes are still important, but planning policies now effectively extract from the development process payments for infrastructure and affordable housing and developers increasingly have to provide open-book economic appraisals to show the degree of policy compliance that may or may not be possible on sites. Given this complexity, planning consultants are normally required for a development of any scale and magnitude. Indeed one of the themes in the chapter is the increasing reliance that developers will typically have on a wide variety of professionals particularly at the feasibility stage of a project.

Towards the end of the chapter the issue of market research was touched upon and this might well be a topic which attracts more prominence in the wake of a banking crisis which illustrated that a more detached analysis of the risks associated with speculative property development may be needed. Cynics would argue that the analysis has always been there but that when markets are coasting along without any problems the word 'no' is not popular and seldom acted upon. The topic of market research is explored in more depth in chapter 10 of the book.

References

Barkham, R. (2002) 'Market research for office real estate', ch. 4 in Guy, S. and Henneberry, J. (eds), *Development and Developers: Perspectives on Property* (Oxford: Blackwell Science).

Communities and Local Government (2006) *Planning Policy Statement 25: Development and Flood Risk* (London: Stationery Office). Available in e-format at: www. communities.gov.uk/planningandbuilding/planning/planningpolicyguidance/ planningpolicystatements/planningpolicystatements/pps25/

Communities and Local Government (2008) *Planning Policy Statement 25: Development and Flood Risk-Practice Guide* (London: Stationery Office). Available in e-format at: www.communities.gov.uk/documents/planningandbuilding/pdf/pps25 practiceguide.pdf

Communities and Local Government (2009) 'Live tables on housing market and house prices – table 511 housing market: simple average house prices by dwelling type, region, United Kingdom from 1986'. Available in e-format at: www.communities.gov.uk/housing/housingresearch/housingstatistics/housing statisticsby/housingmarket/livetables/ [accessed 16.7.09]

Cullingworth, B. and Nadin, V. (2006) *Town and Country Planning in the UK*, 14th edition (London: Routledge).

Environment Agency 'Flood Map and how to use it', web page accessed 19.08.2009 at: www.environment-agency.gov.uk/homeandleisure/floods/31656.aspx

Glasson, J., Therivel, R. and Chadwick, A. (2005) *Introduction to Environmental Impact Assessment*, 3rd edition (London: Routledge).

Homes and Communities Agency (2009) 'Economic Appraisal Tool', web page and downloadable model at: www.homesandcommunities.co.uk/economic-appraisal-tool.htm

London Borough of Camden (2006) *Unitary Development Plan* (Camden Council). Available in e-format at: www.camden.gov.uk/ccm/navigation/environment/ planning-and-built-environment/our-plans-and-policies/camden-s-unitary-development-plan-udp-/

Medway Council (2004a) 'Rochester Riverside Development Brief', Medway Council. Available in e-format at: www.medway.gov.uk/rochester_riverside_development_brief-3.pdf

Medway Council (2004b) 'Outline Planning Application MC2004/2030 regarding land at Rochester Riverside and related Section 106 agreement'. Available in e-format at: www.medway.gov.uk/index/environment/planning/planapp/planonline.htm?cfid=12529&st=1

Office of the Deputy Prime Minister (2003) *Sustainable Communities: Building for the Future* (London: ODPM). Available at: www.communities.gov.uk/documents/communities/pdf/146289.pdf

Ratcliffe, J., Stubbs, M. and Keeping, M. (2009) *Urban Planning and Real Estate Development*, 3rd edition (London: Routledge).

Royal Institution of Chartered Surveyors (2008a) *Valuation Information Paper No. 12: Valuation of Development Land* (London: RICS).

Royal Institution of Chartered Surveyors (2008b) *Commercial Property Forecast* (London: RICS). Available in e-format at: www.rics.org/NR/rdonlyres/631D9200–FADC-48D4-958D-B0C8F5B8773B/0/commercial_forecast_1208.pdf

Royal Institution of Chartered Surveyors (2009a) *RICS Guidance Note: Development Management* (London: RICS).

Royal Institution of Chartered Surveyors (2009b) *RICS Information Paper: Flooding: Issues of Concern to Chartered Surveyors* (London: RICS).

Royal Institution of Chartered Surveyors (2009c) *RICS Information Paper: Planning Act 2008: Delivering Infrastructure* (London: RICS).

Smith, R. E. (2006) *Planning Control – Development Permission and Enforcement* (London: RICS Books).

Syms, P. (2004) *Previously Developed Land: Industrial Activities and Contamination*, 2nd edition (Oxford: Blackwell Science).

Westminster City Council (2007) *Unitary Development Plan* (London: Westminster City Council). Available in e-format at: www.westminster.gov.uk/services/environment/planning/unitarydevelopmentplan/

Westminster City Council (2008) *Supplementary Planning Guidance on Planning Obligations* (London: Westminster City Council). Available in e-format at: www.westminster.gov.uk

Wilkinson, S. and Reed, R. (2008) *Property Development*, 5th edition (London: Routledge).

3

The residual valuation

Aims

This chapter explores the residual valuation technique which is used to value land with development potential. The chapter also explains how this technique can be adapted to identify the profit arising from development where the land value is given. The concept of sensitivity testing in property valuation is introduced and valuation formulas used in the calculation of development value are considered towards the end of the chapter.

Key terms

>> **Initial yield** – the rate of interest which reflects the rental income from a property relative to its capital value at the point when a property is purchased.

>> **Present value** – a sum of money receivable in future discounted by the prevailing rate of interest to reflect its present-day value.

>> **Sensitivity test** – adjustments made to the large value and cost variables in a residual valuation to identify the effect that this has on the residual land value. Where small adjustments to key variables generate a large swing in land value, a volatile and risky scheme may have been identified and risk reduction measures may be required.

>> **S-curve** – a graphic depiction of the cumulative drawn down of a loan facility by a developer to pay for construction work over a contract period.

>> **RICS** – the Royal Institution of Chartered Surveyors which is the pre-eminent organisation for professionals working in the land, property and construction sectors in the UK and around the world.

3.1 Introduction

This chapter explores the residual valuation method which is widely used in practice to determine the value of sites with development potential. The chapter also explores sensitivity testing because a residual valuation can be very sensitive to slight variations in its key variables such as rent, initial yield, construction costs, finance rate and building period. Because of this potential volatility the technique has attracted criticism from the Lands Tribunal in cases as far back as 1965: *Clinker and Ash Ltd* v. *Southern Gas Board*. In that case the Tribunal felt that because the variables could be manipulated on the back of assumptions, that almost any land value could be generated (the case and its implications are discussed at some length by Scarrett, 2008: 117–20). The Tribunal has on a number of occasions since indicated that wherever possible the comparative method should be used as it is more straightforward and transparent.

Despite the Land Tribunal's scepticism regarding the residual method, it continues to be used widely in practice. This is because as discussed in chapter 1 and confirmed by authors such as Dubben (2008: 361) there are limitations in the comparison method when faced with complex development proposals. The comparative method therefore tends to fulfil a secondary role by providing a benchmark against which to check that the outturn figures from a residual are realistic.

The distinction between valuation and analysis

The property crash in the early 1970s focused attention on valuation methods used by the property profession. In the period since, there has been an expectation that valuation professionals would continuously seek to improve the quality and standard of the valuations produced. Large-scale investment for instance has taken place in recent years by the financial institutions and the investment advisers acting for these institutions require more explicit market evidence and analytical techniques to be used in valuation work.

Because in some cases the actual returns on property investments have not reflected the target returns predicted, there has been debate about the validity of the methods used. There is also much more awareness now of the responsibilities of the professional to clients' needs, specifically, that property professionals should not just act as agents but provide, during the buying and selling process, some idea to the client of the forecast of income arising from the investment.

The findings of RICS's Mallinson Report in 1994 suggested that the valuer should obtain clearer instructions from the client and should explain the valuation of property in company accounts. In addition, the report suggested that there should be more comment on valuation risk factors, price trends and economic factors and the use of more refined discounted cash flow techniques. Subsequent editions of RICS's Valuation Standards colloquially known as 'the Red Book' and now in its sixth edition (2007a) have built upon these principles.

The debate resulted in a clearer distinction being drawn between property valuation and property analysis. As previously mentioned in chapter 1, the approach that should be taken is that the overall property appraisal should be clearly divided between property valuation for purchase (that is the valuation for market price) and the subsequent analysis of performance. The former case is defined as valuation and in the latter is defined as analysis, the overall process is generally termed 'property appraisal'.

The valuation of a property is therefore the calculation of the exchange value of a property which is different from the subsequent analysis of the performance of the investment, which is the appraisal of its actual worth. Calculations before and after purchase will not always agree because of the lack of perfect knowledge in the market at the time of the transaction and the inability to predict accurately the future changes in the cash flow and the risk profile of the investment. Thus the techniques discussed later in this book can be used to anticipate the market value or to record and analyse the progress of the investment subsequent to purchase. However, it is still important to understand the difference between these two approaches.

Simplified residual valuation

Returning to the theme of valuation, RICS (2008: 9) confirm that the basis of the calculation for a residual valuation is:

value of completed development
less the cost of carrying out the development (including a profit element)
equals the amount available to pay for the land

In the simplified example below the figures are hypothetical, as market conditions change over time and from location to location. The important elements: the rents, yields, interest rates, costs and fees must be estimated from the market conditions.

A proposed office development on a city centre site has the following project details:

Gross floor area	1,000 m^2
Rental value	£500 per m^2
Building cost	£1,100 per m^2
Profit as a percentage of cost	20%

Appraisal	£	
Gross development value:		
Net lettable floor area (80% of gross)	800	
Rental value £ per m^2	500	
Annual rental income £	400,000	
Yield at 7.5%	13.33 YP	
Capital value		5,332,000

Development costs:

Building cost		
1,000 m² @ £1,100 per m²	1,100,000	
Professional fees estimated @	140,000	
Interest on costs estimated @	<u>90,000</u>	
Total cost		1,330,000
Profit @ 20% of total costs		<u>266,000</u>
Total costs plus profit		<u>1,596,000</u>

Amount left for land purchase   <u>3,736,000</u>

In the above example, the YP is a capitaliser which converts the income flow into a capital sum which represents the purchase price. This is explained in more detail later in the chapter but at this stage it is important to realise that the YP is a capitalisation figure which represents the return that investors would want for the project. YP stands for *years' purchase* but this expression should not give the idea that this is some form of payback approach; it is an investment method which in its simplest form links the rent to the capital value as follows:

years' purchase × annual rental income = capital value

In the simplified approach above the time value of money has been ignored and it is assumed that all values are present values. This is not so and the more detailed calculation later in the chapter will take the time difference into account by discounting a future land value to present value.

The costs in a residual valuation which have to be deducted from the gross development value include:

- building costs, ancillary costs and professional fees;
- fees on letting and advertising;
- interest on costs;
- contingencies;
- purchase costs of land (not the land value as this is the residual) which include legal fees, stamp duty land tax and possibly compensation for tenants to obtain vacant possession.

Some rough estimates have been used above but in practice the professionals associated with the project would provide more detailed estimates for these items.

3.2 Elements in the residual valuation

Gross development value

For commercial developments such as offices, shops, warehouses or factories, where a rent will be passing on the property the gross development value (GDV) is based on the net annual income from the development multiplied by the years' purchase at the investment yield for the type of property in the particular location. The investment yield is therefore derived from comparison with other similar investments in the market in the particular locality. In a mixed-use development which included housing the GDV would be a composite from sales achieved on the housing units plus the capitalised value of the commercial part of the scheme as described above.

The GDV is achieved by the developer when all of the housing units and the commercial element are sold. There is an established protocol which requires that when developers sell commercial properties to financial institutions they deduct the purchaser's costs. The latter includes solicitor's fees for conveyancing and stamp duty land tax. At present these combine to around 5.5% of the GDV of a typical commercial property and so if the GDV were £10 million a developer would actually receive a net development value from a purchasing fund which would be calculated as follows:

$$GDV = £10,000,000$$

Fund's costs of purchase @ 5.5% therefore the net development value is:
$(1/1.055) \times 10,000,000 = £9,478,673$ (rounded up)
Costs of purchase paid as tax and fees to solicitors =
£10,000,000 − £9,478,673 = £521,327

In a residual valuation therefore, the purchaser's costs may be deducted from the GDV at the beginning of the calculation to identify the net development value.

Building costs

The following are selected examples of average building costs from the UK's Building Cost Information Service (BCIS) for the first quarter of 2009. The service, which is available to subscribers at: www.bcis.co.uk, can also provide more detailed cost information against a wide range of building types. There are other sources which provide information on building costs, for example Spons building price guides produced by cost consultants Davis Langdon.

Building type	$£/m^2$
Offices, general	1,249
Offices, with air conditioning	1,403
Offices, 6+ storeys	1,647
Shops, general	777
Hypermarkets, supermarkets up to 1,000m^2	773
1,000–7,000m^2	1,064
Warehouses	557
Retail warehouses	529
Factories, general	590

Costs per square metre are based on gross internal floor area and are the national average tender prices for construction works, exclusive of external works, professional fees and VAT. The regional variation for London is around plus 14%. Value Added Tax is payable on new and refurbishment contracts at 17.5% but can be recovered where developers are registered for VAT.

Gross internal areas are measured from the inside of external walls. This measurement contrasts with others used in the development process. For town planning purposes, buildings are measured on their gross external areas while measurement to determine lettable space for rental purposes is on a net internal basis which excludes common areas, services and access-ways.

To prevent doubt on what should be included in these different measurements and to clarify the context in which each of these measurements should be used, RICS provides a *Code of Measuring Practice* which is now in its sixth edition (RICS 2007b). While the physical attributes of each building will differ, an approximation for converting gross to net floor area may be: 0% for new warehouse buildings, 10% for industrial property generally and 20% for shops, blocks of flats, offices and older industrial units.

Professional fees

A development will require inputs from professionals such as the architect, quantity surveyor, civil engineer and valuer. Historically the fees payable to these professionals were set out by professional bodies such as RICS and RIBA (Royal Institute of British Architects). However, this approach has given way to a more flexible system whereby professional consultants enter into a fee agreement with a client. A pattern has emerged from this process which does provide a benchmark for the magnitude of fees that a client might expect for a major scheme and this is around 12.5% of the total building costs. However as Wyatt (2007: 160) points out there can be parameters for each professional input which he sets out as follows:

Architect	5–7.5%
Quantity Surveyor	2–3%
Structural Engineer	2.5–3%
Civil Engineer	1–3%
Project Manager	2%
Mechanical and Electrical Consultants	0.5%

Of course the total figure for professional fees will increase if the scheme consumes additional professional time from a wider range of specialists and authors such as Ratcliffe *et al.* (2009: 402) suggest that the envelope for professional fees will therefore be between 12.5% and 15% of construction costs. For example the figure will be closer to 15% where a contaminated site requires the advice of specialists on remediation techniques or where there are complicated highways issues requiring traffic modelling or a hydrologist is required to advise on flood mitigation and drainage issues or a business park requires extensive landscape architecture inputs.

Contingency

This is conventionally around 5% of the building costs and may fluctuate depending on the nature of the project, the contract for construction and the possible risk of variation on costs. The contingency is essentially to allow for unforeseen cost overruns which will probably arise for any number of unpredictable reasons.

Finance charges

Given that developers will normally be borrowing money from a bank to pay for a development, finance charges gradually accumulate over the project period against the agreed interest rate between the borrower (the developer) and lender (the bank). The interest charges are rolled up across the development timeline to form one of the cost headings. In a residual valuation finance charges are conventionally calculated on the total building cost for half the building period. This reflects the fact that not all the money for the contract will be required at the beginning of the contract but that money will be drawn down as work proceeds.

The logic underpinning this approach is that at the beginning of the project a team may be busy on demolition followed by the ground works and production of a floor slab. However it is not until a superstructure is in place that other trades and sub-contractors can make their contributions to a project so that the site becomes progressively busier towards the middle and back end of the project. The example below models the principle for illustrative purposes against a hypothetical £15 million building contract.

In reality the precise rate of draw-down month by month will vary from this pristine model and will be contingent on diverse factors such as weather conditions to whether the ground is contaminated and requires heavy upfront costs to remediate it. The credit crunch during 2008–9 has even seen work deliberately slowed in the hope that market values will recover in time for project completion and disposal. However the mathematics below in Table 3.1 has been used to generate the S curve in graphic form in Figure 3.1.

The builder is paid monthly but interest on outstanding amounts could be assessed on a monthly or quarterly basis depending on the loan agreement. In the above example it is assumed that monthly interest applies. The annual interest rate which generates the monthly or quarterly rate results from the bank's assessment of the project risks as reflected in a margin over LIBOR. The latter is normally 20 or 30 basis points above the Bank of England base rate (there are 100 basis points in 1%).

In August 2009 the Bank of England base rate was at a historic low point of 0.5% as the Bank's Monetary Policy Committee was trying to stimulate the economy by ensuring that companies could borrow at competitive rates. A broad package of measures under the umbrella term *quantitative easing* was used to try to bring the economy out of recession. At that time the three-month LIBOR rate was 30 basis points above the base rate, so a bank could obtain money from the interbank system at 0.53% to lend onwards. However many of the banks had become overexposed to property loans, some of which had become toxic, requiring the banks to write off significant debts. Thus there was diminished enthusiasm by banks to lend, particularly against speculative property developments.

If a bank were to be enticed into lending against a proposed development then it would want a significant return above LIBOR to reflect the risks and so

Table 3.1 Developers' finance charges

Annual interest = 8%
Monthly equivalent = 0.643%
Construction cost = £15,000,000
Interest calculated by the traditional method = £588,457
Interest calculated by the S curve method below = £512,454
Difference between the above methods = £76,003

Month	Monthly spend %	Amount (£)	Cumulative construction spend (£)	Cumulative %	Monthly interest payments (£)	Total monthly expenditure	Brought forward
1	2	300,000	300,000	2		300,000	300,000
2	4	600,000	900,000	6	1,929	601,929	901,929
3	6	900,000	1,800,000	12	5,799	905,799	1,807,728
4	8	1,200,000	3,000,000	20	11,624	1,211,624	3,019,352
5	10	1,500,000	4,500,000	30	19,414	1,519,414	4,538,766
6	14	2,100,000	6,600,000	44	29,184	2,129,184	6,667,950
7	16	2,400,000	9,000,000	60	42,875	2,442,875	9,110,825
8	14	2,100,000	11,100,000	74	58,583	2,158,583	11,269,408
9	10	1,500,000	12,600,000	84	72,462	1,572,462	12,841,870
10	8	1,200,000	13,800,000	92	82,573	1,282,573	14,124,443
11	6	900,000	14,700,000	98	90,820	990,820	15,115,263
12	2	300,000	15,000,000	100	97,191	397,191	15,512,454
Totals	100	15,000,000			512,454		

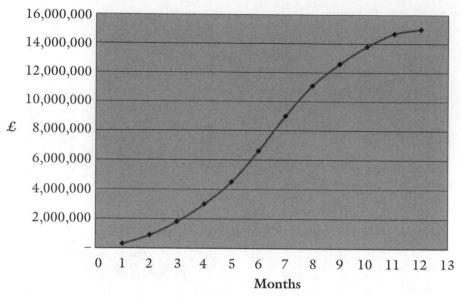

Figure 3.1 'S' curve of building costs

developers as borrowers were unlikely to see loan rates very much below 7%. However by historical standards that rate of interest would not be an impediment were a developer to take on the risks of developing at what was a difficult time. Developers are more familiar with servicing double digit interest rates on their borrowing for schemes.

The professional fees are conventionally front-end loaded in a residual valuation to reflect design activity by the architect, cost estimates, ground condition surveys and negotiations with the local authority to obtain planning and building regulations approvals. The interest charges on professional fees are therefore estimated as being on the total fee over two-thirds of the building period.

Letting and sales fees

Generally the letting fees are 10% of the initial annual rent but if there are joint agents as on a larger scheme, they will operate jointly for a total fee of 15% of the rents. In some circumstances, agents may be asked to bid for the contract and thus a developer might be able to secure a lower fee structure.

Where there is residential in a scheme there will typically arise agent's fees to achieve sales and these might be between 1% and 2% of the unit value. Where the scheme is entirely residential and the sales are being conducted by the housebuilder this cost heading would be internalised into the company overhead.

Advertising budget

The advertising budget includes the cost of advertising the property and preparing and distributing particulars. An advertising consultant would be asked to prepare a budget for the advertising campaign. The extent of advertising and promotion will depend on the project, the locality and the state of the market, although it is conventional in a residual valuation to estimate the budget as a spot figure of between 0.5% and 1% of the gross development value.

Ancillaries

The main building contract sum will seldom cover every eventuality and there will inevitably be other minor costs which the developer will have to meet. These could include for example the costs of connecting the site to underground services and which will need the attendance of service providers, temporary insurance policies will need to be paid for and there will be planning application and building regulations fees to pay to the local authority.

Developer's profit

The developer's profit is dependent on the nature of the project and the type of developer but fundamentally it should represent the risk involved in the project. Reward will vary directly with the level of risk, additional risk being compensated by additional reward.

The developer's profit is a point figure as a percentage of cost or GDV but for security there may be a minimum threshold based on rental cover. This cover means that there is an ability to pay the rental, if lettings are difficult, from the profit where guarantees to funders have been made. A pre-let or presale will reduce the risk. If an institution has provided the presale and perhaps the short term finance for construction of the project, it will look to reduce the developer's profit by purchasing the property at a higher yield, i.e. a discount which reduces the gross development value at purchase.

Given that the developer's profit may be geared to a percentage of the GDV or a percentage of the total costs (TC) it is worth briefly exploring the difference by way of a simple example in which it can be seen that a profit aspiration expressed as 20% of total costs will be virtually the same as expressing the profit as 17% of GDV.

$$GDV - TC = Profit$$
$$\text{if Profit (P)} = 0.2\,TC, \text{ then } TC = P/0.2$$
$$\text{inserting this value in the original equation: } GDV - (P/0.2) = P$$
$$GDV = P + (P/0.2) = \frac{0.2P + P}{0.2} = \frac{1.2P}{0.2}$$
$$\text{thus } P = GDV/6 = 16.5\%\ GDV$$

From a purist perspective it is more logical to benchmark profit against GDV as this provides an incentive for a developer to achieve a high-quality scheme and thus by securing the envisaged value is rewarded at the end of the project. To benchmark profit against costs might suggest that there was no incentive to control cost increases.

However this is more of a semantic than practical point as the real issue is that a developer who overestimates the profit whether benchmarked against costs or GDV will be in danger of inflating this cost heading. The result will be that the residual land bid will be depressed allowing another, less self indulgent developer, to acquire the site with a superior land bid. There is theoretically therefore an in-built mechanism which prevents developers from over-rewarding themselves.

Development period

Although not an explicit heading in the residual valuation a view has to be formed by the appraiser on the length of the development period in order to provide parameters for the calculation of interest charges and the time over which the land value has to be discounted to present value.

The development period includes the planning period, the building contract and the void period. The planning period is the time required to obtain planning permission and when drawings and bills of quantities are prepared. In the simplified representation below this time is assumed to be six months, although on major schemes requiring the completion of legal agreements this period could well be longer.

The simple example in Figure 3.2 below assumes a 15-month building contract although this period will obviously vary between projects depending on their complexity and for a project of any magnitude this period is likely to be longer.

The void period is the time to let the property and over which interest is charged on the whole cost of the project. The length of the void period will vary depending on circumstances. In the simple example in Figure 3.2 below six months has been allowed, which is likely to be optimistic. During periods when companies are not expanding or looking for additional space it can take up to two years to fully let a speculative office development and even then tenant inducements such as rent free periods may have to be offered.

Of course the opposite may be true when the economy is strong and when a developer may have been able to secure at least some pre-lets on a scheme. Some developers may be in the fortunate position to be able to phase the development of a large site in a good location, so that a phase is only activated when a pre-let is secured. The More London development on London's South Bank was developed on this basis, so that void periods are avoided.

Residual land value

In practice the residual value will have to be discounted back over the period of the development and void period to reflect the interest paid on the land cost. This would provide the land cost at the time of purchase being the beginning of the development.

VAT implications

One of the budget headings which does not normally appear in a residual appraisal is VAT (Value Added Tax) which is payable in the UK and European Union. However this is not to say that VAT is of no concern to a developer. Indeed a developer should obtain specialist advice on the implications of VAT on any site acquisition or intention to dispose of a completed development. As a general principle, Havard (2008: 156–8) points out that developers in the UK

Total development period – 27 months (or 9 quarters)								
3	6	9	12	15	18	21	24	27
Planning period: six months		Building contract: 15 months					Void period: six months	
Interest on Land Purchase for 27 months								
		Interest on building costs @ ½ × 15 months					Interest on total building costs for six months	
		Interest on professional fees @ ⅔ × 15 months					Interest on total professional fees for six months	
							Interest on total advertising, contingency and letting agents fees for six months	

Figure 3.2 Development period (six-month void period)

are required to pay VAT at the standard rate of 17½% on construction costs and interests in rights over land and licences to occupy land. The requirement only applies to commercial buildings and not to residential buildings. A vendor, in the case of selling an interest in land or buildings, or landlord in the case of leases and licences, has to opt to charge tax.

In the majority of cases, VAT has an impact only on the cash flow of the development project as developers may be able to recover all VAT paid on land transactions and construction costs if they charge VAT on the sale of the completed building or on rents from the letting of the completed building. Thus the cash flow implications are that there may be a delay between the payment of VAT and its recovery. An approach to this is to allow a lag of approximately four months between the charge and recovery of VAT within a residual calculation.

There are some important exemptions such as when a completed commercial building is to be let or sold for occupation to a bank, insurance company or other VAT exempt body. In those circumstances those organisations cannot claim VAT charged to them and so the developer may have to write off any VAT already paid during the construction of the project or effectively make the building 17.5% more expensive to the purchaser. There are other detailed caveats in the VAT regime which can prevent VAT recovery and which underline the importance of developers obtaining specialist tax advice.

Ground rents

The residual calculation can be extended to devise a ground rent calculation in situations where there are partnerships between developers and landowners and the developer takes a lease of the site, these calculations are discussed in more detail in chapter 4.

3.3 Detailed residual valuation

The simplified residual calculation earlier in the chapter served to illustrate the general principle; however, residual valuations will typically contain more variables as the following example shows. In the example below a 0.3 hectare city centre site has been identified by a developer who wishes to develop a six-storey building (ground floor plus five upper floors) whose footprint covers 2,000m^2 of the site. The developer envisages a 1,000m^2 basement for plant and some car and motorcycle parking bays plus cycle storage.

The developer's investigations reveal that a mixed-use development containing some housing, offices and retail would be supported by the local authority. Taking into account that the site abuts a secondary street in retail terms but in which there is some retail presence, the developer proposes that only half of the ground floor be devoted to retail. The remaining half of the ground floor and the entire first to fourth floors will be devoted to offices and the top floor will be residential (flats). The local authority has stipulated that they expect at least 30% of the flats to be affordable and transferred to a registered provider under an s.106 agreement. The agreement will also secure £250,000 to pay for a green travel plan, school places and improvements to the public realm around the site.

The current owners of the site are a primary healthcare trust which has relocated the services previously provided on the site to a new multi-purpose building nearby. The redundant four-storey building on the site has little potential for conversion and is not listed and nor is it in a conservation area, so could be demolished. The developer could acquire the site with vacant possession from the healthcare trust which is inviting bids from potential purchasers.

The developer has consulted market databases such as Focus and has spoken to agents to ascertain comparable rents and yields for the office and retail elements and the sales values likely to be achieved on the one, two and three-bedroom flats. A registered provider has been approached and the 30% affordable flats in the scheme can be transferred to the provider at a value reflecting 70% of the open market value of the flats.

The developer envisages that a scheme like this would take 18 months to complete and has an in principle agreement with a bank that funds could be secured at 8% for this scheme. The developer has also identified building costs for the different elements in the scheme and these have been fed into the residual appraisal below (in Figure 3.3) along with the developer's profit expectation which is 17% of GDV to reflect the project risks.

Assumptions

All residual valuations will be based upon assumptions of one sort or another and as RICS point out (2008: 17) the valuer must make these explicit to the

	Gross floorspace m²	Net m², 90% for retail and 80% for offices	Rental value £ m²	Annual rental value £	YP @ 7.5% yield for retail and 6.5% for offices	Capital value
Retail on ½ ground floor	1,000	900	350	315,000	13.3333	4,199,990
Offices on 4½ floors	9,000	7,200	500	3,600,000	15.3846	55,384,560
Subtotals				3,915,000		59,584,550

Net development value of retail and offices reflecting 5.5% purchaser's costs = 56,478,246

Flats on the top (5th) floor	No.	Net unit size m²	Gross floorspace m²	Unit value £	Sub total value £
1 bed open market	4	50	250	200,000	800,000
2 bed open market	7	65	569	260,000	1,820,000
3 bed open market	6	80	600	300,000	1,800,000
1 bed affordable	2	50	125	140,000	280,000
2 bed affordable	3	65	244	182,000	546,000
3 bed affordable	2	80	200	210,000	420,000
Subtotals	24		1,988		5,666,000

Gross Development Value		62,144,246

Construction and all other costs

Demolition costs		250,000	
Construction costs	£ m²		
1,000m² gross retail floorspace ×	800	800,000	
9,000 m² gross office floorspace ×	1,350	12,150,000	
1,988m² gross floorspace for flats ×	1,000	1,988,000	
1,000 m² basement ×	600	600,000	
Ancillary costs		100,000	
Subtotal		15,888,000	
Professional fees @ 12.5%		1,986,000	
Section 106 agreement		250,000	
Interest on building and section 106 costs over ½ × 18 months @	8%	958,906	
Interest on professional fees at ⅔ × 18 months @	8%	158,880	
Interest on total for void period of 3 months @	8%	373,801	
Subtotal			3,727,587
Contingency	5%	794,400	
Letting fees @	15%	587,250	
Residential sales agents fees @ 2% of open market flat sales		88,400	
Advertising @ 1% of GDV		621,442	
Developer's profit @ 17% of GDV		10,564,522	
Subtotal		12,656,014	
Total development costs		32,271,601	

Value of site in 1¾ years = GDV–Total development costs =			29,872,645
Present value of £1 in 1¾ years @ 8%	0.8740		26,108,692
Less land acquisition costs and stamp duty @ 5%		1,243,271	
Site value today			24,865,421

Figure 3.3 Residual valuation for a six-storey mixed-use development on a 0.3 ha city centre site

client. A summary on the types of assumptions that might be expected to support the above valuation might be as follows.

1 It is assumed that the retail and office elements in the scheme are sold to a financial institution at the end of the development period and that the purchaser's costs are then assumed to be 5.5% as shown deducted above from the capital value of those elements of the scheme.

2 Assumptions have been made regarding the setting of key cost variables such as:
   (a) professional fees which are benchmarked at 12.5% of building costs;
   (b) finance charges on professional fees have been set at two-thirds of the building period and on building costs over half the building period;
   (c) the contingency sum has been set at 5% of the construction and demolition subtotal to reflect the redevelopment of a complicated city centre site;
   (d) the letting fees at 15% of the annual rental income from the offices and retail element assumes a joint letting agency arrangement.

3 A void period of three months is assumed for letting of the commercial element and sales of the flats and over which time interest is calculated on the total sum. This assumption would normally be justified against evidence of similar lettings and sales in the locality.

4 The gross to net floorspace relationship for the flats is assumed to be 80% and thus 20% of the space is given over to common area such as hallways and stairwells. The build costs for the open market and affordable flats are assumed to be identical to ensure a tenure blind development.

5 Demolition costs are based upon tenders obtained by the developer.

6 The ancillary costs are estimates based upon the developer's experience on similar schemes.

7 The site acquisition costs are made up of agents' fees, valuation fees, survey fees, legal fees and stamp duty land tax. In the example 5% is assumed to include 1% for various fees and 4% for stamp duty. Thus the land cost is 'netted' by the deduction of the acquisition costs as follows:

Value of site now	£26,108,692
Net site value = (1/1.05) × site value	
Net site value =	£24,865,421
Site acquisition costs @ 5% therefore =	£1,243,271

3.4 Sensitivity and risk

As can be seen from the above example, there are numerous variables in a residual valuation and inaccuracy can therefore easily occur. Changes in the items which have a large monetary value such as the gross development value and build costs can dramatically alter the residual land value. Rather than presenting the findings as one single land value figure, valuers may alter some of the key variables to determine the outcome as a form of sensitivity analysis, an approach which is supported by RICS (2008: 17):

It may be appropriate to present an appraisal based on provable values alongside a sensitivity analysis to show the effect on the land value of differing assumptions as to the future rent and yield. The aim is to assist the client in assessing the likely land value by reference to present and future market trends, and the likely shifts in supply and demand. Wherever possible, the treatment and presentation of these issues is to be discussed with the client.

In conducting a sensitivity analysis there is little point in focusing upon dependent variables which have a relatively small monetary value and which do not have knock-on effects in the overall valuation. For example in the above valuation there is little point in exploring the effects on a £24.9 million (rounded up) site value of an increase in the residential agent's sales fees shown benchmarked at 2% of the sales values on the open market flats. Even in the unlikely event that this item was to double in cost from £88,400 to £176,800 it would make very little difference to the viability of the scheme.

A sensitivity analysis is however useful where it explores small but possible changes in the large value items which could have a disproportionate effect on the land value. Some judgement is required to determine the realistic order of magnitude that key variables might change by over a development period which in the example is 18 months excluding the void period. Thus building costs are a potentially sensitive variable to be included in a sensitivity test and a judgement therefore needs to be made on the likely extent of change in this variable over the project timeline.

In recent years building costs have been increasing slightly above the rate of inflation which was averaging around 4%. However during the 2008–9 credit crunch there was deflation in building costs simply because contractors had to cut their prices during a period when there was little demand for their services. This said, it would not be unreasonable to explore a +5% and +10% increase in building costs as those potential changes would not be beyond probability with a +5% increase perhaps being much more likely than a 10% increase over 18 months.

Generally when conducting a sensitivity test the client is looking at the downside possibilities to establish the risk. Thus although building costs could be less than budgeted for this would be a windfall to add to any profits. A developer would be more interested in what would happen in a worst case scenario where building costs increased combined with an increase in the interest (borrowing) rate and a decrease in rental and capital values at the end of the project. A development which was still viable if all of these changes occurred in combination might be considered to be robust, while a scheme where such a combination of changes extinguished the developer's profit and generated a negative land value would be considered a high risk and volatile development.

Therefore it is the 'big ticket' independent variables which are normally subject to sensitivity testing in a residual valuation and a cursory glance at the above valuation will reveal these to be the commercial development value (£56.5 million), the residential sales value (£5.7 million), the combined building costs (£15.9 million) and possibly the combined interest charges (£3.7 million). The developer's profit and land value are also high-value items but they are dependent variables which are affected by changes in the above. Some further comment is now warranted on what appear to be the most sensitive variables in this scheme culminating in a simple sensitivity analysis.

Changes to rental income

The rental income is an estimate of the rent that will be achieved when the development is completed at the end of the development period. The convention is that appraisals are based on today's rental values without allowing for inflation or real increases over the period of the development. The rental income directly determines the developer's yield and indirectly the developer's profit which is related to capital value. In a scheme such as the one explored in this chapter where the mixed-use development is dominated by the commercial floorspace element, changes in rental value assumptions would need to be explored explicitly. The table below therefore explores falls of 5% and 10% for both the office and retail rents.

Changes to the investor's yield

The capital value of the commercial part of a completed project is arrived at by capitalising the income at the appropriate investor's yield making allowance for the cost of disposal. Yields however, vary over time and, unless the investment is to be pre-sold, the developer has to form a view of what yields will be at the end of the project, perhaps some 18 months on.

Because of the difficulties of forecasting, it is not unusual to adopt current yields and thus a sensitivity analysis would look at potential negative changes from the developer's perspective. This would mean looking at situations where the yield is said to slacken, i.e. the investment market has become less interested in the product and the capital values fall, reflecting rising yields. For example a prime retail property generating a net annual rent of £50,000 might be capitalised at a yield of 5% at the top of the market and thus its capital value would be in the order of: years' purchase (YP) in perpetuity = $1/0.05 = 20$ generating a capital value = $20 \times £50,000 = £1,000,000$. However several years later retail property is not seen as such a good investment and the yield on the subject property slackens to 6% so that the YP is now $1/0.06 = 16.67$ (rounded) generating a revised capital value of $16.67 \times £50,000 = £833,500$.

Thus in the table below the yields for the office and retail element in the scheme have been adjusted by +5% and +10%. So for example the office yield in the residual valuation above is 6.5% reflecting what would be prime offices. A 5% increase in this yield would therefore be $6.5\% + (6.5\% \times 5\%) = 6.825\%$ and a 10% increase in the yield would be $6.5\% + (6.5\% \times 10\%) = 7.15\%$.

Changes to the building costs

Building costs could increase because of the nature of the development and the problems which may arise on the contract. If increases in building costs do arise, they may to some extent be absorbed by the contingency allowance in the residual valuation. However a sensitivity test would normally explore increases in this variable as construction cost is usually the single biggest cost element in a residual valuation. Increases in building costs may be driven by increases in the cost of building materials and/or increases in the cost of labour. In a sensitivity test it is possible to model foreseeable increases in building costs by reference to indices for the year ahead produced by BCIS. This degree of sophistication is not employed in the example below which simply explores +5% and +10% changes in the building costs.

Changes in the interest rate

Interest rate changes may occur over the development timeline and in the UK these are decided upon by the Bank of England Monetary Policy Committee in the context of overall economic performance. If the developer has borrowed on a variable rate then subsequent rate changes will affect interest charges arising on the scheme. Where significant sums are being borrowed on a variable rate without cap or collars to limit the range of interest rate changes then it would be valid to explore changes in this variable in a sensitivity test. In the residual example in this chapter the rate of 8% is assumed to be a variable rate and therefore could be subject to change and the simple sensitivity analysis therefore explores a +5% change which is:

8% + (8% × 5%) = 8.4% which is the same as 8% plus 40 basis points = 8.4%

and a + 10% change which is:

8% + (8% × 10%) = 8.8% or 8% plus 80 basis points = 8.8%

Changes to housing sales values

The example in this chapter contains housing on the top floor and which contributes £5.7 million to the development value and so would attract some attention in a sensitivity test. During the credit crunch housing values fell in all parts of the UK sometimes in dramatic fashion but it was not unusual to see housing values fall between 5% and 10% per annum for both 2008 and 2009. Thus in the simple example below those figures have been adopted to gauge the effect that such falls might have on the scheme.

The summary in Table 3.4 below captures the above changes to identify the effect that each individual change would have on the land value. The land value is shown as the constant because where a developer had purchased the site at its core valuation of £24,865,421 any subsequent variation would have a direct consequence for the profit margin in the scheme. The profit margin therefore becomes the elastic dependent variable once the site value has been committed to.

Table 3.2 sets out the degree of sensitivity of the variables in descending order, so that it is clear that changes in the rental values and yields would have the most effect on what a developer might make from the scheme. For example if the rental values achievable on the offices and retail element fell by 10% the developer's profit would be eroded by 36%. However the figure only considers each change in isolation and perhaps a developer would really want to know the outcome of a worst-case scenario where all of the negative possibilities combined as shown below.

Of course it would be a very unfortunate developer that saw all of the key variables move against the scheme as shown in Table 3.3 by say 10% and which would see an 88.6% reduction in the profit margin. However even in that

Table 3.2 Simple sensitivity test exploring the effects of 5% and 10% changes to selected variables

Variable	Change £	New land value £	Change in land value £	Change in land value %	Profit erosion assuming the land purchased at £24,865,421	Remaining profit £
Rental value of offices and retail	−5%	22,962,393	−1,903,028	−7.7%	−18.0%	8,661,494
	−10%	21,059,366	−3,806,055	−15.3%	−36.0%	6,758,467
Yield on offices and retail	+ 5%	23,029,741	−1,835,680	−7.4%	−17.4%	8,728,842
	+ 10%	21,360,936	−3,504,485	−14.1%	−33.2%	7,060,037
Construction, demolition and ancillary costs	+ 5%	24,027,213	−838,208	−3.4%	−7.9%	9,726,314
	+ 10%	23,189,007	−1,676,414	−6.7%	−15.9%	8,888,108
Interest rate	+ 5%	24,644,335	−221,086	−0.9%	−2.1%	10,343,436
	+ 10%	24,424,041	−441,380	−1.8%	−4.2%	10,123,142
Value of open market and affordable housing	−5%	24,672,053	−193,368	−0.8%	−1.8%	10,371,154
	−10%	24,478,687	−386,734	−1.6%	−3.7%	10,177,788

Table 3.3 Combined changes in key variables to reflect a pessimistic scenario

Variables and % change	New land value £	Change in land value £	Change in land value %	Profit erosion assuming the land purchased at £24,865,421	Remaining profit £
A combination of a +5% on yields, +5% building costs, +5% interest rate, – 5% rental values, –5% values for flats.	19,992,768	–4,872,653	–19.6%	–46.1%	5,691,869
A combination of a +10% on yields, +10% building costs, +10% interest rate, –10% rental values, –10% values for flats.	15,504,322	–9,361,099	–37.6%	–88.6%	1,203,423

'melt-down' scenario the developer would still have a slim profit providing one indicator that this was a financially robust development. While some of the variables might move in the wrong direction as far as the developer were concerned other variables might remain unchanged or possibly move in a positive direction for the developer providing a degree of compensation.

During the credit crunch rents, yields and sales values have moved against developers but there has been some compensation in that building costs have reduced marginally and interest rates have reduced significantly. However the negatives from a developer's perspective far outweighed the positives and the result was that work on a number of sites stopped and some schemes went into receivership.

The probability that the 5% and 10% changes might occur could be modelled using statistical techniques. However the coverage of that topic is beyond the scope of this chapter but is looked at in chapter 5 when sensitivity testing is revisited in the context of cash flow appraisals.

Other variables which could be modelled in a sensitivity analysis

The development timeline

A sensitivity analysis could model not only changes in the monetary value of variables, it could also explore different assumptions on the duration of a development while interest charges are accumulating but when there is no project income. There are a number of different influences on how a development timeline might change.

To begin with the period for which the land will be held and therefore the period for which it has to be financed, is made up of three parts. First, the period between the purchase of the land and the start of construction, may be easy to assess if planning permission is already available. When no planning permission exists, the contract of purchase may be made subject to planning permission being granted and the greater part of the land costs therefore will not be incurred until that time.

The second period which has to be financed is the period of construction and thus assumptions around the length of the building period are important in determining project value given the exposure to short term building finance.

The third period is the period for letting and selling. If the property is speculative, it would need to be assumed that there is no rental income receivable before the completion of construction and that an additional period of somewhere between three months and up to 18 months (depending on market conditions and the locality) would need to be allowed to secure a tenant and arrange for leases to be granted. The void period will also need to take into account any rent free periods offered as tenant incentives or in respect of fitting-out periods.

Floorspace assumptions

It is assumed in the residual valuation example in this chapter that the developer has explored the maximum envelope for floorspace on the site in discussions with the local authority and that this quantum of development would ultimately be reflected in a planning consent. However this will not always be the case and there may be some scope to model different assumptions regarding the overall quantity of floorspace in a scheme and/or the way that the floorspace is distributed between different uses.

In the example in this chapter 9,000 m^2 gross floorspace of offices generated a capital value of £55,384,560 and thus notionally each m^2 of offices in the scheme contributed £55,384,560/9,000 = £6,154 of value. However each m^2 of offices had to be built at a nominal cost of £1,350 per m^2 and so the nominal surplus value added by each m^2 of offices in the scheme would be £4,804. Given this perspective, an unconstrained developer might well deliver only offices on the site because as Table 3.4 below shows, offices have the highest added value £ per m^2 rate in the scheme. However there were policy limitations in the scenario which required a mixed-use development including housing and retail. In reality there would be some policy parameters on the extent to which a developer could engage in 'what if' modelling which explored the substitution of one use with another within the overall building envelope.

Table 3.4 Developers' modelling (relative to different uses)

Use	Nominal value £ per m^2	Nominal cost to build £ per m^2	Nominal surplus value added £ per m^2
Retail	4,200	800	3,400
Offices	6,154	1,350	4,804
Flats	2,850	1,000	1,850

Inflation

Rents and building costs could inflate or deflate over the development timeline and that is why a sensitivity analysis might explore movements in those variables. However it is possible for a sensitivity test to model inflation systematically and for instance:

1 the rental levels used in the calculation of the gross development value could be inflated over the development period from existing rent levels using an Amount of £1 calculation (see section 3.8 in this chapter) to represent the anticipated growth in rental values over the development period;
2 the yield could be adjusted to a quarterly in advance calculation to reflect more accurately the future income flow;
3 the cash flow could be extended from the development period into the investment period once the development has been completed and a subsequent analysis carried out. The investment part of the valuation can take into account contemporary techniques such as short-cut discounted cash flow (DCF) approaches and reflect inducements and voids.

Use of valuation software packages in sensitivity testing

Given that there is almost an infinite number of combinations regarding changes to variables in a residual, some valuers find that the use of software packages such as Prodev can bring time savings and a systematic approach to sensitivity testing. These off-the-shelf valuation packages incorporate sensitivity matrices which enable different combinations of variables to be played off against one another at differing step changes to identify the effects on either a scheme's profit margin or land value.

Some rules of thumb in sensitivity testing

We have seen that relatively small changes in sensitive variables may have a large effect in the outcome of a residual valuation. There is also a broader perspective to consider when undertaking these exercises and this relates to the context of the site and the scale of value and costs involved. A simple example is set out below which shows the effect of changes on two different development appraisals, one with a low land value and the other with a high land value.

Simple sensitivity testing

Development on a prime site (land cost is high in relation to costs)		Development on a sub-prime site (land cost is low in relation to costs)
GDV	£1,000,000	£1,000,000
Total costs	700,000	900,000
Land value	300,000	100,000

Three scenarios could be assumed for the above appraisals:

1 value and cost increase by same percentage;
2 value increases more than cost;
3 cost increases more than value.

Value and cost increase in the same proportion
In this case land value will increases in the same proportion.

Value increases by 30%, cost by 10%

	Prime site	Sub-prime site
GDV	£1,300,000	£1,300,000
Total costs	770,000	990,000
Land value	530,000	310,000
% change	+77%	+210%

Thus, if value increases by more than cost, it affects land value more in the case where the land value is small in proportion to the total value of the development.

Value increases 10%, cost by 20%

	Prime site	Sub prime site
GDV	£1,100,000	£1,100,000
Total costs	840,000	1,080,000
Land value	260,000	20,000
% change	− 13%	− 80%

The effect on the land value in this case where the land value is a small proportion of total value is again more dramatic, illustrating the concept of gearing which is discussed in the later chapters on finance.

Sensitivity analysis and risk mitigation measures

One of the purposes of carrying out a sensitivity analysis is to identify those variables in which a relatively small change will bring about a disproportionately large change in the core valuation. Once these variables are identified the developer is at least in a situation where some consideration can be given to whether a degree of control or mitigation might be possible to soften the impact of damaging change in a sensitive variable.

Generally the developer will have more potential to control changes in costs than values. For example it may be possible for a developer to negotiate a fixed-cost building contract which effectively transfers the risk to the building contractor. Other cost items such as professional fees can be controlled to some extent by monitoring and staging payments related to performance. An effective project manager may also be able to anticipate problems and prevent cost escalation during construction.

Values on the other hand are largely determined by the interplay of market forces and this dynamic is largely beyond the scope of an individual developer to control. Perhaps the best alternatives are to work from market forecasts which if they predict a difficult market ahead for sales or lettings might focus the attention of a developer on trying to achieve pre-sales or pre-lets perhaps by offering discounts. Forecasts of volatility might also suggest a partnership approach to a development in which a landowner shares some of the risks but would therefore expect to share in the rewards from a scheme. On larger sites schemes may be broken down into phases so that the cash flow from an earlier phase will help to fund subsequent phases thus reducing exposure to borrowing. Phasing also enables slower production to harmonise with a slower sales or lettings rate in a difficult market.

Thus there are some risk reduction measures available but they can only mitigate rather than eliminate the main risks to a development. This is why the returns from property development will need to be significantly higher than on risk-free investments such as gilts or fixed-rate bonds.

3.5 Calculation of the development profit

The residual valuation indicates how much should be paid for a site. However, if the site value is already known, then this can be incorporated into the valuation to work out the developer's profit. Using the figures from the residual example above, the profit on completion can be calculated by using the costs and capital values as shown below.

Profit on completion

Gross development value:		£62,144,246
Total costs excluding profit:	£21,707,079	
Land cost inclusive of 5% purchase costs:	£26,108,692	
Finance on land cost over 1¾ years @ 8%	£ 3,764,160*	
Subtotal:		£51,579,931
Residual profit =		£10,564,315

*This is calculated by compound interest, i.e. [£ 26,108,692 × $(1 + 0.08)^{1.75}$] − £26,108,692. This is based on the Amount of £1 formula sometimes referred to as the compound interest formula which can be found in section 3.8 of this chapter.

Thus instead of the traditional residual calculation to find the site value, which is based on:

Gross development value less (building cost plus profit) equals land cost:
GDV − (BC + P) = LC

This is rearranged to:

Gross development value less total cost (which includes land cost) equals profit:
GDV − (BC + LC) = P

From the calculation:

$$\text{Profit as a percentage of total costs} = \frac{£10,564,315}{£51,579,931} = 20.5\%$$

$$\text{Profit as a percentage of capital value} = \frac{£10,564,315}{£62,144,246} = 17.0\%$$

Rental cover

Taking the expected annual income on the commercial element of the scheme = £3,915,000 and the residual profit calculated above = £10,564,315 then the rental cover is the profit: rental ratio which = £10,564,315: £3,915,000 = 2.7 times.

This indicates the cover available from the profit if the rent is guaranteed and has to be paid by the developer if there is no letting of the property. It suggests that the developer could cover 2.7 years of void with the profit from the scheme.

3.6 Alternative approaches

The traditional residual technique is not adequate to deal with a more complex development situation where expenditure and income are being made and received at different times over a long-time scale. Greater accuracy can be achieved by using cash flows and three such approaches are as follows:

1 A period by period cash flow in which interest can be charged against outstanding debt in each period.
2 A discounted cash flow (DCF) in which cash flows are discounted back to the present rather than interest added.
3 A DCF approach but building inflation into costs and growth into rents.

Improved techniques do not solve all the difficulties encountered in the residual valuation in that changes to key variables in the calculation can still affect the final site value – sometimes dramatically. Sensitivity analysis therefore also has a role to play in cash flow approaches and these issues are explored in chapter 5.

When using the residual method, an appraiser will sometimes express profit as a percentage of the total development cost, including interest (the profit yield), the other criteria that may be adopted include:

1 *Initial yield*: the net rental return calculated as the full annual rental on completion of the letting expressed as a percentage of the total development value. This is useful for assessing whether the developer could service a long-term mortgage loan on the development.
2 *Cash-on-cash (or equity yield)*: the capital uplift or (more usually) net income (after interest charges on any long-term mortgage loan) expressed as a percentage of the long-term equity finance provided by the developer.
3 *Discounted cash flow methods*: the income stream is projected with explicit assumptions about rental growth and discounted back to a net present value (NPV) using an appropriate discount rate; the scheme is deemed viable if NPV exceeds the total development cost. The discount rate allows for a profit margin reflecting the risk and reward elements of the project.

4 *Equated yield (or internal rate of return – IRR)*: a variant of 3 (above) the
   IRR is the yield which equates the discounted value of the project with
   discounted cost (NPV = 0), strictly the equated yield is the same as the IRR
   but where there is inflation/growth allowed for in the costs and values (see
   Isaac and Steley 2000: chapter 5).
5 *Amount of cover*: the extent to which the rent or sale price can be reduced or
   the letting or sale period extended without suffering an overall loss on the
   scheme.

3.7 Calculating value using the investment method

This section provides an introduction to the investment method to be used in
the residual valuation to calculate the gross development value. It looks at the
valuation tables used to carry out basic calculations and examines the
compound rate of interest formula which is used in the residual valuation.
Readers familiar with valuation principles may therefore wish to omit this
section.

Most investors seek to obtain a return on their invested money either as an
annual income or a capital gain, the investment method of valuation is traditionally concerned with the former. Where the investor has a known sum of
money to invest on which a particular return is required the income can be
readily calculated from:

$$\text{Income} = \text{Capital} \times \frac{i}{100} \text{ where } i = \text{the rate of return required as a percentage.}$$

For example if £10,000 is to be invested with a required rate of return of 8%
the income will be:

$$\text{Income} = £10,000 \times \frac{8}{100} = £800$$

In this type of problem the capital is known and the income is to be calculated.
In the case of real property the income (rent) is known, either from the rent
passing under the lease or estimated from the letting of similar comparable
properties and the capital value is usually calculated. The formula above has to
be changed so that the capital becomes the subject:

$$\text{Capital} = \text{Income} \times \frac{100}{i}$$

For instance, what capital sum should be paid for an investment producing
£800 per annum when a return of 8% is required?

$$\text{Capital} = £800 \times \frac{100}{8} = £10,000$$

This process is known as 'capitalising' the income, in other words converting an annual income into a capital sum. It is essential that the income capitalised is 'net' that is clear of any expenses incurred by the investor under the lease. The formula can be modified to:

$$C = NI \times \frac{100}{i} \text{ where } C = \text{Capital}$$
$$NI = \text{Net Income}$$
$$i = \text{Rate of Return}$$

For given rates of return 100/i will be constant, for example:

Rate of return	100/i
10%	10
8%	12.5
12%	8.33

This constant is known as the present value of £1 per annum in perpetuity or more commonly, the years' purchase in perpetuity (abbreviated to YP). The formula can thus be finally modified to:

$$C = NI \times YP$$

The YP calculated by using 100/i will only apply to incomes received in perpetuity which are those received from freehold interests let at a full market rent, sometimes referred to as the 'rack rent'. Incomes to be received for shorter periods use a YP which must be calculated using a more complex formula, but tables of constants are available and *Parry's Valuation and Investment Tables* are most commonly used (Davidson 2002). Parry's Tables enable either an assumption that rental income is received annually in arrears or that income is received quarterly in advance to reflect actual market practice. However, whatever income basis is used, the two essential inputs required for the calculation are: (a) the period of time the investment is to last; and (b) the rate of return required, usually known as the yield.

To summarise, to estimate the capital value of an interest in real property using the traditional investment method, three inputs are required:

1 The net income to be received.
2 The period for which the net income will be received.
3 The required yield.

1 and 2 will be obtained from the lease of the subject property or if the property is unlet, an estimate of the rental value will be obtained from lettings or comparable properties. The required yield will be obtained from analysis of sales of comparable investments. A valuer must therefore have knowledge of two separate markets: the letting and investment markets.

Simple investment valuation

Assume prime shops in a certain location have a yield of 5%. The income from the shop you are interested in is £200,000 net per annum (pa). How much would you pay for the freehold?

Net Income	£200,000 pa
Years' purchase @ 5% in perpetuity	× 20 YP*
Capital Value	£4,000,000

$$*YP = \frac{1}{5\%} = \frac{1}{0.05} = 20$$

3.8 A summary of the valuation tables

In order to understand the basis of the traditional method and the calculation of compounding and discounting in investment calculations, we need to consider the tables which underpin the appraisals. In dealing with investment situations, we are considering the purchase of an asset to generate an income stream over a period of time, thus we are converting the value of an income stream in the future into a present capital sum. *Parry's Tables* (Davidson 2002) deal with the conversion of present and future sums and the conversions of capital and income streams. For instance, the Amount of £1 table will add compound interest to an initial sum to give a future capital sum. The six main options of conversion are:

1 capital to income and vice versa;
2 present sums to future sums and vice versa;
3 the compounding of sums into the future, and discounting back to the present.

Amount of £1

This table provides the amount £1 will accumulate to over n years at an interest rate of i% pa. It thus compounds up from a present capital sum to a future capital sum. The approach is commonly known as compounding and the formula is:

$$A \text{ (Amount of £1)} = (1 + i)^n.$$

PV of £1

The present value of £1 gives the sum which needs to be invested at the interest rate i to accumulate to £1 in n years. i discounts a future capital sum to a present capital sum; it is the process of the Amount of £1 in reverse and the formula is:

$$1/A.$$

Amount of £1 pa

This is the amount to which £1 invested annually will accumulate to in n years. It is thus compounding a present income stream to a future capital sum and the formula is:

$$(A - 1)/i.$$

Annual sinking fund (ASF) to produce £1

This is the amount which needs to be invested annually to accumulate to £1 in n years at an interest rate $i\%$. It thus discounts back the future capital sum to a present income stream. The formula is:

$$i/(A-1).$$

Annuity £1 will purchase

This is the income stream that will be generated over n years by an original investment of £1. The income produced will be consumed as part capital and part interest on capital. Assuming the rates of consumption are the same, a single-rate approach gives an equation: $i/(1-PV)$. If the rates differ, then the formula $(i + s)$ needs to be used, where s is the annual sinking fund formula (see above) at a different interest rate from i. Note that this is the way a mortgage is calculated: a building society provides the initial capital sum and expects repayments of equal amounts throughout the loan period (assuming fixed-rate money), but the repayments consist of interest and capital (that is, the sinking fund).

PV of £1 per annum

The present value of £1 pa is the present value of the right to receive £1 pa over n years. The future income stream is discounted back to the present value and is the opposite of the annuity calculation. Thus the formulation for a single rate is $(1 - PV)/i$ or for the dual rate, $1/(i + s)$, where s is the annual sinking fund at the sinking fund rate. This approach is commonly known as the years' purchase and gives the present value of a future stream of rental income.

The compound interest formula

As can be seen from the valuation table summary below in Figure 3.4, the formula for compound interest is the same as the Amount of £1 formula (A) where:

$$A = (1 + i)^n$$
Where i is the interest rate for a period and n is the number of periods.

These must coincide, that is if the formula is calculating on an annual basis, then n is the number of years and i the annual interest rate, so interest is compounded

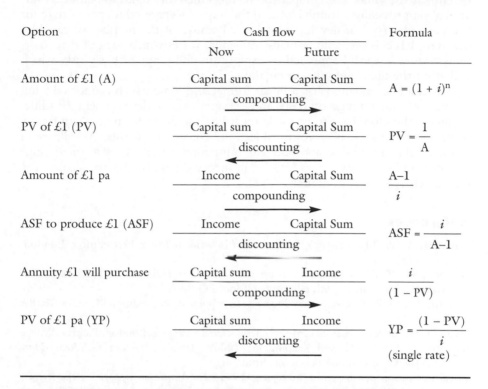

Option	Cash flow		Formula
	Now	Future	
Amount of £1 (A)	Capital sum	Capital Sum	$A = (1 + i)^n$
		compounding	
PV of £1 (PV)	Capital sum	Capital Sum	$PV = \dfrac{1}{A}$
		discounting	
Amount of £1 pa	Income	Capital Sum	$\dfrac{A-1}{i}$
		compounding	
ASF to produce £1 (ASF)	Income	Capital Sum	$ASF = \dfrac{i}{A-1}$
		discounting	
Annuity £1 will purchase	Capital sum	Income	$\dfrac{i}{(1 - PV)}$
		compounding	
PV of £1 pa (YP)	Capital sum	Income	$YP = \dfrac{(1 - PV)}{i}$ (single rate)
		discounting	

Figure 3.4 Summary of valuation tables (from Isaac and Steley 2000: 22)

annually. If n is the number of months and i the monthly interest rate then the calculation is compounding monthly.

Thus on an *annual* basis:

The future value of £1 in 2 years at an interest rate of 10% pa =
£1 × $(1 + 0.10)^2$ = £1.21

On a *quarterly* basis:

The future value of £1 in 8 quarters at a quarterly rate of 2½%, interest being compounded quarterly =
£1 × $(1 + 0.025)^8$ = £1.22

Note that 2½% compounded quarterly gives an annual rate greater than 10%:

£1 × $(1 + 0.025)^4$ = £1.1038, interest is £0.1038 = 10.38%

3.9 Summary

Despite criticism of the residual valuation technique, it remains useful in development situations as no two sites or the development proposals upon them can be entirely the same. The comparison method therefore tends to play a secondary role in providing a rough check in the way of average values per hectare for the particular type of development land. Because of the number of variables involved, RICS is one among many influential voices which suggest that sensitivity testing is a valid approach to explore the full range of likely risks which will affect the final land value calculation.

The residual valuation has a linear format and logic which cannot take full account of the timings of costs and receipts over a development timeline. Estimates therefore have to be made regarding the draw-down of a loan facility to pay for items such as professional fees and construction costs. We will see in chapter 5 that a cash flow approach can bring more transparency to the timings of costs and income over a project and in theory should be able to calculate the interest charges more accurately.

References

Davidson, A. W. (2002) *Parry's Valuation and Investment Tables*, 12th edition (London: EG Books).

Dubben, N. (2008) 'Development properties', ch. 13 in Hayward, R. (ed.) *Valuation: Principles into Practice*, 6th edition (London: EG Books).

Havard, T. (2008) *Contemporary Property Development*, 2nd edition (London: RIBA Publishing).

Isaac, D. and Steley, T. (2000) *Property Valuation Techniques* (London: Palgrave).

Ratcliffe, J., Stubbs, M. and Keeping, M. (2009) *Urban Planning and Real Estate Development*, 3rd edition (London: Routledge).

Royal Institution of Chartered Surveyors (1994) *The Mallinson Report – Report of the President's Working Party on Commercial Property Valuation* (London: RICS).

Royal Institution of Chartered Surveyors (2007a) *RICS Valuation Standards* ('the Red Book') 6th edition (London: RICS).

Royal Institution of Chartered Surveyors (2007b) *Code of Measuring Practice*, 6th edition (London: RICS).

Royal Institution of Chartered Surveyors (2008) *Valuation Information Paper No. 12: Valuation of development land* (London: RICS).

Scarrett, D. (2008) *Property Valuation: the Five Methods*, 2nd edition (London: Routledge).

Wyatt, P. (2007) *Property Valuation in an Economic Context* (Oxford: Blackwell).

4

Ground rents and partnership schemes

4.1 Introduction
4.2 The calculation of ground rents
4.3 Equity sharing and partnerships

4.4 Advantages of partnerships
4.5 Summary

Aims

This chapter introduces the concepts of ground rents and partnerships in commercial property development. Partnerships are analysed on different bases and the balance of risk and reward is considered in each case. Detailed examples are provided and the advantages of partnerships discussed.

Key terms

>> **Ground rent** – the payment to the owner of land used in the development process which recognises its contribution to the final development value.
>> **Partnerships** – arrangements for development where a landowner, funder and developer agree to work together to realise a scheme.
>> **Equity-sharing arrangements** – the division of the rental income from the development to land owners, funders and developers, respectively *ground rent*, *finance rent* and *developer's profit* and consideration of the sharing of any excess amounts.

4.1 Introduction

Particularly in town and city centre locations where large retail or mixed-use developments are envisaged there will often be a complex interplay between a landowner (who may be the local authority) a developer and a funding institution. Each may wish to retain a long-term interest in the completed development because historically well-planned shopping centre development has tended to be commercially successful. Thus a landowner may want to retain an ongoing interest in the scheme rather than disposing of a valuable freehold site for a one-off capital payment to a developer. Similarly the developer may need a site of sufficient size in the right location to realise a profitable development and may therefore be willing to share in some of the anticipated financial returns if such as site can be made available for development. The funding institution may also want to share in the longer-term capital and rental growth rather than acting as a passive lender of debt finance. Sharing in the longer-term capital and rental growth of a development also requires that parties accept a share of the risks involved, ideally on a *pro rata* basis relative to the rewards.

As Havard (2008: 142) points out partnerships can comprise two or more organisations combining to carry out a development project. Indeed the term 'joint venture' is often used in an interchangeable manner with the term partnership when property development is the objective, however for simplicity in this chapter the term 'partnership' will be used. In a commercial property development context such as the development of a town centre retail scheme the two principal parties would normally be the local authority (as landowner) and a private developer. However, partnerships could equally comprise private sector-only organisations such as a landowning pension fund combining with a private developer with no direct local authority involvement.

Other partnership models might see a local authority landowner partnering a private developer and a funding institution. There is potentially a four-party model where a regeneration agency also becomes involved because of the additional risks which might arise in the context of the redevelopment of a challenging brownfield site. Given varied locations and change within the property market, it is perhaps not surprising that a number of different partnership models have therefore evolved to deal with sharing the risks and rewards from development. This chapter will look at some of the partnership models which have emerged since the concept was first used on a large-scale commercial basis in the context of shopping centre developments in the 1960s and 1970s.

4.2 The calculation of ground rents

The capital value of a development site as calculated in the previous chapter can be used in situations where the freeholder of the land wishes to retain a longer-term interest, rather than disposing of a site to a developer. In these situations a development partnership is formed involving the landowner, a developer and possibly a financial backer. The landowner may be a local authority with a land bank or a statutory authority with surplus property or a large financial institution or charitable foundation which manages its estate for longer-term investment purposes. In these cases the landowner may feel that the development expertise required does not exist within the organisation to carry out a development and therefore an appropriately experienced developer and possibly a funder are sought to form a development partnership.

As Morley (1988: 37) describes large-scale commercial development partnerships first came to prominence in the 1960s and since then they have evolved to suit the needs of partner organisations. By 2010 variants of development partnerships had been used by local authorities and regeneration agencies in the UK in order to realise redevelopment in situations where it would be too risky for one organisation to carry out the large complex schemes required. However in more conventional town centre development scenarios a common form of development agreement will see a landowning local authority retain the freehold of a well-located site and thus an interest in the development enabling it to share in the future financial growth of the scheme.

In the above scenario the landowning local authority will normally grant a long lease of, say, 125 years to the developer to carry out the project. The landowner thus receives an annual ground rent for the land rather than taking a capital sum for outright disposal. This arrangement has enabled major landowners historically to develop their lands while maintaining an ongoing return and a degree of control. This approach is particularly useful in town and city centres where land assembly is often difficult and risky.

Partnerships also lend themselves to development situations where the nature of the market has not yet been established and where the risks may deter developers or funders or both. In these situations partnerships offer the potential to balance risks and rewards to a degree which is acceptable to all parties. Partnership arrangements also provide an opportunity to use more innovative funding arrangements such as sale and leaseback (a concept which will be investigated further in chapter 7).

In order to remove the element of risk from the equation, local authorities may take a lease and leaseback arrangement or an overriding lease of the property to give guarantees to the rents and thus enable the developer to obtain funding. In these situations the local authority grants a 125-year lease to the developer, who then leases back the property at a guaranteed rent for, say, 25 years to the local authority. The local authority then lets the premises on occupational leases and this arrangement is shown below in Figure 4.1.

By guaranteeing the rent in this way, the developer can obtain finance. The local authority has control over the leases and can use the space to further policies of local economic regeneration or employment if necessary. If successful, there will be an excess of rent received over the guaranteed rent to be paid to the developer. The principles governing the calculation of the ground rent are illustrated in the example below.

Example 4.1: Ground rent calculation for a 125-year lease with 5-year rent reviews.

Estimated annual income	£500,000
Yield	7% freehold: long lease (say) 7.5%
Finance costs	9%
Estimated costs	£5,000,000 (all development costs except land)
Profit	20% benchmarked against costs

Calculation:

	£	£
Annual income		500,000
Development cost excluding land	5,000,000	
Yield @ 7.5%, decapitalise by	0.075	
Return for risk and profit (20% of 7.5%)	0.015	
Sinking fund: long lease therefore	Nil	
Total development yield		0.09
Developer's costs and profit		450,000
Annual ground rent available		50,000

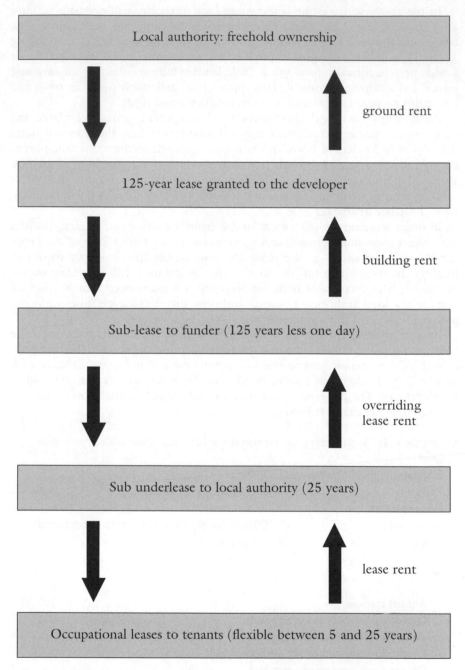

Figure 4.1 Example of a lease structure in a partnership arrangement

The future rent is divided up on the original proportions as follows:

Future growth apportioned: <u>£50,000</u> to local authority/landowner <u>ground rent</u>
£500,000 total income
= 10%

Developer's return is: £<u>450,000</u> = 90%
£500,000

At the next rent review, the income is divided in the same proportions.
Return to local authority/landowner:
Assume historic site purchase costs to be £750,000 including fees and disturbance costs.

	£
Site purchase cost	750,000
Interest during development period of 3 years @ 9%	221,272
Total cost on completion	971,272

Return = £<u>50,000</u> = 5.15%.
£971,272

Interest on total cost of £971,272 for one year @ 9%[*] =	£87,414
Less ground rent received	£50,000
Initial deficit	£37,414

[*]cost of borrowing

4.3 Equity sharing and partnerships

Participation arrangements involve the sharing of the additional return which arises over a period from the estimated outcome to the actual outcome on completion. In this case, let us assume that there has been growth in rental income over the development period as well as inflation in building costs and that the landowner and developer will share equally in the growth in the net income over the development period.

Example 4.2: Participation arrangement

	£
Estimated annual rental income	500,000
Actual rental income given that an uplift of 20% has occurred	600,000
Estimated costs	5,000,000
Actual costs given that an uplift of 10% has occurred	5,500,000

The original annual ground rent was £50,000 but now there is agreement that any excess of return over the estimated position is shared equally between the two parties. The calculation would look as follows:

	£	£
Actual annual rental income		600,000
Actual cost	5,500,000	
Decapitalise by the development yield	.09	
		495,000
Residue		105,000
Less ground rent		50,000
Excess		55,000
Thus 50% excess to local authority		27,500
Plus original ground rent		50 000
Revised ground rent		77,500

Future growth apportioned to the local authority is therefore: 77,500/600,000 which equals 12.9% and so the developer receives the balance of 87.1%.

With regards to equity-sharing arrangements the main differences are to do with the number and way that slices are made to the income. One of the early academic discussions regarding slicing in a commercial property context was provided by Morley (1988: 37–66) and this has influenced subsequent thinking and discussions on the topic by authors such as Dubben and Williams (2009: 183–224) who explore the topic in some depth and Wyatt (2007: 388–91). The slicing concept described by these authors and which has evolved in practice can be considered further as follows.

A four-slice arrangement

Where a four-slice approach is taken to the income as illustrated below in Figure 4.2 the priority of order of charges on the total income arising from occupational leases is as follows:

- The first charge is the ground rent payable to the local authority or landowner.
- The second charge is to the developer's costs also known as the 'building rent' (0.075 on costs in the example above).
- The third charge is to the developer's profit (0.015 on costs in the example above).
- The fourth charge is the residue or 'top slice', which is any additional profit generated by the scheme and which may be split 50:50 between the parties as the diagram below illustrates.

Dubben (2008: 374–5) discusses a variation on the horizontal four-slice approach shown below in Figure 4.3 in which a funding organisation becomes involved to create three parties. The scenario here is that the funder who might be a pension fund or insurance company agrees to meet the development costs excluding the land, the latter being made available on a long lease by the local authority in return for a safe ground rent. The funder then takes a predetermined percentage return which represents the second slice or charge on the

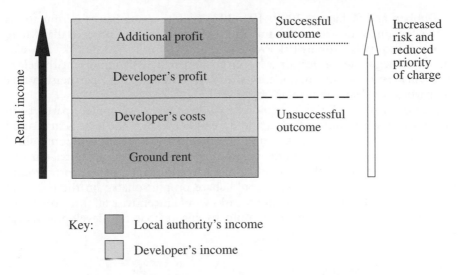

Figure 4.2 Equity sharing: four-slice approach

rental income generated by the occupational tenants. The third slice is the developer's profit and the fourth slice (should there be any) is shared equally between all three parties.

Given that the developer's return would be in the third and relatively risky slice with a potential bonus in the most risky fourth slice, there would be sufficient incentive for the developer to use all reasonable endeavours and expertise to ensure that the scheme was a success. Conceptually the four-sliced arrangement described by Dubben would look as follows.

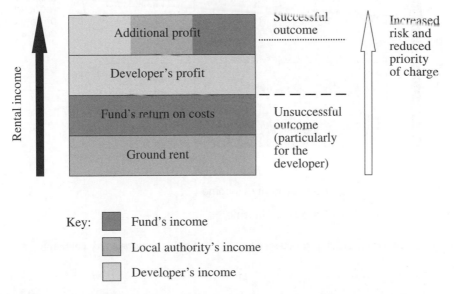

Figure 4.3 Equity sharing: four-slice approach (with funding organisation, based on Dubben (2008))

Dubben and Williams (2009: 191–203) explore a number of permutations of this 'ground rent with premium' approach to slicing and observe that where a local authority is strongly risk averse it might wish to forgo the risky top slice share but negotiate harder for a larger ground rent. It is important therefore that when entering into negotiations to form a development partnership that the parties are clear about their objectives.

Shapiro *et al.* (2009: 343) also discuss a three-way development partnership involving a local authority, funder and developer in which the lease is structured so that the income is shared on a side-by-side basis without any horizontal slices or priority order of charges on the income generated from occupational tenants. In these circumstances the ground landlord would grant a peppercorn ground rent and then all three partners would share proportionately in the risks and rewards. Again this direct exposure to risks would incentivise all three parties to contribute in whatever way they could to ensure that the development was successful.

A three-slice approach

Where a three-slice approach is taken to the income and where a funder is not directly involved as an equity partner, the slice earmarked for the developer's profit is removed. In this situation the developer is taking a substantial risk and will probably negotiate for a lower ground rent to be payable to the local authority. The concept is illustrated in Figure 4.4 below.

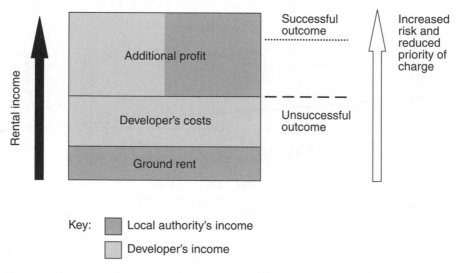

Figure 4.4 Equity sharing: three-slice approach (funder as non-equity partner)

The calculation for the three-slice approach shown above would be as follows:

	£	£
Actual annual income		600,000
Actual cost	5,500,000	
Decapitalise by the developer's costs	0.075	
		412,500
Residue		187,500
less ground rent		20,000
Excess		167,500
thus: 50% excess to local authority		83,750
plus original ground rent		20,000
Equity rent payable		£103,750

The future growth is apportioned £103,750/£600,000 which equals 17.3% and which is the local authority or landowner's share of the income and the remaining 82.7% is the developer's share. The priority of order of charges on the rental income is as follows:

- The first charge is the ground rent payable to the local authority or landowner.
- The second charge is the developer's costs, also known as the 'building rent' which in the example represents 0.075 of the costs of the scheme.
- The third charge is the residue (if there is any) remaining after the first and second charges above and which is shared equally between the partners.

Although the landowner stands to receive a slightly higher share of the income than in the standard equity participation arrangement, the landowner bears more risk in this model as the ground rent is reduced and more reliance is placed on a share of the riskier top slice income.

A two-slice approach

Here the local authority or the landowner is taking all the risk if something goes wrong, so they may ask the developer to take less profit by perhaps reducing the development yield to 8.5%. The priority of order of charges on the rental income in this scenario is as follows:

- The first charge is to the developer's costs and profit.
- The second charge is the residual payable to the local authority or landowner.

Conceptually the two-slice arrangement is represented below by Figure 4.5.

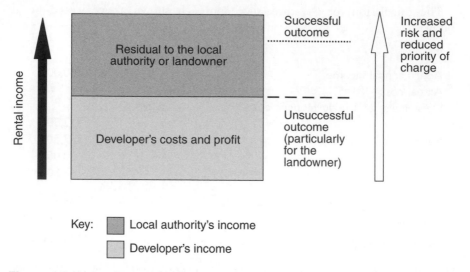

Key: Local authority's income

Developer's income

Figure 4.5 Equity sharing: two-slice approach

An example of a calculation in this two-slice scenario is as follows:

	£	£
Actual income		600,000
Actual cost	5,500,000	
Decapitalise by the development yield	0.085	
		467,500
Residue to the local authority or landowner		132,500

The future growth is apportioned £132,500/£600,000 which equals 22.1% and which is the local authority or landowner's share of the growth. The remaining 77.9% is the developer's share. Thus the landowner's return apparently increases over that attainable in the three slice approach however there is considerably more risk for the landowner to bear given that if the scheme is unsuccessful there will be little or no return. The developer in this scenario appears to be achieving a high return for bearing little of the risk and from this safe position there is little incentive to ensure that the scheme is successful beyond achieving the bottom slice of income. It is most unlikely that a professionally advised local authority would enter into such an agreement.

Observations on equity-sharing arrangements

The risk element will always affect the top slice of the income stream first if anything goes wrong as can be seen in the priority of charges and figures depicting the slicing arrangements above. On rent growth the returns have been worked out on apportioned returns, as at the date of completion of the scheme. So, in the participation arrangement (example 4.2 above) the proportionate share was 12.9% to the local authority/landowner and 87.1% to the developer. This arrangement then serves to divide the proceeds at subsequent rent reviews.

If the four-slice method was used and the proportions were recalculated at each rent review, then there would be a gearing effect on the review as the residue increases in proportion to the total income. Thus the local authority's/landowner's 50% of the top slice would increase and the developer's share would decrease as the following calculation illustrates.

Original position on completion of the scheme: 12.9% of income to the local authority/landowner and 87% to the developer.

Rent reviews at five-year intervals see the scheme's rental income increase by 50% thus:

	£
New annual rental income	900,000
Development yield	495,000
Residue	405,000
Less ground rent	50,000
Excess	355,000
50% of excess to the local authority	177,500
Plus ground rent	50,000
Total local authority income	227,500

The new proportion of income to the local authority is now therefore: £227,500/£900,000 = 25.3% and the remaining 74.7% to the developer. A gearing effect has therefore established itself in favouring the local authority, although it was dependent on the large rental uplift at the five-year rent review.

Of course not all town centre retail schemes will show the impressive rental performance at rent reviews assumed above and a number of town centre retail developments have suffered from retail impact cause by the development of large out of town retail centres. The latter were developed in the late 1980s and early 1990s and have since traded very successfully and they include Bluewater and Lakeside on the edge of London, Meadowhall near Sheffield and the Metro centre near Newcastle. In 2009 the Westfield Centre opened in West London and the quality and quantity of the retail offer there inevitably poses threats to the continuing viability of suburban shopping centres nearby. While some town centres close to these schemes are robust enough to withstand this type of retail competition, a number of secondary centres have seen poor rental performance from retail schemes over the last ten years while some recognised national retailers have pulled out altogether. The resulting voids have proved difficult to fill and are prone to temporary Christmas lettings or are leased to 'no frills' bargain basement retailers and charity shops.

A number of secondary shopping centres have therefore lost their vitality and viability and while planning policy in the UK has subsequently created a virtual embargo on the building of further out-of-centre comparison retail centres, it is unlikely that some secondary town centres will ever recover the footfall necessary for them to regain their position in the town centre retail hierarchy. The 2008–9 credit crunch which affected commercial property values quite dramatically in the UK has further exposed the weak trading position of some secondary centres. In these centres it is now questionable whether some of the large vacant retail units will ever again see retail tenants.

While there are various equity-sharing and slicing permutations for local authorities and landowners to consider there are always fundamental decisions to make on the trade off between risk and reward. Thus a local authority which seeks to expose itself to top-slice and riskier income tranches from developments should only do so after looking at the wider picture and assessing the strategic project risks. Arm's length advice should also be sought from suitably experienced consultants who may assist on structuring an appropriate slicing arrangement to suit particular circumstances.

4.4 Advantages of partnerships

Recognising that there will always be risks involved in complex mixed-use developments there remain a number of advantages stemming from a partnership approach to such developments. McCarthy (2007: 18) when discussing the wider concept of partnership working identifies a number of themes which apply to development partnerships, including 'synergy' which combines assets and resources so that partners can achieve more together than they could have individually. Partnerships also bring about budget enlargement and more subtly, but of some importance McCarthy cites 'transformation' whereby:

> partners are exposed to different modes of working, resulting in the objectives and cultures of different partners converging towards a mutually acceptable, and potentially innovative strategy. (McCarthy, 2007: 18)

Returning to the more prosaic level of property development Wilkinson and Reed (2008: 147) confirm that the sharing of risk is also an important principle in bringing parties together. The advantages of partnerships for the main parties are summarised in the following paragraphs.

Advantages for the developer

A developer may need the involvement of a local authority who may already part-own a large site which has development potential or who will be able to complete the site using compulsory purchase powers. The involvement of a local authority in this respect would certainly reduce the development period and if the local authority owns or takes possession of a site there will be no site acquisition costs or finance charges on the site for the developer to meet until development. The direct involvement of the local authority in a scheme can assist on planning, environmental impact assessment, building regulations and highways matters.

A partnership also provides greater certainty around a project and this may be an important factor in attracting development loans from funders at competitive rates. There is also the prospect of creating positive publicity and marketing where the local authority is a key stakeholder. While most commercial property development ventures would be expected to be self financing and not reliant upon public grant or subsidy, the involvement of the local authority can be helpful in introducing a regeneration agency where a market is untested and/or where infrastructure works may be needed to make a site developable.

Advantages for a local authority

The local authority can use partnership arrangements to encourage development on difficult sites and to initiate schemes which help to achieve wider regeneration objectives. The local authority also has more control over what is being developed if it is actually involved directly in a development. This control is greater than can be achieved by planning legislation. As the slicing concepts discussed above reveal, with careful business planning a local authority can share in the future financial returns from a successful scheme and this money can be used to meet a whole variety of social objectives which the authority may have.

Partnerships may allow developments to be funded in the market as funders may be attracted to a partnership scheme whereas they may not be as interested in a local authority scheme. One of the criteria for choosing a private sector partner may in fact be that they have expertise in raising funds. Partnerships complement the skills of the two parties. The local authority can provide backup on engineering matters, sewers, roads, transport and planning whereas the private partner can provide project management, financial expertise and development know-how. The developer can also take some of the risk out of the development. Similar advantages may be available for other types of landowner besides the local authority.

A development partnership scenario

An example of the financial structuring of a partnership arrangement for development can now be considered in a little more detail in the context of a development scenario in which a local authority owns a town centre site of 1 hectare. The buildings on site have no value and the local authority want the site redeveloped. A detailed planning consent is in place which allows for the development of the following mixed-use scheme:

6,000 m^2 of offices
20 shop units each of which is 120 m^2
A 3,500 m^2 supermarket
200 basement car parking spaces

The local authority wishes to participate in the scheme and requires an initial annual ground rent of £100,000 with a premium. The rents are likely to increase over the period by 10%. The appraisal is set out below showing the calculation of the residual value for the land and details of a suitable equity-sharing arrangement. The figures in the appraisal have been rounded up to the nearest pound for simplicity.

Assumptions		
Rents £ per m^2 per annum	Offices	200
	Shop units	250
	Supermarket	210

Investment yield:	7.00%		Long leasehold yield:		7.50%	

Building costs £ per m²	Offices	1,300	
	Shop units	1,000	
	Supermarket	950	

Cost to provide each of the 200 basement parking spaces: £2,000

Short-term finance annual rate:	9%	

	Months	
Planning period	0	
Building period	18	
Void period	6	

Site appraisal

Gross development value

Offices gross area m²		6,000	
Net area @	80%	4,800	
Rent £ per m²	200	Total office rent therefore:	960,000
Shop units gross area m² each		120	
Net area @	90%	108	
Rent £ per m²	250		
Number of units	20	Total shop rents therefore:	540,000
Supermarket gross area m²		3,500	
Net area @	90%	3,150	
Rent £ per m²	210	Total supermarket rent therefore:	661,500

Total rental income from scheme			2,161,500

Years' purchase in perpetuity @	7%	YP =	14.29	
Gross development value				30,887,835

Less costs

Building costs	Gross m²	£ per m²	£		
Offices	6,000	1,300	7,800,000		
Shop units	2,400	1,000	2,400,000		
Supermarket	3,500	950	3,325,000		

	No.	£ per space			
Parking spaces	200	2,000	400,000		
Demolition and site costs			200,000		
Total building costs			14,125,000		
Professional fees @ 12.50% of building costs			1,765,625		
Interest on ½ building costs for 18 months @ 9%			953,438		
Interest on ⅔ fees for 18 months @ 9%			158,906		
Total cost			17,002,969		
Interest on total for 6 month void @ 9%			765,134		
Contingency on total cost @ 3%			533,043		
			18,301,146		
Letting fees @ 15% of total annual rent			324,225		
Advertising @ 1% of GDV			308,878		
Total development costs			18,934,249		
Plus developer's profit @ 17% of GDV			5,250,932		
Costs plus profit				24,185,181	
Value of the site in 2 years				6,702,654	
Present value of £1 in 2 years @ 9% =			0.8417		
Value of the site now				5,641,624	
less acquisition costs @ 5% of site value			268,541		
Site value therefore				5,373,083	
Equity participation					
Assuming no increase in costs, allow for an equal participation in increased income.					
Original position					
Expected annual income				2,161,500	
Costs:					
Development costs less profit			18,934,249		
Developer's yield					
Investment yield		7.50%			
Annual profit @ 20%		1.5%			
Total yield required on costs therefore:			9.00%		
Rent to developer				1,704,082	
Balance of rent available for landowner				457,418	
Ground rent to local authority			100,000		
Balance on ground rent			357,418		

Premium = balance/development yield		9.00%		
		3,971,311		
Actual position				
Actual annual income is 10% above original			2,377,650	
Costs				
Development costs less profit		18,934,249		
Premium		3,971,311		
Total costs		22,905,560		
Developer's yield				
Investment yield	7.50%			
Annual profit @ 20%	1.5%			
Total yield required on costs therefore:	9.00%			
Rent to developer			2,061,500	
Ground rent to local authority			100,000	
Residue			216,150	
split 50:50 therefore 108,075 to each party				
Income to local authority = ground rent plus 50% of the residue =			208,075	
Income to the local authority as a proportion of income therefore		8.8%		

Income on review determined on a proportional basis with 8.8% to the local authority and the balance of 91.2% to the developer.

4.5 Summary

Partnership schemes can be employed in various ways by the parties involved in a development project. For example local authorities can offer long building leases and in return receive ground rent, but perhaps more importantly retain some control over the future of a site by virtue of the lease covenants that are agreed. In other cases landowners can negotiate a share of the profits in a scheme, in return perhaps for adjustments in the negotiated price. The amount of capital put at risk by the various parties can be reflected by slicing of the equity stakes held. Partners can be included for their expertise in and access to funding for example and such measures are helpful in reducing risk to a project.

References

Dubben, N. (2008) 'Development properties', in R. Hayward (ed.) *Valuation: Principles into Practice*, 6th edition (London: EG Books).

Dubben, N. and Williams, B. (2009) *Partnerships in Property Development* (London: Wiley-Blackwell).

Havard, T. (2008) *Contemporary Property Development*, 2nd edition (London: RIBA Publishing).

McCarthy, J. (2007) *Partnership, Collaborative Planning and Urban Regeneration* (Aldershot: Ashgate).

Morley, S. (1988) 'Partnership schemes and ground rent calculations', in C. Darlow (ed.), *Valuation and Development Appraisal*, 2nd edition (London: Estates Gazette).

Shapiro, E., Davies, K. and Mackmin, D. (2009) *Modern Methods of Valuation*, 10th edition (London: EG Books).

Wilkinson, S. and Reed, R. (2008) *Property Development*, 5th edition, Routledge, London.

Wyatt, P. (2007) *Property Valuation in an Economic Context* (Oxford: Blackwell).

5

Cash flow methods

5.1 Introduction
5.2 Cash flows in development appraisal
5.3 Spreadsheets

5.4 Sensitivity analysis
5.5 Risk
5.6 Summary

Aims

This chapter explores the advantages that cash flow methods have over the residual method in development appraisal. Through worked examples a number of different types of cash flow which are used in development appraisal work are explored. The chapter also examines risk and expands upon the basic concept of sensitivity analysis first looked at in chapter 3 by investigating how statistical techniques can play a role in appraisals.

Key terms

>> **Period by period cash flow** – the division of a development timeline into months or quarters and the modelling of cash into and out of the project over that timeline in order to identify a site value or profit margin.
>> **Discounted cash flow** – the adoption of a discount rate to reflect project risk and against which future income and expenditure is discounted back to present value to ascertain if the risk rate has been achieved. A positive net present value indicates that the target rate has been achieved while a negative net present value indicates that it has not.
>> **Risk-free rate** – the rate of interest achievable on safe investments such as government securities or bonds.
>> **Risk premium** – the increase on the risk-free rate to reflect the additional risk on a project or investment as perceived by the investor or developer.

5.1 Introduction

This chapter investigates the use of cash flow methods in property development appraisal. Cash flows deal with future costs and revenues and in that sense they are technically forecasts. Valuations and forecasts are fundamentally different as a valuation seeks to determine market price at a specific time which is the valuation date. A valuation may be based on assumptions as to what will happen in the future but it is not a forecast. A forecast will be concerned entirely with the future. In development appraisals assumptions need to be made about project costs, future rents and capital values and potential changes can be incorporated. Where formal forecasting is used in property development appraisals it tends to play a supporting rather than leading role. This is because of the volatility which characterises the development process and which makes forecasting a hazardous process in this field. Forecasting also becomes problematic because there are sometimes practical difficulties in obtaining reliable local or project-specific time series data to use in the forecasting process. There are however some forecasts available at a national level and for example RICS (2008) publishes commercial and housing market forecasts which are highly regarded. However where a cash flow's projected costs and revenues are discounted back to present value to determine a site value the distinction between what is a forecast and what is a valuation becomes blurred if not semantic.

The traditional method of residual valuation is the most commonly used approach in the financial analysis of development proposals. However, the sophistication of investment markets and the size and complexity of development projects has led to the adoption of more transparent techniques of analysis. The momentum towards greater detail and analysis in appraisal lies with the practices of the major funders of commercial development: the financial institutions which include insurance companies and the pension funds. Their demands for better analysis when they are providing funds stems from the quality of analysis used in-house when they are project managing or dealing with their own portfolio.

Other lenders such as banks, individuals and organisations in joint ventures have established their own standards to ensure that their money does not get into trouble. Economic analysis, providing a wider setting to the microeconomic financial analysis used in property development has been applied both in the valuation to ensure the outcome is appropriate to the market and in the subsequent analysis of the investment.

At a basic level, the traditional valuation can be developed by using a cash flow approach which divides up the timescale of a development into periods to which interest charges can be applied. The simple application of interest charges to building costs and professional fees for one-half and two-thirds of the building period respectively is therefore flawed. This is because the 'S curve' of building costs suggests that a greater proportion of the overall costs will tend to arise in the later stages of development, for instance in relation to the high cost of services and finishes in buildings. In this case the residual calculation can overestimate the interest charges. In a competitive situation a cash flow approach will generate lower costs and assuming other elements are equal, a higher site value will be identified than is possible with a residual valuation.

Cash flows enable more explicit assumptions to be made in an appraisal particularly with the timing of costs and revenues. These subtleties cannot be accommodated in the traditional residual valuation. In a period of inflation or deflation explicit adjustments can be made to various costs and revenues arising at various points along the timeline of the development. The cash flow can make allowance for the timing of one-off cash injections such as a grant or capital allowances and/or contractor retention payments or tax.

Cash flows also provide a means to monitor progress against projections. If for example the maximum point of indebtedness in a development timeline was projected to be in month 16 when a scheme was predicted to have drawn down £20 million from the bank, then alarm bells would ring and corrective action could be considered if in fact the scheme had achieved £21 million of debt by that stage.

The arguments for using cash flow approaches (including discounted cash flow) in preference to the traditional years' purchase approach to valuation are persuasive. Problems can arise using the traditional approach because the price paid in the market may not reflect the present worth of the future cash flow. A discounted cash flow approach is a realistic way to approach this issue particularly in regards to over-rented property where the rent passing under the lease is higher than the existing market rental. During a recessionary market, such as that of 2008–9 in the UK the use of traditional techniques becomes questionable as they cannot adequately nor explicitly cope with rent-free periods, reverse premiums, tenant incentives, bad debts, deflation in rents and capital values and over-rented properties.

5.2 Cash flows in development appraisal

Cash flows adopt the same basis as the residual method in that a scheme's costs are being compared with development value to determine the value of a site. The cash flow approach however gives a more detailed calculation of the scheme's total costs and thus the finance costs. In a period-by-period cash flow, all development costs and revenues are divided into monthly or quarterly amounts. The net cash flows are calculated and short-term finance allowed for each period. Cash flows can model the build-up of construction costs over the contract period and this should capture the back-end loading of construction costs depicted by the S curve (discussed and illustrated in chapter 3).

There are thus two weaknesses in the traditional residual approach:

1 It is assumed that the total money borrowed will bear interest over half the building period. This is inaccurate because:
   (a) it bears no relation to the actual incidence of costs which will differ from month to month over the development period;
   (b) interest compounds monthly or quarterly over the period depending on the arrangements with the lender, the simple interest formula of the traditional residual, or even compounding interest annually is an oversimplification.
2 The build-up of building costs as represented by the S curve suggests that costs are more heavily loaded after the half way stage and typically only 40% of the costs are incurred half-way through a construction contract. This is because ground and initial works tend to involve less labour and it is only when a building's superstructure is in place that numerous subcontractors can begin work on installing expensive mechanical and electrical services such as lifts, sprinkler systems, telecoms and air-conditioning systems. The traditional method will thus allow for too much interest.

To summarise, cash flows are more versatile than the residual approach as they can:

1 model the effects of inflation in rents and building costs over time;
2 incorporate sensitivity analyses more explicitly to examine the effect of changes on the elements of cost and value;
3 include the effect of tax in the calculation;
4 take into account the phasing or partial disposal of a development;
5 show the extent of debt outstanding at any point; and
6 they can identify the time of peak cash outlay and thus the point of maximum financial exposure.

Cash flows are an obvious choice for developments such as residential estates where the phased construction and then disposal of dwellings can be used to fund the next phase of the development. Cash flows also lend themselves to the appraisal of complex retail schemes where discrete phases are completed and let to retailers and then opened to the public for trading while the next phase is undertaken. Large industrial estates and business parks with a programme of plot completions, lettings and then disposals are also candidates for cash flow appraisal. In the past commercial development schemes did not readily allow for phasing because tenants did not welcome occupying premises with construction continuing around them. This can affect a business and its profitability. However, business and retail parks and industrial estates do lend themselves to phasing which can considerably reduce the funding requirements as well as the risk to the developer which increases the longer a scheme takes to complete (Isaac and Steley 2000).

There can be problems of retaining a development while there is no income as in the case of a speculative development which has not been presold or pre-let. This increases the risk to the developer and to the financier. An obvious way of reducing the funding problem and the risk of voids is to phase developments as discussed above.

Large atypical developments such as eco-towns which involve phased implementation and early delivery of core social and physical infrastructure also lend themselves to cash flow analysis. In these cases there is often heavy up-front expenditure by regeneration agencies or local authorities on green infrastructure and/or compulsory purchase to assemble a site and kick start the project. It is therefore reasonable for these organisations to model with private sector stakeholders overage or claw-back agreements so that early investment is recouped from increases in site value that are subsequently achieved by a development partner.

When considering the finance of a project, discounted cash flow techniques can be useful if the scheme is to be retained and financed by a commercial mortgage as the net return can be identified. Authors such as Fraser (2004) have thoroughly explained the mechanics of the different types of cash flow appraisal which can be used in various property contexts. It is not necessary to review all of the techniques here, however given the concerns of this book there are three approaches which warrant further investigation and these are: the period-by-period cash flow, the net terminal value approach and the discounted cash flow. The advantages and disadvantages of the three approaches are summarised below in Table 5.1.

The three types of cash flow discussed above can now be modelled in Table 5.2 using a development scenario in which the costs of building plus fees breaks down as follows, excluding finance.

Table 5.1 Type of cash flow and their respective advantages–disadvantages

Period by period	*Net terminal value*	*Discounted cash flow*
Purpose Identifies explicitly the quarterly or monthly spend and interest charges arising. Interest on the previous quarter/ month is rolled up i.e. added to the next period.	**Purpose** It rolls up interest on the outstanding amount to the end of the construction period and then identifies the project's value.	**Purpose** It converts future payments and revenues to present day value.
Advantages The debt is shown for each period and it copes with interest rate changes.	**Advantages** Quicker, logical extension to the traditional residual.	**Advantages** Quickest approach, the net present value and internal rate of return can easily be identified.
Disadvantages Can be time consuming to produce as a meticulous approach is required.	**Disadvantages** Not flexible nor widely used nor quickly understood.	**Disadvantages** Not related to how costs have evolved. Does not show the total debt.

Table 5.2 Quarterly cash flow and building costs

Year 1	*Costs £*	*Year 2*	*Costs £*
Quarter 1	200,000	Quarter 5	270,000
Quarter 2	220,000	Quarter 6	275,000
Quarter 3	230,000	Quarter 7	280,000
Quarter 4	255,000	Quarter 8	270,000

The builder is usually paid monthly, although in the scenario in Table 5.2 the developer uses a quarterly cash flow against which interest is charged on a quarterly basis.

Income from the scheme is £260,000 and it could be sold at an 8% yield for £3,250,000 on completion of the works. Finance is 2% per quarter which is equivalent to 8.24% per annum. Applying the formula $((1 + i)^n) - 1$ to the quarterly rate demonstrates how the annual rate is derived as follows: $((1.02)^4) - 1$ = 8.24% rounded to two decimal places. The return for risk and profit is 20% of the capital value.

If the above data were used in a residual valuation it would appear as shown in Figure 5.1.

Having identified the site value produced by the residual method it can now

Traditional residual valuation method		
Annual income £		260,000
Years Purchase in perpetuity @ 8% = 12.5		
Gross Development Value (GDV) =		3,250,000
Less Costs		
Building costs plus fees	2,000,000	
Finance on costs for ½ × 2 years @ 8.24%	171,590	
Total costs		2,171,590
Return for risks and profit @ 20% of capital value	650,000	
Total costs plus profit =		2,821,590
Site value on completion (GDV – Total costs plus profit)		428,410
Present Value of £1 in 2 years @ 8.24% = 0.8535		
Site value today		£ 365,648

Figure 5.1 Cash flow methods: traditional residual

be compared with the site values generated by three cash flow approaches to establish which would generate the most competitive site bid.

The debt shown in Table 5.4 on page 109 is virtually the same as for the period-by-period cash flow shown in Table 5.3 with a very slight difference due to rounding. The completion of the valuation would therefore arrive at a virtually identical site value of: **£396,286**.

There is a slight difference in the outcome shown in Table 5.5 on page 109 when compared with the net terminal value approach due to rounding.

It can be seen that the three cash flow approaches generate very similar outcomes all of which are more competitive than that achieved by the residual method. The main differences between the cash flow approaches are really in the way that the data is processed over the time periods. The main procedural differences are summarised in the following paragraphs.

Table 5.3 Period-by-period cash flow

Quarter	Total costs £	Income £	Net cash flow £	Capital outstanding from previous	Interest on capital outstanding @ quarterly rate of 2%	Capital outstanding
	a	b	c = b − a	d	e	f = c + d + e
1	200,000	0	−200,000	0	0	−200,000
2	220,000	0	−220,000	−200,000	−4,000	−424,000
3	230,000	0	−230,000	−424,000	−8,480	−662,480
4	255,000	0	−255,000	−662,480	−13,250	−930,730
5	270,000	0	−270,000	−930,730	−18,615	−219,345
6	275,000	0	−275,000	−1,219,345	−24,387	−1,518,732
7	280,000	0	−280,000	−1,518,732	−30,375	−1,829,107
8	270,000	0	−270,000	−1,829,107	−36,582	−2,135,689

Capital value   3,250,000

Less outstanding debt   2,135,689

Return for risk and profit @ 20% of GDV   650,000

Site value on completion   464,311

PV of £1 in 2 years @ 8.24%   0.8535

Site value today   £396,289

Table 5.4 Net terminal value

Quarter	Net cash flow as above £	Interest until completion @ 2%	Net outlay on completion £
1	−200,000	1.1487	−229,740
2	−220,000	1.1262	−247,764
3	−230,000	1.1041	−253,943
4	−255,000	1.0824	−276,012
5	−270,000	1.0612	−286,524
6	−275,000	1.0404	−286,110
7	−280,000	1.0200	−285,600
8	−270,000	1	−270,000
Outstanding debt therefore =			−2,135,693

Table 5.5 Discounted cash flow

Quarter	Net cash flow as above £	PV of £1 @ 2%	PV of cash flow £
1	−200,000	0.9804	−196,080
2	−220,000	0.9612	−211,464
3	−230,000	0.9423	−216,729
4	−255,000	0.9238	−235,569
5	−270,000	0.9057	−244,539
6	−275,000	0.8880	244,200
7	−280,000	0.8706	−243,768
8	−270,000	0.8535	−230,445
Total costs			−1,822,794
Profit	650,000	0.8535	−554,775
Value	3,250,000	0.8535	2,773,875
Site value today			£396,306

Period-by-period cash flow

The interest is assessed quarterly on the outstanding amount from the previous quarter. This is a more accurate statement of cost plus interest, the total cost is deducted from the gross development value to obtain the site value which is discounted back to the present in this calculation.

Net terminal value

The interest per quarter is assessed to the end of the project but in other respects it is similar to the period by period cash flow approach.

Discounted cash flow

The cost, value and profit are all *present valued* and the site value emerges in its present value form.

Example of a development appraisal using a cash flow

An office development has been proposed which will have a gross floor area of 1,100 m² and the net lettable area will be 80% of the gross floor area. An investment yield of 8% is expected to be obtained on a net rental value of £450 per m². Construction is planned to commence six months after the site is acquired and building will take 15 months to complete. The premises will be let and sold as an investment six months after completion. Funding can be obtained at an interest rate of 8% per annum.

The conventional residual valuation is shown below in Figure 5.2 which the net development value is based on the capitalised rent, less the purchaser's fees of 5%. The building costs will be estimated on the gross internal area and the professional fees are taken at 13% of building costs. Ancillary costs are estimated to be 5% of building costs and a contingency allowance of 5% is made against professional fees, building and ancillary costs. Finance on construction costs is taken for one-half of the construction period and for professional fees over three-quarters of the construction period. This is a minor variation on the two-thirds times construction period mentioned in earlier chapters for the calculation of finance on professional fees and reflects a scenario here where more up front professional input is required. Over the void period of six months' interest is charged on the total costs plus accumulated interest charges.

The amount for the site will have to be financed from the date of purchase and therefore the final sum is discounted for 27 months that being the total development period for the project. The resulting present value of £1,443,761 is available for the purchase of the site at the beginning of the project.

The cash flow approach is then set out below the residual. In the cash flow, interest is charged at the end of each quarter. It is usual for a retention sum to be held by the developer, part being released on completion and the remainder at the end of the defects liability period, generally six months. This retention allows for any minor defects to be remedied. Had the development been let before being sold as an investment, the rent received would have been entered as an income with a corresponding reduction in borrowing. On the basis of the cash flow approach an improved offer of £1,499,373 could be made for the site.

The two treatments of the example in Figure 5.2 illustrate that the basis of the residual valuation for development purposes remains unchanged in that there is a deduction of development costs from development value to identify a site value. However, the cash flow approach gives a much more accurate valuation by requiring the valuer to give detailed consideration to the timing of all the cost elements likely to arise during the project. Cash flows produced on spreadsheets do not provide an easy solution – they only enable otherwise tedious and repetitive calculations to be avoided.

Sometimes the purchase price of the site is known, in which case a developer will try to identify the profit to be made from a project. In using the cash flow,

Gross floor area m²	1,100			
Net floor area m²	880			
Net income £ per m²	450	Annual income £ =	396,000	
Years Purchase in perpetuity @ 8%			12.5	
Gross Development Value =			4,950,000	
Less purchaser's costs at 5%			247,500	
Net Development Value				4,702,500
Development costs				
Cost to build 1,100m² @ £1,250 per m²		1,375,000		
Ancillary costs @ 5% of build costs		68,750		
Professional fees @ 13% of build costs		178,750		
Subtotal		1,622,500		
Contingencies @ 5% of subtotal above		81,125		
New subtotal			1,703,625	
Finance costs on:				
Construction, ancillaries				
and contingency	1,524,875			
over ½ × 15 months @ 8%	0.0493	75,176		
Professional fees	178,750			
over ¾ × 15 months @ 8%	0.0748	13,371		
Letting period for accrued amount	1,792,172			
over 6 months @ 8%	0.0392	70,253		
			158,800	
Letting cost				
Letting agent's fees @ 10% of annual rent		39,600		
Legal fees @ 2% of annual rent		7,920		
			47,520	
Developer's profit @ 20% of GDV			990,000	
Total development costs				2,899,945
Amount for site on completion (net development value less total costs)				1,802,556
Present value of £1 for 2.25 years @ 8%			0.8410	
Present value of amount for site acquisition				1,515,949
Less stamp duty @ 4% plus 1% acquisition fees			72,188	
Amount for site				1,443,761

Figure 5.2 Residual valuation of the project

the acquisition costs can be included as a development expense and thus the resulting residue is the profit. Viability statements showing profit expressed as a return on gross development value or total cost can also be prepared and are valuable for monitoring a development project; changes in interest rates, delays in construction programmes and variations in cost and sales forecasts. There is no doubt that the traditional residual valuation still has a role, especially where a quick appraisal is required, but in a competitive market where the dividing line between success and failure can be fine, then detailed consideration with a cash flow is important.

Table 5.6 Period-by-period cash flow (of the same project)

Quarterly period	1	2	3	4	5	6	7	8	9
Expenditure									
Contractor			137,500	240,625	288,750	343,750	364,375		
Ancillary costs at 5%			6,875	12,031	14,438	17,188	18,219		
Less retention @ 5%			−7,219	−12,633	−15,159	−18,047	−19,130		
Release retention								36,094	36,094
Professional fees	26,813	26,813	17,875	17,875	17,875	17,875	17,875	17,875	17,875
Contingency at 5%		10,141	10,141	10,141	10,141	10,141	10,141	10,141	10,141
Developer's required profit									990,000
Letting and legal fees @ 12%									47,520
Balance brought forward		27,333	65,534	235,182	512,983	845,111	1,239,609	1,662,732	1,760,343
Total monthly expenditure	26,813	64,287	230,706	503,221	829,028	1,216,018	1,631,089	1,726,842	2,861,973
Income									
Sale									4,950,000
Less purchaser's costs @ 5%									247,500
Total net income	0	0	0	0	0	0	0	0	4,702,500
Outstanding balance	−26,813	−64,287	−230,706	−503,221	−829,028	−1,216,018	−1,631,089	−1,726,842	1,840,527
Interest on balance	−520	−1,247	−4,476	−9,762	−16,083	−23,591	−31,643	−33,501	35,706
Cumulative balance c.f.	−27,333	−65,534	−235,182	−512,983	−845,111	−1,239,609	−1,662,732	−1,760,343	1,876,233
Balance at end of project =				1,876,233					
PV of £1 @ quarterly rate of 1.94% over 9 quarters				0.8412					
Present amount for site =				1,578,287					
Stamp duty plus acquisition fees @ 5%			78,914						
Site value					1,499,373				

The use of predicted values and costs

In property appraisal the use of current estimates of costs and revenues can easily be overtaken by time as illustrated by stalled housing projects in 2009 whose predicted completion values were based upon sales values achievable two years earlier. Average housing values fell by around 15% per annum in the two years following 2007 and construction costs experienced marginal deflation during 2009 following a number of years when they increased above the rate of inflation as measured by the retail price index (RPI). However the use of predicted values in appraisals by the application of inflation (or deflation) to the costs and forecasted growth rates for the rental levels are also subject to the risk of errors in estimation. Thus there are risks in whichever approach is taken particularly during periods of economic turmoil.

Property developments have a long timescale over which the economic context is bound to change and this raises a danger that current estimates will be inaccurate. But consider the danger of taking no action. It is normal for businesses and individuals to review and update their financial position from time to time and this will sometimes lead to revised decisions. Indeed in a rapidly changing economic environment to avoid review and decision making may well invite financial disaster. The explicit approach of looking to the future and making adjustments accordingly may be flawed but is likely to be the only option. The problems of forecasting changes can be alleviated to some extent by the application of better techniques, the use of data arising from research and the use of software to handle the demands of the techniques and the weight of data.

Strictly speaking, if a market rate of interest is used to discount and compound the elements within the residual valuation, then these elements should then reflect market rates. A market discount rate will include an inflation element and therefore should be applied to a current cost, not an historic one envisaged at the time of appraisal. The current cost will have the inflation allowance built in.

An approach to building in predicted costs and values into a cash flow would involve a breakdown of each cost element and an appropriate inflation rate applied. The 'inflation revised' costs would then attract interest charges to completion. Finally, the building and finance costs can be incorporated into a residual valuation with a rental figure in which a growth rate has been applied as shown in the simplified example below. There will need to be a refinement in the cash flow to allow for the delay of payments to the contractor (say, four weeks) and a retention allowance of 3–5% deducted from each monthly payment with half repaid on completion and the other half six months after completion.

A project with the following criteria has been adopted to illustrate a cash flow with inflated costs and expected rents.

    Gross development value:
        Full rental value: £100,000
        YP in perpetuity @ 5% = 20
        Capital value therefore =   £2,000,000

Table 5.7 Development period and cash flow (quarterly periods)

Period	Building costs £	Fees £
1st quarter	200,000	
2nd quarter	200,000	
3rd quarter	200,000	50,000
4th quarter	200,000	50,000

The development period is assumed to be one year and the cash flow divided into four quarters as shown in Table 5.7 with Figure 5.3 on page 115 showing related inflated costs and expected rents.

Growth rate for rent: 1% per quarter
Inflation rate for building costs: 3% per quarter
Inflation rate for fees: 2% per quarter
Interest rate: 2.5% per quarter

5.3 Spreadsheets

Computer software is a necessity for property development appraisals. In addition to databases to provide the market evidence for valuation and property transactions, the spreadsheet is the tool that valuation surveyors rely on most when conducting calculations.

Most readers will be familiar with Excel spreadsheets which are widely used in a business context. For those who are less familiar there are numerous generic texts such as Day (2007) which advise on, for example, cell reference and formula construction when using spreadsheets. In a surveying context sources such as Fawcett (2003) and Bowcock and Bayfield (2000 and 2003) provide guidance on how to build spreadsheets for different types of property appraisal.

The power of the spreadsheet lies in its ability to recalculate instantly when one or a number of the inputs are changed so that 'what if' scenarios can be conducted on residual, cash flow and investment calculations. Spreadsheets are also very useful for complex valuation methods particularly when dealing with discounted cash flow calculations and attempting to apply growth rates or risk probabilities to variables as discussed earlier. There are also a number of specialised functions such as Goal Seek and statistical tools such as correlation and regression as well as graphics functions which can be called up to interrogate data in a spreadsheet.

Because of the versatility of Excel spreadsheets they form the basis for development appraisal software packages which can be purchased off the shelf such as Prodev and companies such as Argus offer a range of products for property development and property investment analysis. Development appraisal toolkits such as the Three Dragons model and the Homes and Communities Agency's Economic Appraisal Tool are also based upon linked worksheets in an Excel spreadsheet.

Where calculations such as a residual valuation follow a structured format, spreadsheet templates can be set up so that data can be inserted into the

Step 1: Apply inflation to costs (£)

Quarter	Current estimate: Building costs	Inflation @ 3% per quarter	Inflated cost: Building costs	Current estimate: Fees	Inflation @ 2% per quarter	Inflated cost: Fees	Total cost
1	200,000	1	200,000				200,000
2	200,000	1.03	206,000				206,000
3	200,000	1.0609	212,180	50,000	1.0404	52,020	264,200
4	200,000	1.092727	218,545	50,000	1.061208	53,060	271,605

The above assumes that costs are incurred at the beginning of the period thus inflation applied to remaining periods: e.g. for period 2 inflation = $(1 + i)^n$ where i is the growth rate per quarter and n is the existing period less 1.

Step 2: Include interest

Quarter	Total cost	Interest @ 2.5% per quarter	Cost to completion (rounded up)
1	200,000	1.076891	215,378
2	206,000	1.050625	216,429
3	264,200	1.03	270,805
4	271,605	1	271,605
Total			974,217

Step 3: Valuation with growth rate applied to rent:

Present estimated rental value £	100,000
Rental growth 4 quarters @ 1%	1.040604
Future estimated annual income £	104,060
YP in perpetuity @ 5%. 20	
Capital value £	2,081,200

Less cost and finance	974,217	
Risk and profit @ 20% of capital value	416,240	
Total	1,390,457	
Site value (capital value less total costs)		690,743
PV of £1 in 4 quarters @ 2.5%: 0.9060		
Site value today (including acquisition costs)		625,813

Figure 5.3 Cash flow with inflated costs and expected rents

appropriate cells and the required result is immediately obtained. It is good practice to lock cells containing essential formulae thereby preventing any accidental alteration to the structure of the program. Indeed one of the dangers with spreadsheets is that they can create 'snow-blindness' in the operator in that it becomes difficult to see errors. Ideally companies or individuals who use spreadsheets on a regular basis for high-value projects should have in place an arm's length quality control procedure as there are considerable professional and corporate risks from undetected errors in spreadsheets which may distort decision making.

As was noted above, the spreadsheet can instantly conduct 'what if' calculations and this is particularly useful because, as in residual valuations, relatively minor changes in the sensitive variables can produce considerably greater change in the resulting land value. Appraisers therefore need to pose questions such as what if the interest rate changes? What if the building costs increase? What if the yield changes? One of the functions available in Excel is a *what if analysis* under which there is a *scenario manager* in which changes to single or combined variables can be assessed in terms of their effect on the residual outcome.

An example of a spreadsheet which was used to develop a cash flow analysis is shown below. The sensitivity analysis was used to vary the exit yield by +/−0.5% and the rental value which was assumed to follow inflation as measured by the RPI. The inflation rate was adjusted by +/−0.5% and the two changes combined in a simple best-case–worst-case comparison. The scenario manager in Excel is able to tackle far more complex combinations of variables and readers who are not familiar with this function are encouraged to experiment with it to explore its potential.

The cash flow reflects a scenario in which a developer has purchased a plot on a business park and has developed it for a modern B1 unit on a speculative basis. For those readers who are not familiar with categories in the UK's use classes, a B1 building may lawfully be used as offices or for light industrial or research and development purposes. Following completion of the building there was an eight-month void period before a business tenant could be found to take on a 20 year FRI lease with five-year rent reviews. The developer had by that stage accumulated debt of £5,500,000 and had been paying 10% per annum interest on this debt.

On securing a tenant the developer now had a valuable capital asset which was income producing. On that basis the developer was able to refinance the debt at 8% and planned to retain the building for five years up to the first rent review when the building would be sold and remaining debt paid off. Over the five-year holding period the developer would use the rental income to service the loan on an interest only basis, thus the debt of £5,500,000 would have to be repaid from the capital received when the building is sold after five years. The developer has a minimum target rate of return of 15% on this scheme and has therefore decided to model the permutations on a spreadsheet to see if the plan will achieve the desired return.

Among the benefits of using a spreadsheet for this type of analysis is that variables can be altered over the cash flow's time period. For example the growth rate of the rent can be changed and so can the yields and interest rates. Also the spreadsheet can incorporate quite complex calculations in a single cell, for

Developer's target rate = 15.0%	Gross internal floor area m^2 = 2,500
Net floor area m^2 = 2,125	Rent £ per m^2 = 210
Initial rent commencing in 2009 = £446,250	Quarterly in advance = £111,563
Exit yield = 8.0%	Refinancing loan = £5,500,000
Refinancing annual loan rate = 8.0%	Quarterly equivalent loan rate = 1.9427%
Average annual inflation measured by the RPI over the previous 10 years = 2.82%	

Figure 5.4 Variables for the business park development scenario

example the capital value at the point of sale in the first quarter of 2014 is calculated in a single cell which is referenced to cells containing the reviewed rent and the exit yield (see Figure 5.4).

The disposal of the building is assumed to take place at the commencement of 2014 thus the purchaser begins receiving the reviewed quarterly rent in advance at that point. A 1% allowance has been made against rent for management costs and this is included in the expenditure column along with interest payments on debt. The exit yield is set at 8% to reflect some loss of competitiveness by that stage. The forecast annual rent at that stage is benchmarked against average RPI and this is used to calculate the capital of the building on rent review and disposal. Exit costs are assumed to be 3% of the capital value at the point of disposal and these have been added to the loan repayment in the expenditure column. No allowance has been made for costs which might arise due to rent reviews although in reality some professional fees would be consumed around that time. For clarity of presentation, monetary sums have been rounded up to the nearest pound and the PV of £1 has been rounded up to four decimal places.

One of the interpretations arising from this simple test might be that this is a financially robust scheme which even in the worst case scenario still achieves a positive NPV, i.e. it achieves the developer's target rate of 15% with a modest margin of £93,600 on top. However in reality a valuer would factor in other variables in order to examine the downside risk a little more in the worst-case scenario.

Table 5.8 Scenario summary

Variable	Current values	Best-case scenario	Worst-case scenario
Exit Yield	8.0%	7.5%	8.5%
Inflation rate (RPI)	2.82%	3.32%	2.32%
NPV Result £	325,114	588,417	93,600

Table 5.9 Discounted cash flow with rent received quarterly in advance to evaluate the net present value of a business park development

Year	Beginning of:	Project time in years	Expenditure (£)	Income (£)	Net cash flow (£)	PV of £1 @ 15%	Discounted cash flow (£)	Notional effect on annual rent (£) of applying average RPI from previous 10 years	Comments
2009	1st quarter	0	107,964	111,563	3,599	1	3,599	446,250	Development is let and rental income begins. Outstanding debt refinanced.
	2nd quarter	0.25	107,964	111,563	3,599	0.9657	3,476		
	3rd quarter	0.5	107,964	111,563	3,599	0.9325	3,356		
	4th quarter	0.75	107,964	111,563	3,599	0.9005	3,476		
2010	1st quarter	1	107,964	111,563	3,599	0.8696	3,130	458,834	
	2nd quarter	1.25	107,964	111,563	3,599	0.8397	3,022		
	3rd quarter	1.5	107,964	111,563	3,599	0.8109	2,918		
	4th quarter	1.75	107,964	111,563	3,599	0.7830	2,818		
2011	1st quarter	2	107,964	111,563	3,599	0.7561	2,721	471,773	
	2nd quarter	2.25	107,964	111,563	3,599	0.7302	2,628		
	3rd quarter	2.5	107,964	111,563	3,599	0.7051	2,538		
	4th quarter	2.75	107,964	111,563	3,599	0.6809	2,451		
2012	1st quarter	3	107,964	111,563	3,599	0.6575	2,366	485,077	
	2nd quarter	3.25	107,964	111,563	3,599	0.6349	2,285		
	3rd quarter	3.5	107,964	111,563	3,599	0.6131	2,207		
	4th quarter	3.75	107,964	111,563	3,599	0.5921	2,131		
2013	1st quarter	4	107,964	111,563	3,599	0.5718	2,058	498,756	The forecast annual rent for this year is used to calculate the exit value.
	2nd quarter	4.25	107,964	111,563	3,599	0.5521	1,987		
	3rd quarter	4.5	107,964	111,563	3,599	0.5332	1,919		
	4th quarter	4.75	107,964	111,563	3,599	0.5149	1,853		
2014	1st quarter	5	5,687,034	6,234,450	547,416	0.4972	272,175		Building sold and debt repaid.
						NPV =	325,114		

5.4 Sensitivity analysis

Risk is related to return but it is important to distinguish between risk and uncertainty. Whereas risk can be assessed in terms of its probability and therefore insured against or allowed for, this is not possible with uncertainty. Risk also needs to be distinguished in its application to an individual asset or to a portfolio of assets. Risk relating to a portfolio is more concerned with investment strategy and portfolio analysis and this is discussed later.

Allowance for risk can be applied in a number of ways, firstly it can be applied to the discount rate used in the calculation or secondly it can be applied to the cash flow which arises from the investment. In the first case for instance, if a risk free rate is 5% and the risk premium is 2% then this premium could be added to the risk free rate to give a discount rate of 7% which is therefore appropriate for the risk taken. If the risk is applied to the cash flow, then this flow has to be varied within a range of acceptable values and thus the output of the calculation can be assessed accordingly. The result can be found by using a statistical analysis assigning probability to the incidence of the cash flows and thus the result can be more accurately defined.

The aim of sensitivity testing is to examine the effects of changes in variables on the residual value and the basic method involves changing one variable at a time, recalculating the value and analysing the result. The percentage change in the variable is compared with the percentage change in the residual amount. If a small percentage change in the variables produces a large percentage change in the residual amount, then this variable is deemed to be sensitive and an example was provided in chapter 3 where the rent and yield were found to be the most sensitive variables. To widen the perspective on this concept further examples of sensitivity analyses are now considered.

Simple sensitivity testing

Here the individual variables are changed one at a time and the effect of these changes on the result is seen in Figure 5.5. Percentage changes in the result or output can be seen relative to the changes in the input variables for example as shown below in Figure 5.5. to produce a matrix of site values where two variables have been adjusted. Site value 5 in the matrix would reflect the core value while site value 3 would reflect the lowest site value and site value 7 would reflect the highest site value.

		Variable 1: Investment capitalisation rate		
		5%	6%	7%
Variable 2:	£100 per m²	site value 1	site value 2	site value 3
Estimated rental	£110 per m²	site value 4	site value 5	site value 6
value	£120 per m²	site value 7	site value 8	site value 9

Figure 5.5 Matrix of site values for different variables

Variation

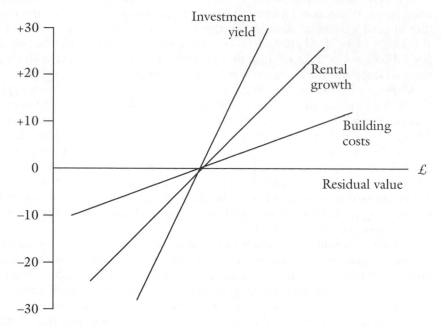

Figure 5.6 Spider diagram

Or alternatively, as illustrated in chapter 3 individual variables can be focused upon to determine the effects of say a +10% or –10% change in the variable on the residual value or developer's profit.

A spider diagram as shown in Figure 5.6 could also be produced to show changes in the variables plotted against the residual value or level of developer's profit as shown above.

Scenario testing

This involves changing a combination of inputs and the output is then calculated. This can be done in a number of ways, for instance a combination of factors which are the expected variables can be used, and for instance the expected rental and yield of a future deal. In addition to the expected outcome, an optimistic scenario and a pessimistic scenario can be assessed as represented by Table 5.10 below.

Probability

Where an appraisal contains several or many uncertain inputs, the output becomes problematic and a more sophisticated form of sensitivity analysis is required which takes probability into account. This approach assesses the probability of the inputs achieving certain numerical values. The probabilities are assigned to the input variables according to how likely it is that they will achieve the particular numerical values. For instance, if subjectively the analyst feels that

Table 5.10 Scenario testing: optimistic–pessimistic

Variable	Optimistic	Expected	Pessimistic
Rental growth	e.g. 7%	5%	3% etc...
Investment yield			
Building cost			
Finance cost			
Building period			
Development period			
RESULTS			
Profit			
Residual value			

there is a 30% chance of the rent being £220 per m², then the probability is assigned at 0.3 and included in the calculation accordingly.

By running a computer program with the assigned probabilities which picks up the inputs on the basis of the probability, for instance, a 30% chance of picking a rent of £220 and then by running the program a number of times, an average output can be assessed. This approach is called a Monte Carlo simulation and while it is not necessary to explore this in depth here readers who are particularly interested in this concept could refer to Baum and Crosby (2008: 253–9) or Sayce et al. (2006: 180–1).

A basic approach to probability which explores changes in rental growth is shown by Figure 5.7 below.

The weighted probability of rental growth = 0.7% + 3.0% + 0.9% = 4.6%. This figure can then be used in a scenario test instead of the single estimate figures (Isaac and Steley 2000: 186).

Analysing risk requires that the distribution of returns be defined in some way and this requires that the range and distribution of the inputs must be defined. The analysis, as described by Wyatt (2007: 291–6) used is probability modelling, where the value of a variable cannot be predicted with certainty but that it is possible to set a range within which it will almost certainly fall. Furthermore it will be possible to say that some values for the variable are more likely than others.

Probability modelling generally falls into two categories; algebraic and simulation. The algebraic approach normally used is the Hillier method but this has limitations and simulations have been found to be more useful. A Monte Carlo simulation is the model most referred to and it can be run on a

Rental growth	(a)	7%	5%	3%
Probability	(b%)	10%	60%	30%
Chance	(b)	0.1	0.6	0.3
Expected outcome	(a × b)	0.7	3.0	0.9

Figure 5.7 Probability of rent growth

spreadsheet software add-in called @RISK which is produced by the Palisade Corporation (www.palisade.com). This software enables Monte Carlo simulations to be more easily carried out and the results can be displayed graphically if required.

The key feature of the Monte Carlo simulation is that input variables which cannot be stated with certainty are treated as distributions rather than single values. When the simulation is run, a value for each variable is selected at random from the range of possible values to generate a possible value from the output. Through a process of iteration this is repeated many times thus simulating the range of possible outcomes. So long as sufficient iterations have been undertaken, a distribution of the possible outcomes can be produced to provide a measure of risk for the project.

This then gives a range of results, say for the residual value or profit. The mean is then calculated for the value or profit and the standard deviation is calculated. Assuming that the range of results is a normal distribution in statistical terms, there is a 95% likelihood that the result will fall in the range of the mean ± 2 standard deviations. The standard deviation is an indication of the variability of the results and therefore represents risk. A developer who wishes to limit the downside possibilities may then try to manage variables so that the outcome falls within an acceptable range of values.

5.5 Risk

The analysis of return without consideration of risk is pointless, as the return will vary with risk and an individual or company's expected return on a venture will normally be higher in a risky situation. Thus a housebuilding company which embarks upon a modest housing development in a popular suburban area where the developer's product has a ready market will probably accept a lower rate of return than for embarking upon a complex mixed-tenure and mixed-use development in a regeneration area where the housing market has historically been fragile.

The risk encountered and accepted by the developer or investor will also need to be considered against the backdrop of other projects or investments. Thus a company which has a portfolio of low risk projects (or investments) which achieve commensurate and therefore modest rates of return might wish to seek some additional risk exposure. Conversely a company which already has a portfolio or risky projects might wish to seek some risk diversification by looking for some low-risk ventures whose modest returns might provide a guaranteed income stream needed as ballast against an overtly volatile portfolio. In business analogy the latter investor/developer would be looking for a 'cash cow' rather than a 'problem child'.

The decision maker's attitude to risk has been discussed by Lumby and Jones (2001: 185–6) who note that as a general rule investors are risk averse but that some may be able to accept more risk than others given certain circumstances.

For example an investor who is already a successful multimillionaire might 'take a punt' on investing £50,000 in a high-risk small business. The business might have a product which requires some marketing and although high risk, the small business could be the next success story. The investor in this role is essentially acting as a venture capitalist. There is a high risk to the investor that there will be a total loss of the £50,000. However this investor is able to take that risk and may be looking for this type of risk exposure given that the loss would be insignificant to a multimillionaire who in all probability already had a portfolio of low-risk investments. The loss would however be highly significant to an investor who only had £50,000 of savings. This investor simply cannot afford to lose £50,000 as it would represent a 100% loss of assets and thus the investor will be considerably more risk averse than the risk seeking multimillionaire. The risk-averse investor might however be quite content to invest the £50,000 in a high street savings account where the capital is safe and where the rate of return is modest but known.

Organisational or individual variations in tolerance to risk could be depicted as shown below in Figure 5.8 in a trade-off between risk and return. The upper curve represents the more risk-averse investor who may have limited and undiversified assets and thus will require the promise of significant above normal rates of return to tempt them to move away from the risk-neutral path which by analogy might be a high street bank's savings account. The lower curve represents the diversified and asset rich investor who might accept a lower than normal rate of return in the short term by perhaps investing in the risky small business but which shows potential for longer-term growth. Organisations will also have policy and legislative parameters within which they operate and which to some extend will temper the degree to which assets can be exposed to risk. It is said of long-term institutional investors that because they have to meet the maturation of insurance policies and pensions, the bulk of their investment portfolios must be relatively safe so that financial obligations can be met when required.

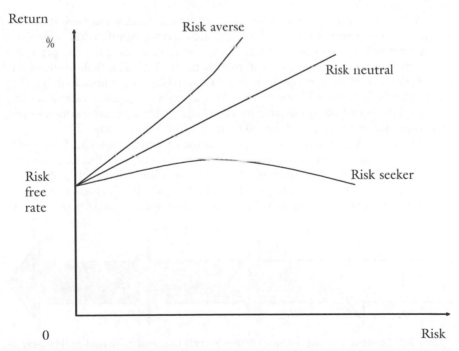

Figure 5.8 Risk–return trade-off

Investment behaviour (and here development is considered to be a form of investment) could therefore be thought of as a spectrum between *risk aversion* through to *risk seeking* with a central spine or *risk neutrality*. As noted above this translates in property development where developers will generally require more reward for more risk bearing, although this is tempered to a degree by the scale of existing assets and characteristics of projects already committed to.

Definition of risk

Investment is and developments are considered risky because the investor/developer is unsure about the actual return which will be realised from the investment. There is according to some commentators a spectrum of uncertainty which extends from the present when values are certain (the left-hand side of Figure 5.9 below) to the future when values become increasingly uncertain. Forecasters face the same dilemma as the further a forecast extends into the future the more uncertain it becomes.

Certainty represents precise knowledge of the outcome; risk is a situation where alternate outcomes are identified together with a statement of the probability of such outcomes. Partial uncertainty is where alternative outcomes can be identified but without the knowledge of the probabilities of such outcomes. Total uncertainty is where even the alternative outcomes cannot be identified.

If risk is regarded as the extent to which the actual outcome of an action or decision may diverge from the expected outcome, an action or decision is risk-free when the consequences are known with certainty. To a rational developer, the possibility of a lower than expected return has more importance than the possibility of a higher than expected return. The former case is therefore termed the downside risk.

Definitions of risk may be descriptive or analytical. Descriptive definitions are related to sources and elements of risk and are used for classification of projects on the basis of the risk associated with them and to determine the risk premium for use in a discount rate (see later in this chapter). Analytical definitions of risk provide definitions in terms of probability or variability, i.e. the probability that the developer/investor will not receive the expected or required rate of return;

Portfolio theory also tells us that total risk will have two components, systematic and unsystematic risk as shown in Table 5.11 on page 125.

Systematic risk may have a number of elements which might include variations in the market, business cycles, inflation, interest rate fluctuations and technological change. Unsystematic risk will cover elements such as business risk (associated with the product, markets or strategy), financial risk (associated with financial structure), liquidity risks and other specific risks related to the

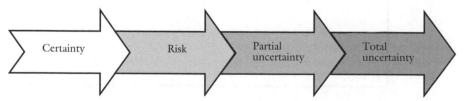

Figure 5.9 Spectrum of uncertainty: certainty–total uncertainty (based on Hargitay and Yu (1993: 35))

Table 5.11 Components of risk from portfolio theory

Systematic risk	*Unsystematic risk (or specific risk)*
Caused by factors which affect all projects/investments and over which the investor/developer has little control and which could be:	Factors which affect only a particular investment/development and over which the investor/developer has limited control and could be:
• Changes in the economic, political, social and technological environment.	• Choice over the way a project has been financed, for example more debt would mean more risk.

industrial sector in which the project takes place, the nature of the property and its location.

Risks in development projects are concerned with future events which by their nature are uncertain. A rational approach to risk associated with the development process should therefore include a strategy for dealing with risk such as:

1 recognition and definition of risk and its various components;
2 quantification and measurement of risk;
3 the analysis of risk; and
4 a response to risk.

In a risk–return trade-off, the risks associated with a development project must be adequately compensated for by the expected returns. A suitable combination of discounting and probability criteria is the best solution according to Hargitay and Yu (1993: 155). In investment decision making, risk is defined as the extent to which the actual outcome of a decision may diverge from the expected outcome. Statistical measures such as measures of standard deviation and variance can be used as the absolute measure of variability of the actual outcome and the expected outcome. The methods of risk analysis indicated can thus be classified as shown in Table 5.12.

Table 5.12 Risk analysis

Methods which attempt a description of the riskiness of a project	*Methods which attempt the incorporation of perceived risk in appraisal models*
• Expected value/variance methods (mean variance method). • Sensitivity analysis. • Scenario testing. • Simulations. • Beta analysis.	• Risk-adjusted discount rate method (RADR). • Certainty equivalent method. • Sliced income approach.

The descriptive methods of risk analysis have been outlined elsewhere in this text in relation to sensitivity testing, scenarios and simulations. The mean-variance rule is used in projects and suggests that project A is preferred to project B where at least one of the following situations arise:

1 the expected return of A is greater than B and A's variance is less than or equal to B (expected return A > B, variance A ≤ B);
2 the expected return of A is equal to or greater than B and A's variance is less than B's (expected return of A ≥ B, variance A < B).

The variance is a statistical measure of dispersion around the mean value and is a measure of risk as discussed earlier. Finally, among these descriptive measures is beta analysis, this concerns portfolio theory and the earlier discussion of systematic and unsystematic risk. Detailed analysis of these approaches is beyond the scope of this book and you are referred to Baum and Crosby (2008), Byrne (1996), Sayce *et al.* (2006) and Wyatt (2007) where more coverage is devoted to this topic. However to bring to a close consideration of risk appraisal models in this chapter the risk-adjusted discount rate (RADR) will be explained followed by an example which shows how the certainty equivalent technique may be used in appraisals.

Risk-adjusted discount rate (RADR)

The market interest rate or discount rate:

$$I = (1 + i)(1 + d)(1 + r) - 1$$
Where i is the time preference allowance
d is the inflation premium
r is the risk premium (see Isaac and Steley 2000: 111–12).

The risk-free rate (RFR) is a function of i and d only so that:

$$I = (1 + RFR)(1 + r) - 1$$

In practice the equation used is $I = RFR + r$ (risk-free rate + risk premium).

The use of the risk adjusted rate implies more return is required to compensate for more risk but the problem is the estimation of how much.

Certainty equivalent techniques

This approach uses the statistical mean and standard deviation of a distribution to indicate the position where a risk averse investor/developer would be happy. Taking a normal distribution as shown below ± 1 standard deviation from the mean will incorporate 68% of the range of outcomes and the downside risk is defined as the area below the curve, more than 1 standard deviation less than the mean. This area will incorporate only 16% of the distribution. Using this distribution enables a developer/investor to explore an 84% chance of bettering the position (Figure 5.10).

The certainty equivalent approach uses the characteristics of the normal distribution and the standard deviation in a five-stage process as follows:

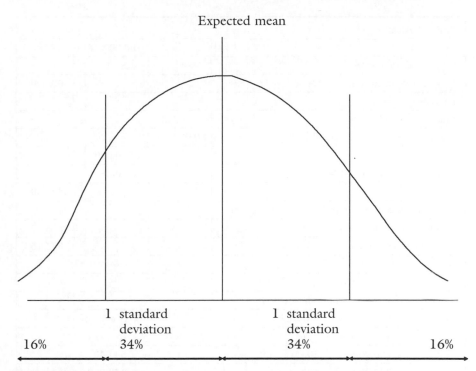

Expected mean

1 standard
deviation
34%

1 standard
deviation
34%

16%

16%

Figure 5.10 Distribution under a normal curve: the downside risk is the 16% of outcomes on the left-hand side of the diagram below the curve

1 Calculate the expected value:
   $\bar{a} = \Sigma(p \times \hat{a})$
   where p = the probability of the sample
   and $\hat{a}$ = each sample outcome
2 Calculate the variance:
   $\sigma^2 = \Sigma(p) (\hat{a} - \bar{a})^2$
3 Calculate the standard deviation:
   $\sqrt{\text{variance}} = \sigma$
4 Calculate certainty equivalents
5 Redo the calculation with certainty equivalent variables.

The example which follows in Figure 5.11 shows how the above five-stage process can be applied in a development appraisal context.

Sliced income approach

This approach develops risk adjustment and certainty equivalent techniques to provide an overall method which may be suitable in property appraisal. Like the hard-core method or layer approach (see Isaac and Steley 2000: ch. 6), it distinguishes layers of income which are less risky (core income) and more risky (top slice). The guaranteed income could thus be valued at a risk free rate while the top slice income is then discounted at a higher or risk-adjusted rate. The top

Residual valuation			
Income £		200,000	
YP in perpetuity @ 8%		12.5	
Gross development value			2,500,000
Less costs			
Building costs plus fees	1,000,000		
Finance costs for ½ × 2 years @ 8%	80,000		
Total costs		1,080,000	
Return for risk and profit @ 20% of GDV		500,000	
Costs plus profit			1,580,000
Site value on completion (GDV– costs and profit)			920,000
PV of £1 in 2 years @ 8%			0.8573
Site value today therefore			788,716

1. Calculate the expected value				
Assume two variables: income and yield				
Income:	Outcome	Probability		Sample outcome
	â	p		(p × â)
	180,000	30%		54,000
	200,000	60%		120,000
	220,000	10%		22,000
Expected value: â = Σ (p × â)			Total	196,000

Yield:	Outcome	Probability		Sample outcome
	â	p		(p × â)
	7%	10%		0.7%
	8%	50%		4.0%
	9%	40%		3.6%
Expected value: â = Σ (p × â)				8.3%

2. Calculate the variance						
Income						
Outcome â	Expected value ā	(â − ā)	(â − ā)²	Probability p	p(â − ā)²	
180,000	196,000	−6,000	256,000,000	30%	76,800,000	
200,000	196,000	4,000	16,000,000	60%	9,600,000	
220,000	196,000	24,000	576,000,000	10%	57,600,000	
Variance: σ² = Σ (p)(â − σ)²					144,000,000	

Figure 5.11 Application of certainty equivalent approach

(continued opposite)

Yield					
Outcome â	Expected value â	$(â - ā)$	$(â - ā)^2$	Probability p	$p(â - ā)^2$
7%	8.3%	−1.3%	0.0169%	10%	0.00169%
8%	8.3%	−0.3%	0.0009%	50%	0.00045%
9%	8.3%	0.7%	0.0049%	40%	0.00196%
Variance: $\sigma^2 = \Sigma\,(p)(â - â)^2$					0.00410%

3. Calculate the standard deviation	
Income standard deviation = $\sqrt{}$ variance = σ	12,000
Yield standard deviation = $\sqrt{}$ variance = σ	0.64031%

4. Calculate certainty equivalents				
	Expected value		Standard deviation	
Income	196,000	minus	12,000	= 184,000
Yield	8.3%	plus	0.64031%	= 8.9403%

For the yield the risk is of a higher yield and lower YP producing less value and so it is the upper end of the range that we do not want. Thus it is the expected value plus the standard deviation.

5. Reinsert the values in the calculation			
Residual valuation (certainty equivalent)			
Income £		184,000	
YP in perpetuity @ 8.9403%		11.1853	
Gross Development Value			2,058,095
Less costs			
Building costs plus fees	1,000,000		
Finance costs for ½ × 2 years @ 8%	80,000		
Total costs		1,080,000	
Return for risk and profit @ 20% on GDV		411,619	
Costs plus profit			1,491,619
Site value on completion (GDV −costs and profit)			566,476
PV of £1 in 2 years @ 8%			0.8573
Site value today therefore			485,640

Figure 5.11 *continued*

slice income is calculated by comparing the expected value of the total income stream with the level of the risk-free core income. Baum and Crosby (2008: 91–112) explain the derivation of this method which is sometime used in situations where a core rental is guaranteed but where an addition income is possible but not guaranteed. In development valuations the concept could be

Table 5.13 Risk analysis steps: advantages–disadvantages

Type of analysis	Examples	Advantages	Disadvantages
Sensitivity analysis	Scenario testing, probability and simulation.	Investor/developer retains decision responsibility.	No simple decision rule, a range of results is provided.
Risk-adjusted discount rate	RADR, certainty equivalent techniques, sliced income approach.	Provides objective decision rule.	Decision made by subjective risk adjustment.
Mean-variance analysis	Coefficient of IRR/NPV variation.	Has separate measures of risk and return; investor can be more subjective about risk–return trade-off.	Deals with individual project risk only.
Portfolio analysis	Beta analysis.	Deals with the effect on portfolio of carrying out the project.	Difficult to estimate betas (measures of systematic risk).

applied in partnership arrangements where the various slices would have differing risk levels.

A summary of the possible advantages and disadvantages of the various steps of risk analysis drawn from Baum and Crosby's work are summarised in Table 5.13 above.

5.6 Summary

The chapter began by looking at how cash flows offer a more complete picture across a development timeline than is possible with a residual valuation. It was noted however that both methods work on the same principle that a site's value may be found by comparing development costs against the value of a completed scheme. Alternatively the profit may become the residual element where the land value and other costs are known relative to the completed development value.

A cash flow maps the events in the development process over time and it enables modelling of the inflows and outflows of cash likely to occur on a project. In theory this should enable a developer to identify a more competitive site bid than is possible under the broad assumptions used in a residual valuation.

Discounted cash flows (DCFs) can also be used for development appraisal however they are more commonly used to appraise longer time-spans when a completed development may be held as an investment for a number of years prior to disposal. DCFs therefore really come into their own when incorporating an investor's discount or target rate against which the income and capital growth of a property can be assessed.

Cash flows are explicit about the timing and magnitude of costs and revenues which are likely to arise in the future on a project and thus they cannot avoid the necessity for judgements to be made today about the calibration of variables which may be subject to change in the future. This has led analysts to explore the use of risk appraisal techniques involving probability so that developers can see an array of most likely outcomes. Given that most developers are risk averse they might then at least be able to consider how to take action to avoid the down side risk. In the final analysis this might mean taking a more cautious view on what to pay for a site.

There has been progress made in the quantification of risk and advances in software have enabled techniques such as Monte Carlo simulations to become more widely available and easier to use. Thus project level sensitivity and scenario testing has raised some interesting possibilities for valuers, albeit that there is still the requirement for expert subjective input.

Despite the apparent sophistication of these techniques developers can never entirely remove or tackle all aspects of project risk. For example the global economy during 2008 and 2009 experienced an unheralded credit crunch which began in the sub prime residential mortgage market in the United States. The ripple effects triggered a loss of confidence in the banking system across the world and in the UK saw a run on a bank for the first time in over 100 years with the bank subsequently being nationalised. The knock-on effects impacted upon an overvalued residential property market in the UK and this coincided with an economic downturn based upon a lack of consumer confidence and spending. In effect a negative multiplier had set in which few forecasters had been able to predict.

In the commercial property sector the downturn resulted in, for example, prime office rents in London's West End falling by over 30% in two years. These global-level risks provide a broader perspective for the worthy but delicate project-related statistical risk identification techniques discussed in this chapter.

References

Baum, A. and Crosby, N. (2008) *Property Investment Appraisal*, 3rd edition (Oxford: Blackwell).

Byrne, P. (1996) *Risk, Uncertainty and Decision-Making in Property Development*, 2nd edition (Abingdon: Taylor & Francis).

Bowcock, P. and Bayfield, N. (2000) *Excel for Surveyors* (London: Estates Gazette).

Bowcock, P. and Bayfield, N. (2003) *Advanced Excel for Surveyors* (London: Estates Gazette).

Day, A. L. (2007) *Mastering Financial Modelling in Microsoft Excel* (London: Prentice Hall).

Fawcett, S. (2003) *Designing Flexible Cashflows* (London: EG Books).

Fraser, W. D. (2004) *Cash Flow Appraisal for Property Investment* (London: Palgrave Macmillan).

Hargitay, S. E. and Yu, S. M. (1993) *Property Investment Decisions: A Quantitative Approach* (London: Spon).

Isaac, D. and Steley, T. (2000) *Property Valuation Techniques*, 2nd edition (London: Macmillan).

Lumby, C. and Jones, C. (2001) *Fundamentals of Investment Appraisal* (London: Thomson Learning).

Royal Institution of Chartered Surveyors (2008) *Commercial Property Forecast* (London: RICS). Available in e-format at: www.rics.org/site/scripts/documents_info.aspx?documentID=548&pageNumber=2

Sayce, S., Smith, J., Cooper, R. and Venmore-Rowland, P. (2006) *Real Estate Appraisal: from Value to Worth* (Oxford: Blackwell).

Wyatt, P. (2007) *Property Valuation in an Economic Context* (Oxford: Blackwell).

6

Financing property development

Aims

This chapter examines the various methods of financing property development and looks at both corporate and private funding methods. Of particular concern are the difficulties in raising finance in times of recession and events in the early 1990s and between 2007–9 are reflected upon. Lenders need reassurance that the proposed borrower is able to meet loan repayments and we discuss the need for detailed business plans to support loan applications as well as the requirements by banks to ensure that their underwriting (lending) decisions are sound. This is achieved by careful vetting of an applicant's business background.

Key terms

>> **Lending criteria** – the most important criteria from the lender's perspective is the ability of the borrower to be able to meet repayments on a loan. This is a judgement by the lender and depends primarily upon the financial status of the borrower, whether a corporate or a private entity.

>> **Sources of finance** – for property development in the UK the majority of lending is provided by domestic clearing banks supplemented by loans provided by overseas banks. However the latter will tend to withdraw from domestic markets during periods of economic turmoil such as between 2008 and 2009. Other sources of finance for property development include insurance companies, pension funds and private investors.

>> **Lending structures** – these can be negotiated to reduce the risk of adverse interest rate changes or to assist cash flow by deferring or rolling

up interest until a development is let or sold. The number of years over which the loan can be repaid is also a matter for negotiation.

6.1 Introduction

A property or building can be owner-occupied or an owner may grant a lease to a tenant who will pay rent thus creating an investment. The property may of course be vacant and surplus to the owner's requirements or a poor investment, where perhaps a tenant has defaulted on rental payments leaving an empty property producing no income. A large proportion of property is owner-occupied but most of the conventional property texts and theories, especially those related to valuation are applied to the commercial investment market. It is acknowledged however that there are many similarities in terms of valuation methods for both owner occupied and investment property.

Finance is needed to purchase property for investment, occupation and development and property finance is money raised on the back of existing prop-erties or raised for the purpose of expenditure on properties. The property becomes the security for the loan and can be repossessed by the lender if the borrower defaults by not meeting the loan payments. The arrangements for possession by the lender in the event of default are set out in the lending agree-ment between the parties and are governed by English law.

Whether a property is developed for an owner-occupier or as an investment property will have a bearing upon the criteria for raising the funds, but the fundamental concepts of finance will be similar. For instance, funds could be raised internally or externally by an organisation but the criteria for the internal loan or transfer of funds may well need to match those in the market. In this book, the discussion is mainly about the application of funds to property in the commercial development market and funds are considered to be private rather than public sector monies. This is to make the analysis simpler but the princi-ples and concepts of finance for a variety of property transactions could well be similar.

Finally it is important to realise the significance of property and its finance to the economy. The importance can be shown in three different ways: as a factor of production, as a corporate asset and as an investment. As a factor of produc-tion, property provides the space in which economic activity and production takes place, the efficiency and costs of such space will affect the cost of goods and services produced. As a corporate asset, it forms the major part of asset value in a company's balance sheet and the majority of corporate debt is secured against it. As an investment, it is one of the major types of investment held by individual investors and as Fraser (2004: 133) points out:

> The low correlation of property's returns with both gilts and equities, and property's record as a hedge against inflation, are qualities that make prop-erty attractive to institutional funds.

6.2 The structure of the property investment market

The investment market for property cannot be seen in isolation from other investment markets. The application of funds to property has to reflect competition from other forms of investment. The decision to invest in a particular market will be a comparison of return and security and thus knowledge of alternative investments and how finance is applied to other investments could be very important. This can clearly be seen in the securitisation and unitisation of property which are discussed in chapter 8. Another important point to be made concerns the nature of the lender and the property against which funding is sought. At its simplest, the financial arrangement may deal with an individual purchasing a single property with a single loan, but it is rarely this basic. Finance is generally raised by corporate entities such as property companies, using existing property and other assets as collateral for additional purchases.

Ignoring gold, commodities and works of art, there are three major areas of traditional investment opportunity which are fixed-interest securities, company stocks and shares and real property. The Stock Exchange provides a market for listed shares and certain fixed interest securities such as those issued by the government, local authorities and public bodies. The market in real property contrasts with that of company shares and other securities. The commercial property market is fragmented into various sectors such as shops, offices, industrial, warehousing and leisure and within that there are widely different qualities reflecting prime, secondary, new, second-hand and converted buildings and the market is geographically dispersed. In contrast, the market for shares and other securities is highly centralised. The London stock market is an example of this centralisation. The centralisation of markets assists the transferability of investments, as does the fact that stocks and shares can be traded in small units thereby assisting transferability.

Compared with other traditional investment opportunities, real property investment has the distinguishing features of being heterogeneous, generally indivisible and posing ongoing management challenges. Investors in property can be confronted with high barriers to entry in terms of capital cost and there may also be ongoing management responsibilities such as collecting and reviewing rents, dealing with repairs and renewals and lease negotiation. These problems may mean that real property is likely to be an unattractive proposition for the small or inexperienced investor. Furthermore, the lack of a centralised marketplace means that transaction data are not freely available although companies such as CoStar do provide up-to-date online market data via their Focus subscription service. However advice on valuation and other specific property matters is acquired through consultation from professionals, but at a cost. For the layperson, the problems of valuation relate to difficulties of trying to relate comparable transactions to properties being valued or even trying to assess what transactions could be considered comparable.

Because of the nature of the real property market, investment in commercial property is perhaps not as popular as investment in the private rented residential sector, especially for small investors. Investment in residential property grew in the 1990s and reached a peak in 2007. It was fuelled by cheap finance, rising rents and rising asset prices although the market subsequently slowed with the recession of 2008–9. Mortgage finance products were withdrawn and there were fewer active lenders. Those lenders remaining in the market became more selective by choosing only to do business with well-capitalised customers. As the economy deteriorated, repossessions increased and asset prices fell, confirming that like any other investment market there are risks that asset values can fall as well as rise.

Indirect investment in commercial property has grown in the 1990s and into the 2000s through vehicles such as unit trusts, property company shares and Real Estate Investment Trusts (REITs) which are discussed later. A number of property funds have been very successful. However the aforementioned fall in asset prices after 2007 and increasing tenant default have adversely affected this sector, with some funds being closed or taken over. Other indirect investment in property would be in less tangible media such as pension funds and insurance companies whose large investment portfolios contain a proportion of property assets.

Property company shares

Property company shares provide a medium for indirect investment in property and to some extent negate some of the disadvantages of direct investment discussed above. Shares are available in smaller units and can be easily traded and of course have low-management and transfer costs when compared to direct property investment. Property shares specifically, have been viewed as an effective protection against inflation because of the durability of property over time. But property company shares can be more volatile than the property market and reflect stock market movements on a short-term basis which may have no direct link to the property market itself. However, shares in a property investment company, where most of the revenue to the company is derived from rental income, can provide the investor with a high degree of income security and potential for capital growth, as rent will tend to increase in the medium to long term. Thus traditionally property shares were seen to provide both an element of protection against the effects of inflation and greater security to the investor.

Two types of property company are discernible. The investment company normally holds property for long periods and takes its revenue from rental income. Regular revaluations of the portfolio will either increase or decrease the value of the company's balance sheet and this will of course influence share values dependent upon the market at the time. On the other hand, the trading company will develop and sell property, earning revenues on disposal of the property rather than through income. Because of different tax positions, the functions are often kept separate, but the most extensive developers will also often be investment companies which may retain completed developments within a company investment portfolio.

In January 2007, property companies who were listed on the Stock Exchange were able to convert to REIT status and well-established companies such as British Land, Hammerson, Land Securities and SEGRO (Slough Estates Group) took the opportunity. REITs offer certain tax advantages to investors and provide the opportunity to participate in diversified and liquid real estate investment. It is expected that interest from a wide variety of investors will grow in this media once economic conditions improve.

6.3 A brief history of commercial property funding

In the 1950s and 1960s, the modern property developer emerged and property companies established themselves. The stimulation to development was based on the shortage of commercial property in a period of low inflation. This meant that rental levels of developments such as offices, shopping centres and industrial units rose dramatically during a period when building costs were static. The other major stimulants to development were fixed-interest rates and the ability to finance projects with 100% debt finance without any equity input. The growth of property companies continued on the back of a strategy of refinancing the completed development on a fixed-interest mortgage for 20 to 30 years. The financial institutions provided finance for developments during this period and there was some link-up between developers and financial institutions. Subsequently, the institutions, mainly insurance companies, started to insist on a greater share in the equity returns available. They thus purchased shares in the property companies and also made their mortgage debenture loans convertible to shares so that an increased equity stake could be obtained in development schemes which were successful.

However, the taxation structure in the late 1960s affected these arrangements. The financial institutions at the time were termed gross funds (not paying tax), but they suffered from the taxation of income and dividends under these arrangements and thus new financial structures emerged. In the late 1960s and early 1970s developers began using sale and leaseback arrangements enabling projects to be financed at the development stage using short-term bank finance and then sold on completion. As time wore on, a shortage of schemes became apparent and the institutions (insurance companies and subsequently pension funds) purchased development sites directly from property developers and then tied them to a building and lease agreement such that the developers were responsible for the completion and letting of the development. In this manner the institutions obtained growth in the investment without the associated risk.

The 1974–5 property crash underlined how economic conditions had changed since the 1950s and 1960s. High interest rates reduced demand and inflation of costs meant that profit levels were not achieved because of increased capital costs and income voids during which interest arrears accumulated.

From the 1980s and into the 2000s one successful way to fund major property developments was that the funder was invited to purchase the site and provide funds for the building contract. Interest would be rolled up during the development period and added to the development costs. On completion and letting of the building, the profit on development was paid over. On this basis developers built up a large turnover basically matching their site finding, development and project management skills with the aspirations of institutional investors. Such approaches greatly reduced the risk exposure of the developer to a project. Forward funding meant that the project was financed for the development period at a lower-interest rate than market levels but subsequently the capital sum received by the developer at the end of the project was reduced as the funder would value the asset at a higher yield to recoup the interest lost.

As Wilkinson and Reed (2008: 128–9) point out banks became the main providers of finance for property development in the 1980s as institutions reduced their exposure to rebalance their portfolios in order that they contained a higher proportion of better performing assets such as shares and gilts. There was a property recession in 1990 which exposed a number of highly geared property companies and left some banks with project-related losses. However this did not diminish the banks' enthusiasm for property lending and when the economy recovered in the early 1990s the banks again became the principal lenders to property developers.

The 2008–9 credit crunch found a number of high street banks overexposed to property debt and having to write off property-related losses on loans made prior to 2007. While this inevitably created a period of caution on lending against new property projects, it is likely that the banks will continue to see the property developer as a legitimate customer where project appraisals and risk assessments have been carefully worked out and risks properly mitigated. Financial institutions will also be active during a recession in acquiring prime investment-grade properties at discount prices as longer-term investment prospects. Thus institutions can act as counter-cyclical investors (buying low and selling high) by acquiring completed projects in a market downturn rather than instigating the development process.

6.4 Methods of property funding

Methods of funding property development are outlined below and this overview includes debt finance, joint venture arrangements and mezzanine finance. The private finance initiative (PFI) and related public private partnerships (PPP) are also considered briefly.

Debt finance

Clearing banks and, to a lesser extent, merchant banks have been prepared to provide loans for property development. Generally large projects loans have been secured on collateral beyond the property to be developed, which could include other property assets. For smaller schemes, personal property owned by directors of the company looking to raise the finance can be offered as security. Interest on the loan is charged on a fixed or variable basis. Non-recourse finance may also be available, depending upon the status of the borrower. A non-recourse loan is a loan on property unsupported by outside collateral. Effectively non-recourse finance depends upon the strength of the borrower's balance sheet and it follows that this type of funding is normally only available for substantial and well-capitalised developers with successful track records.

Finance is normally available from banks for up to 70% loan to value ratio (LTV) without outside security being provided. Higher LTVs can be available for substantial companies but market conditions will dictate the movement of LTV rates and it follows that the poorer the market, the lower the LTV rate. The rationale for the LTV rate at around 70% is to ensure that if the market falls it is the borrower's stake which is eroded first, leaving the bank's stake immune from any downturn. During periods of financial uncertainty lenders will review their lending ratios and it is not uncommon for banks to revert to loan to cost ratios (LTCs) which effectively reduces a lender's risk exposure as the costs of development are normally significantly less than the values of completed schemes. The use of LTC ratios will also increase the need for equity funding from the borrower or mezzanine finance (discussed further below).

Banks are naturally wary of lending to companies which already have high borrowing and are therefore highly geared. The American term for gearing is leverage. Strictly, in academic texts it is defined as the ratio of debt to *total* capital but gearing is often defined as: the ratio of interest bearing debt to the shareholder's funds, basically the ratio of debt to equity ('debt to equity ratio') which gives an indication of the financial standing of the company.

Banks normally take first charge over a developer's site before advancing monies against a project. Interest rates are normally set at a margin over the London Inter Bank Offered Rate (LIBOR) of between 1% and 2% in a settled market, but this is reduced with pre-let or presale. During the 2007–9 recession, margins rose above this due to problems of liquidity and higher perceived risks. Interest rate margins also depend upon the availability of money on the wholesale markets, inflation and the state of the economy, as well as the status of the borrower.

Interest rates can be finely honed by using what are known as basis points where one basis point is one hundredth of 1%, therefore 50 basis points is 0.5%.

Borrowing rates may be fixed or variable and where a variable rate applies, various arrangements can be negotiated to hedge the risk of a rise or a fall in borrowing costs. Rates can be capped which means that a ceiling is set for rates on a variable loan. One way of providing an interest rate ceiling is by the use of an insurance policy, although there will be a premium for the borrower to pay at the outset and this cost has to be offset against the risk and consequences of a rate increase over the term of the loan.

Loans generally have limited recourse with developer undertakings to:

- pay cost overruns;
- inject equity stakes either upfront or side by side;
- pay interest post-completion; and
- complete within certain time and cost limits.

Banks will normally allow interest to be rolled up during the construction period and developers therefore generally include this in appraisals as a capitalised cost, thus not affecting profits during the development process.

Some of the main types of debt finance available are covered in the following paragraphs.

Commercial mortgages

These are straightforward loans where the interest rate is either paid currently or capitalised. The principal is either amortised over the term of the loan or repaid by a single payment at the end. The interest rate can be fixed or variable and other capital market instruments can be used including caps (compensating for interest rate rises over a certain rate) and floors (preventing interest rate falls below a certain level). These instruments are used to minimise interest rate fluctuations thereby reducing risk and obtaining finer pricing of the loans. The length of loans will vary and could be anything between three and 30 years.

Equity participation or convertible mortgages

This structure allows the lender to share in the uplift of the value of the property for a reduction in the interest rate payable. The mortgage loan outstanding can be converted into the ordinary shares of the company which is borrowing and the lender takes shares in lieu of repayment of the outstanding debt on the mortgage.

Mortgage debenture issue

This is a traditional method of raising corporate finance. It involves a loan raised on a debenture issue which is secured against the property or other assets and yields either a fixed or index-linked return.

Multi-option facility

In this structure a group of banks agree to provide cash advances to a developer to progress a scheme at a predetermined margin for a certain period. The expression 'syndicated loan' is sometimes used in this context.

Deep discounted bonds

Deep discounted bonds are a method of raising long-term finance with a low initial interest rate. Interest payments can be stepped to accord with future rent reviews once the development is let. Bonds can be placed with institutional investors and can be very finely priced.

Joint ventures

There are different types of joint venture although fundamentally the concept involves the coming together of two or more parties to undertake a transaction. Joint ventures are a useful means of bringing parties together with different interests in order to complete projects. They are often the best solution in times of economic uncertainty because they combine the resources of the partners while spreading risk.

During recessionary periods such as that of 2008–9 joint ventures become an option for property development because at those times banks will typically reduce their lending to the property sector. Similarly property companies may be less able to raise new funds in the stock market and so combining with other partners can be a way of combining resources to a point where the overall costs of a scheme can be met. Overseas investors might also prefer joint venture arrangements as a suitably experienced local development partner will be able to provide the expertise required to progress a scheme on the ground.

Forms of joint venture structure are:

1 limited liability companies;
2 partnership, where one party must have unlimited liability; and
3 profit participation.

The decision on whether to create a joint venture will depend on the opportunities and constraints presented by the particular project and for example:

1 whether the project involves one development or a number of consecutive developments;
2 the tax situation for the parties; and
3 stamp duty considerations.

When negotiating a joint venture agreement, important issues for the parties to consider are:

1 the level of funding to be provided;
2 the development period;
3 who will control the decision-making process;
4 how is the profit going to be distributed;
5 what are the provisions for dissolution in the event of failure; and
6 how are disputes to be settled.

Mezzanine finance

This is effectively 'top slice' lending over and above the normal LTV ratios. There are often gaps between the costs of development and limited recourse loans (sometimes referred to as the senior debt) and this is filled by a mezzanine loan. The amount of mezzanine finance varies but it can take debt up to 95% of project costs. As Wilkinson and Reed (2008: 162) explain mezzanine funders require higher rates for this lending because it is more risky and involves a second charge on the assets following the senior debt. Should the project run into problems, the second priority return that the mezzanine funder has can quickly diminish any profit remaining for the developer. A mezzanine finance package could also include the lender taking an equity stake in the profits of the development, or a share in the surplus over the development costs when the project is complete. Given that mezzanine finance is expensive for developers and risky for the lender it is not perhaps surprising that research by Maxted and Porter (2007: 9) found that mezzanine loans each year only accounted for around 4% of bank lending to commercial property in the UK in comparison to senior debt which accounted for the balance of 96% of lending.

The Private Finance Initiative (PFI) and Public Private Partnerships (PPP)

The main focus of this book is upon private commercial property development and this chapter is exploring the funding of that type of development. However no discussion on the funding of property development would be entirely complete without at least summarising the Private Finance Initiative (PFI) and the Public Private Partnerships (PPP) which it enables. In the context of this book this summary serves mainly to distinguish this particular type of funding method which is applicable to the delivery of buildings which will be used mainly by public authorities in the delivery of their services. Readers who want to explore this specialised area of funding in more depth could look at Dubben and Williams (2009: 66–103) who provide a good overview of the way that PFI has been implemented or Cheung et al. (2009) who explore the reasons why some public bodies in Hong Kong, Australia and the UK have chosen PPP as a procurement route.

Since 1992 when PFI was first introduced in the UK it has become a recognised option for procuring public buildings while avoiding the need for public borrowing to support the capital cost of projects. Essentially the public sector body commissions the resources of the private sector to provide a building and then pays back the costs as a revenue stream over the term of the agreement.

Thus a primary healthcare trust might procure a new hospital or a university a new halls of residence or the Home Office a new prison by entering into a PPP. Private sector partners contribute their development expertise and funding to the project in return for guaranteed repayments from the procuring body which might extend over 25 years for a major scheme.

Under a PPP agreement the public body is essentially paying a rate of interest relative to the capital cost expended by the private sector in providing a new building. While that rate of interest will typically be at least double that achievable from direct public borrowing, supporters of PFI claim that the mark-up is justified in terms of the greater efficiencies and know-how which the private sector can bring to the delivery of projects. It is also claimed in defence of PFI that the higher rates of return from PPPs are justified because of the project risk transfer to the private sector from the public sector.

While PFI can provide new state-of-the-art facilities for a public body at an affordable cost, sceptics have claimed that in some instances the private sector partner may have exploited PPPs by negotiating high rates of return for very little risk transfer. Considerable learning has been done on how to structure PPP deals so that both partners achieve acceptable outcomes. There has also been independent scrutiny by the Audit Commission which has explored whether public bodies are in fact achieving value for money from the PPP deals that they have entered into. The structure of PPP agreements is therefore gradually improving with experience. Given tight financial restrictions and public spending cuts in the public sector in the wake of the credit crunch and the huge sums of public money used to bail out a failing banking system, it is likely that PPPs will continue to be supported by government as an option for providing major public buildings.

6.5 Sources of finance

The main lenders in the UK property market are:

1 high street clearing banks
2 foreign banks
3 building societies
4 merchant banks
5 insurance companies
6 finance houses

High street clearing banks

The clearing banks underwent significant change between 2007–9 as global economic conditions deteriorated and illiquidity problems emerged in the banking sector. Lloyds TSB Bank effectively took over HBOS (Halifax Bank of Scotland) in late 2008 and the government subsequently took large stakes in both the Royal Bank of Scotland and Lloyds TSB. Abbey was taken over by the Spanish group Santander. HSBC and Barclays remained outside government ownership. The problems that led to this crisis stemmed from overexposure in property lending, bad debts and excessive and unregulated trading in complex financial instruments. As a result of the financial crisis banks took a far more

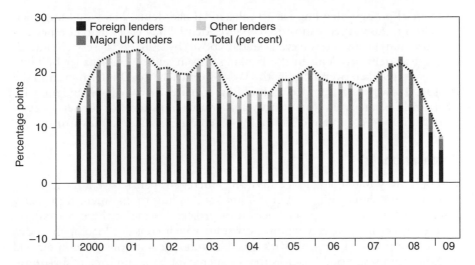

Figure 6.1 Twelve-month growth rates in the stock of lending, 2000–9 (BoE, 2009, adapted)

conservative attitude to risk. Not only did lending volumes drop, but loan to value ratios were reduced. In mid-2009 it was difficult although not impossible to obtain residential mortgage finance at an LTV of 90% or higher. While the number of mortgage products for smaller commercial and residential customers reduced, the demand from borrowers also fell on the back of increased uncertainty, rising unemployment and falling asset prices. The chart above (Figure 6.1) produced by the Bank of England (2009) depicts gross annual lending volumes, and the sharp downturn across 2008 and into 2009 is apparent.

Foreign banks

Maxted and Porter's (2007) research on lending to commercial property confirms that UK lenders still dominate the market, accounting for 71% of all loans made to commercial property in 2006. German banks at that time were the largest single overseas lenders to UK commercial property accounting for 12% of all loans with American lenders accounting for a 2% share. The remaining 15% of lending is made up by a combination of a number of other international banks including those from Japan, Ireland, France, Cyprus, Switzerland and various Arabian countries. The level of lending activity by foreign banks to the UK property sector varies quite considerably, and there have problems in the past with the collapse of BCCI in 1991. In 2008 the Icelandic banking system collapsed and despite an initial pledge by the Icelandic government to repay gradually the debts created by its country's banks, many local authorities in the UK who had made substantial deposits with Icelandic banks were facing significant losses.

Building societies

The building societies fared badly in both the 1990–5 and 2007–9 slumps in the property market. In the late 1980s, initiatives to increase market share in commercial property lending led to substantial bad debts. Many building societies also increased their exposure to the residential buy to let market especially from the mid-1990s. However, as stated above, by 2007–8 there were liquidity and bad debt problems in the banking system and several smaller building societies were taken over, notably the West Bromwich, the Dunfermline and the Skipton. However, a number of building societies remain independent with substantial resources and they are a viable source of finance for property developers with good corporate credit ratings even during a market downturn.

Merchant banks

As reported by Ratcliffe *et al.* (2009: 432) merchant banks have a track record of being quite enterprising when it comes to lending to commercial property developers for the development period of projects. Some of these banks have in-house specialist property lending divisions which consider loan applications from developers and respond with bespoke funding solutions. The latter will probably represent good business for the merchant bank in terms of a requirement for equity participation in the more robust schemes and the levying of a higher interest rate than might be obtainable from clearing banks (should the latter be willing to lend against a scheme). Merchant banks tend to source their funds on the wholesale money markets at a margin above LIBOR and then relend the money to developers at a higher rate, and so in one sense they could be seen as money brokers. Because they have specialist lending divisions, they concentrate on large corporate transactions and are unlikely to be interested in ordinary debt transactions where there would be little opportunity to use their expertise to add value.

Because a merchant bank will tend to be more entrepreneurial and flexible than a high street clearing bank in the structuring of property funding, merchant banks are typically exposed to a higher degree of risk and they are likely to be the first to withdraw and the most badly affected when periodic property crises occur. This was true of the property crash in the early 1970s and again in the recession of 2008–9.

Insurance companies and pension funds

These institutional investors include insurance companies, pension funds, investment trusts and unit trusts. To take a longer-term perspective these institutional investors have since the 1950s increased their share of finance to firms at the expense of private individual investors. Prior to that time individual investors were very important on the stock markets but progressive taxation and increased egalitarianism reduced the differences in income between the very rich and poor and thus enabled the poorer sections of society to accumulate some form of insurance and or pension and thus an ultimate claim on these companies' funds. Thus, with the decline of the large private investors, there has been an increase in the volume of investment from what were traditionally the less affluent sections of society who have tended to invest their money in building societies, unit trusts, insurance companies and banks. In turn, these institutions were increasingly able to reinvest their funds in the stock markets and to selectively fund large prime commercial property developments.

The insurance companies and pension funds thus have a long-term perspective on their investments generally which include property. Morley confirms (2002: 74) that these organisations will therefore reappraise and adjust their overall financial portfolios to align with anticipated liabilities arising on insurance policies and the maturation of pension plans. Whether funding property development and then retaining the finished schemes as investments or purchasing investment grade commercial properties in the open market, this funding activity is very strategic for insurance companies and pension funds. These organisations will thus have property divisions staffed by chartered surveyors, funding and legal experts who deal with acquisitions and disposals and staff who interface with external developers and project managers.

With regards to funding property developments these funds are likely to be very selective in terms of the property developers that they lend to and the location and nature of the schemes. Funds may be provided to developers on a pre-sale basis at what for a developer will be attractive rates of interest, although the conditions of the final sale will limit profitability for the developer as the funds will have predetermined yields while still expecting the developer to shoulder much of the development and letting risk.

Finance houses

In essence, the finance houses have been the principal providers of funding to the secondary leisure and retailing markets, providing finance for the purchase of freehold shops, pubs, restaurants and hotels. Their exposure to small traders makes them particularly vulnerable to recessions when some of their clients will inevitably go into liquidation and when there can be shortages of wholesale money, making it difficult for these organisations to write profitable business.

6.6 Lending criteria

The cost and availability of lending is a function of the value of any particular project and the amount of cost to be financed. The nature of the development is important, as are the design, mix, location and likely demand. The letting status in terms of whether the investment is pre-let or speculative is also a critical consideration. A pre-let scheme is one where a tenant enters a contractual obligation to take a lease before the completion of the project. This is obviously attractive to funders and reduces the risk of income voids and improves the funding position. Therefore a borrower may be able to negotiate a lower-interest rate in such circumstances.

Speculative development is where a scheme is constructed with a view to finding tenants by marketing the scheme to potential occupiers before and during the development period and possibly afterwards if the building remains unlet by that stage. As Sayce *et al.* (2006: 220) point out funders such as banks will tend to focus on the downside risk and will tend to attribute little weight to optimistic forecasts of rental increases when evaluating particularly speculative projects. This cautious approach to lending will be amplified in uncertain markets when there is a high risk that speculative schemes may take many months if not several years to let, putting a bank's capital at risk. These risks may be reflected in lending at higher rates of interest, increased collateral and equity requirements and guarantees.

The quality of the tenant, who will be providing the cash flow to the investment, is crucial in commercial developments. A substantial tenant with a strong business is one of the most important factors in underpinning the capital value of a development scheme. Good-quality tenants are seen as more secure in terms of maintaining income flow from rent and they are less likely to default. A good tenant is known as a 'good covenant', a term which is also used to reflect the financial status of any party involved in a property transaction.

The property investment market has always favoured standard commercial leases often of 20–25 years with regular upward-only rent reviews and repairing obligations imposed on the tenants. However in recent times commercial leases are tending to become shorter and more flexible, with break clauses, allowing tenants the opportunity to end the lease with notice, in certain circumstances. It is the case that the investment market will look more favourably upon a scheme which is let to a blue-chip tenant on a long lease with regular rent reviews, than a similar scheme let to a newly established company on flexible lease terms. Such preferences are reflected in the capital value of the property. Therefore careful lease drafting makes an important contribution to the saleability and value of a property development, but there is a trade-off between what the landlord would like to achieve and what the tenant would accept in terms of their required flexibility.

Other important criteria are the track record of the developer and the strength of security. The duration of the loan will also be important as well as the anticipated regularity of repayments, their size and number prior to redemption.

Most corporate lenders look for the same characteristics in a lending proposal, which in simplified terms are the four 'Cs' and which to some extent are interlinked:

- character
- cash-stake
- capability
- collateral

Character

This relates to the trading history or development experience of a borrower. In respect of a property developer or an investment company the lender will want to know whether the borrower has the experience to complete the development, manage the investment or run the business, if applicable. The lender will also be interested in whether the client is respectable, trustworthy and has an industry reputation for producing quality buildings on time and within budget. There are several ways of assessing this. For example, references may be taken up from business suppliers, recent trading accounts can also be analysed and there are numerous credit check agencies that can provide corporate credit ratings on request. An overall profile of the character of the potential borrower can therefore be established, if the borrower is an unknown quantity to the lender.

Cash-stake

This relates to how much equity (the borrower's own money) is going into the transaction. In addition, the bank will want to know where the equity has come from and for example whether the money is recycled borrowing from another source. The money laundering regulations also come into play and a bank will have to be sure that any equity offered by a borrower has been legitimately earned. A bank will also want to know if the equity offered is simply a paper surplus which has arisen from a revaluation of a property.

Capability

A lender will want to know if the borrower has the capability to service the loan; that is, to pay the interest when it arises and the capital as and when repayment is required. One of the alleged causes of the credit crunch in 2008 was that banks and building societies had become too blasé regarding the ability of borrowers to meet loan requirements. This ultimately led to a crisis of confidence in a financial sector which was too willing to get individuals and companies into debt beyond their means to repay. A prudent lender however, will want to know whether the borrower has accounts or a business plan to show the present financial position and any estimate of future cash flow. Thus it will be very helpful to a potential borrower to have undertaken some financial modelling and to try to demonstrate some involvement in ongoing profitable activities.

Collateral

The lender will want to know what security will be offered for the loan, its value and its saleability. The lender will normally commission a valuation of the proposed collateral assets to ensure that they support the proposed level of borrowing and are not already pledged as security against another loan. The collateral properties could then be repossessed by the lender if the borrower defaults on the loan. Lenders may also ask for personal guarantees to be given by the borrower to underwrite the loan.

6.7 Loan terms and funding of small developers and builders

Once the lender has had the opportunity to examine the risk profile of the proposed borrower against the four Cs above a decision can then be taken in respect of the actual amount and structure of the loan.

For example a project could be deemed to be one which could be funded by deficit financing. This is the financing of a project in such a way that the cash flows in the early years of the project are insufficient to cover the interest on debt payable. The expectation being that future income will accrue at such a rate to cover interest and capital on the loan. Similarly where there may be a period in the development process where no income is received necessitating interest to be rolled up and added to the costs of the project. Repayment will take place when income from sales or rent from the development is received.

The growing importance of financial intermediaries in the market is explained by the complexity and range of choices now available to the property developer seeking to fund a large or small scheme.

There are four main areas to be considered prior to entering into a loan facility to ensure that a suitable structure related to the lender's requirements can be arranged. These are cost, flexibility, risk and accounting presentation.

Cost

The best rates are available for the best-quality covenants (borrowers). Where the lending institution takes more risk, a higher return is required. For a non-recourse transaction the interest rate margin over LIBOR required by the lender is increased when compared to a similar secured loan.

Flexibility

The greater the level of security and recourse, the less likely there is to be any restrictions on management control. Flexibility depends on interest rate structure.

Risk

The greater the lender's risk, the greater the cost to the borrower in terms of loan repayments or the higher the equity stake required by the lender in order to participate.

Accounting presentation

Essentially the best way to represent debt in company accounts relative to company tax and other liabilities.

Finance for small developers and builders

The funding for small development and building firms is important because they undertake developments which fall beneath the threshold which would interest the large publicly listed property companies. Four stages in the financing needs of small companies can be distinguished. These are:

1 *Venture capital* – the funds necessary to meet the start-up costs of a new company.
2 *Development capital* – which is needed to finance expansion once the initial phase of establishing the company has been completed.
3 *Increasing the number of shareholders* – when it becomes necessary to widen the equity base of the company. These situations arise when borrowing may have reached a level where additional borrowing would push the firm's gearing to a point where the continuing financial stability of the company was put in doubt.
4 *Acquiring a Stock Exchange listing* – this might occur where the firm has expanded and has a portfolio of projects which will need shareholder investment.

The smaller firm suffers from a number of disadvantages in the market, such as having to pay higher rates of interest. In addition, many small firms of builders or developers lack knowledge about potential sources of finance. Thus, because of problems related to credit and interest rates, the general condition of the economy will affect smaller firms more acutely than larger ones. The other problems that small firms face in raising finance is that they are very wary of entering into debt arrangements. There are a number of reasons for this including fear of losing control over the company as well as fear of not being able to meet the conditions related to the loans.

Possible sources of funding for small firms include: merchant banks, who provide medium and long-term loans and equity interest; specialist funders such as venture capitalists and other private equity groups. They provide loans and equity interest for venture and development capital while finance houses and leasing companies may provide finance for equipment and vehicle financing. There are also monies available from factoring houses that provide cash for debts and the clearing banks that provide overdraft facilities. Insurance companies provide some financing for property and, finally, there is conditional government funding through a number of intermediary bodies and agencies for financing technological innovation or skills development.

6.8 Case study: finance for the smaller developer/building contractor

The 2008–9 recession reduced the availability of finance for development quite drastically due to problems of liquidity which affected many western economies. However this does not mean to say that financing for property development becomes impossible. It just means that there is less choice for the borrower, lending criteria will be more stringent and borrowing may be more expensive. Traditionally the smaller developer would look to a high street bank, albeit through a commercial lending department which may be a regional office.

First, we consider what is available in terms of financing options and attempt to remove some of the mystique of the financial world and finally outline the ways of properly approaching a lender.

The options available

There are a myriad of ways to raise finance for a particular project including:

- corporate methods
- debt capital
- debenture stock
- unsecured loan stock
- share capital
- preference shares
- ordinary shares
- convertibles
- warrants

However not all of these are open to the smaller borrower who will in all probability not be a listed company and may have limited collateral. For example finance leases are usually only available for larger more complex transactions. The most appropriate source in the scenario being considered here would be a commercial mortgage.

Commercial mortgages

Commercial mortgages themselves offer a wide variety of options and are available from building societies, clearing banks, international banks and insurance companies. There are many types of structure from short-term bridging finance to 30-year terms. A mortgage can be repaid in a variety of ways, and through the use of capital market instruments the interest rate risk can be reduced.

Repayment structures

There are a variety of different structures available. A combination of each can also be used.

- *Capital and interest:* this is the most common type of repayment structure where capital and interest are repaid over a longer period of up to 25 years.
- *Bullet repayment:* this is commonly used in short to medium-term loans where the borrower repays interest only for the duration of the loan. The capital sum is then repaid at the end.
- *Interest only:* interest on the loan is payable with the capital being repaid at the end of the term by, for example, an endowment or pension policy which matures at that point.
- *Pension schemes:* can offer a tax-efficient investment strategy for commercial property purchases. The facility is appropriate for individuals, or people in partnership. Rents on the property are paid into a linked pension fund. Funds from existing pension facilities go towards a deposit on the property with the lending source providing the remainder. The main advantages are that contributions to the plan attract tax relief and any growth in value of property held in the fund is free of capital gains tax.
- *Capital holiday:* interest only is payable for an initial agreed period usually up to five years. Thereafter, capital and interest are repayable for the remainder of the loan. This has obvious attractions in minimising outgoings during the first few years of the loan, which in turn will help cash flow at the most risky time of the project.

Interest rate structures

The rate of interest payable by a borrower will be made up of a base rate plus a fixed margin. The base rate charged can take a number of forms:

- *Variable rates:* the interest rate is normally set periodically at 3, 6, 9 or 12 month intervals. The rate may either be set by the lender (for example finance house or building society base rates) or a variable rate such as the London Inter Bank Offered Rate (LIBOR) may be offered. The Bank of England Monetary Policy Committee reviews interest rates every month and variable rates set by lenders may track the rate set by the Bank of England.

- *Fixed rates:* a fixed-rate mortgage will eliminate any exposure to a rise in interest rates and conversely any benefits from falling interest rates. Lenders who offer long-term fixed rate mortgages will set the figures in the light of anticipated trends in future.

Interest rate hedging instruments

There are a number of capital market instruments available that can reduce a borrower's exposure to interest rate movements.

- *Interest rate caps and collars:* these have been discussed earlier in this chapter. An interest rate collar limits the volatility of future interest rate payments. An interest rate cap is effectively an insurance policy. In return for a premium, a borrower is compensated by a bank or insurance company should interest rates rise above the level at which the cap is agreed.

This arrangement provides both a ceiling, by way of an interest rate cap, and a floor and the interest rate can move between the upper and lower limits agreed between the parties. Should interest rates fall below the floor, the borrower will pay to the bank the difference between the interest payment due at the level of the floor and that due at the prevailing interest rate.

Therefore where interest rates rise above the agreed cap rate, the bank would compensate the borrower. Conversely, where interest rates fall below the agreed floor, the borrower would compensate the bank. By arranging a collar the cost of finance should be significantly cheaper than for a cap alone.

- *Interest rate swap:* is an agreement between two parties to swap their interest payment obligations with each other. Typically, banks act as intermediaries to arrange the swap and this enables a borrower to exchange floating money for a fixed-interest obligation. The main disadvantage of fixing interest rates is that there will be penalty costs if the loan is repaid. These costs can be substantial.
- *Interest rate margin:* is a margin on top of the interest rate (base rate) set by the lender will also be payable. This margin is dependent upon the individual lender's assessment of the borrower's financial strength and reflects the risk to the lender of entering into the transaction. The margin is usually between 0.50% and in some cases over 4.00%. Smaller companies may not be able to borrow at very low margins even in strong markets. During 2009 a 4% margin was not uncommon, reflecting the difficult economic conditions then prevailing.

Servicing

It must be possible for the business to create cash surpluses from its trading activities not only for the repayment of the loan but for tax, living expenses and future expenditure.

As a rule of thumb the net profit figure shown in the accounts should be twice the amount of all interest charges to include bank borrowing, factoring, overdraft charges, etc. However where, for example, a rented property will be replaced by a freehold property, the rental saving should be added back to the net profit figure. The worked example below in Figure 6.2 illustrates the principle of double interest cover in which a ratio of 2.04 is deemed to be an acceptable risk.

Amount of loan sought:	£450,000

Company's latest audited accounts indicate:

Net profit before tax:	£217,000
Add back rent saving:	£19,000
Net profit therefore:	£236,000

This year's finance charges from cash flow:

Bank overdraft interest:	£55,000
Hire purchase interest:	£20,000
£450,000 loan @ 9% interest:	£40,500
Total interest payable:	£115,500

Ratio of net profit to interest payable:	£236,000/£115,500 = **2.04**

Figure 6.2 Double interest cover

Other costs relating to a mortgage

It is likely that the lender will charge an arrangement fee of between 0.5% and 1.0% of the amount of the advance. An independent valuation will need to be undertaken at a cost of between 0.125% and 0.2% of the value and the borrower will also be liable for the lender's legal fees.

Information required when approaching a lender

When a borrower approaches a lender to obtain funds the borrower should be clear on what finance is required and also that sufficient background information is provided to the lender as follows.

- *Amount and purpose:* the borrower should be able to specify the amount of loan required and its purpose such as the acquisition of a property, goodwill, fixtures and fittings.
- *Borrower's details:* the borrowing company should be able to provide confirmation of the trading name and registered address, banker and solicitor, together with the company's authorised and paid-up share capital and a breakdown of shareholders and their respective holdings.
- *Directors'/shareholders' details:* the borrower should be able to provide the CVs of the directors/shareholders and the background or history of any parent company. Where the borrower is a sole trader partnership, the lenders will require CVs together with personal asset and liability statements and copies of partnership agreements where relevant.
- *Accounts:* the borrower will be expected to provide three years' audited accounts which will help the lender to assess the financial strength of the company.
- *Bank borrowing:* a breakdown of all current borrowings, i.e. mortgages, overdrafts will be required. Details of any hire purchase agreements and

leasing will be required, identifying each lender and how each facility is secured. This is important because it gives an indication of the outgoings of the borrower and can assess the ability of the borrower to meet periodic mortgage payments.

- *Development activity:* where the borrower is building or extending premises, the lender will need full details of the development including a description and breakdown of costs, warranties, a copy of the planning consent, details of any contractor and building contract and a full set of drawings.
- *Borrower's equity:* the amount and availability of the borrower's equity will need to be divulged together with cash flow forecasts to support the borrowing request. The use of Excel spreadsheets will allow an applicant to create a sensitivity analysis of their proposals. This can be a useful tool for both the borrower and the lender because it enables the proposed scheme to be assessed for risk at changing borrowing costs, sale proceeds, development timescales and void periods. Off-the-shelf software packages can be used for such an exercise although books by for example Bowcock and Bayfield (2000) and Fawcett (2003) provide advice on how to structure spreadsheets in Excel to fulfil the same function.

6.9 A market overview and select glossary of financial terms

Market overview

In 2009 the UK economy was in recession with poorly functioning lending markets. The foreign banks that did so much to support UK property lending in the period up until 2008 largely withdrew and most domestic banks were nursing substantial bad debt provisions in the commercial property lending sector. Interest rates were reduced by the Bank of England Monetary Policy Committee from 5% in the autumn of 2008 and sustained at 0.5% through 2009 and into 2010. Despite this, banks were charging high arrangement fees and margins on lending to reflect the riskier nature of loans in a poor market. Because there were fewer lenders in the market, there was a lack of competition and this contributed to the uncompetitive pricing of loans and fees.

According to the Bank of England (2009) commercial property prices fell 40% from the peak in June 2007. Lending against new property development fell to virtually zero in 2008–9 but the impact of draw-downs on lending facilities on long-term development projects was still taking place (see Figure 6.3).

The government's policy of quantitative easing in 2009 was designed to stimulate higher bank lending to assist the economy out of recession. Quantitative easing is the term used to describe the buying of corporate or government bonds from banks, by the Bank of England which in theory should provide revenue for banks to lend to businesses. According to Savills (2009) this macro-economic policy approach appeared to be bearing fruit in the commercial property sector towards the end of 2009 when developers were reporting renewed optimism and a gradual return to 'business as usual'.

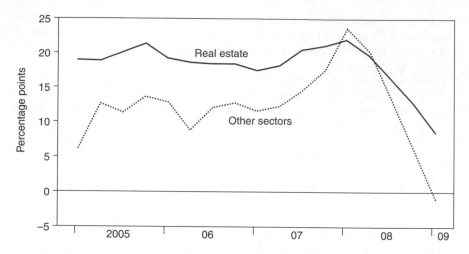

Figure 6.3 Growth in lending to the real estate and other sectors (BoE, June 2009)

A select glossary of financial terms

In this chapter various property funding concepts have been introduced and below selected aspects of that vocabulary are explained briefly for those who may be new to the subject and may wish to consolidate their knowledge.

Finance lease: This involves the sale and leaseback of a site for development with a financial institution. There may be tax advantages in such an arrangement for a developer without the loss of control over the asset.

Ground rent: An annual payment for the inclusion of the land element in a development project and which would normally be the first charge on the income arising from the development on the land.

Joint venture: Two or more parties, working together, sharing the rewards and risks of a development project.

Overage: The growth in capital value over the development period which is available to be shared between vendor and developer when the scheme has been completed or a specified milestone has been reached. Sometimes the term 'claw-back' is used interchangeably with overage, although a distinction is that claw-back is the mechanism used and might for example be a legal agreement containing a trigger mechanism so that the added value (the overage) is 'clawed back' to the vendor. The trigger could be when a certain condition has been met such as the grant of full planning consent or the full letting of a completed building.

Rental void: The period of time a completed development remains unlet and thus not income producing. During this period it is usually difficult to sell the completed project at a competitive price.

Senior and junior debt: These are different levels of debt with different priorities for repayment, security and with different arrangements for repayment. Senior debt usually has first charge on the security. Equity investors may lose all of their money if a development does not perform very well and is only able to meet the repayment of senior and then junior debt.

Swap: An interest rate swap is an agreement between two parties to swap their interest rate obligations, normally from a variable interest rate to a fixed one. A swap option enables a change to a fixed rate in the future at preset terms.

6.10 Summary

Fluctuations in the property market create many challenges for developers looking to raise finance. For example the credit squeeze of 2007–9 led to significant difficulties for many borrowers at a time when base rates were historically low yet lending margins remained high and unaffordable for many borrowers. Banks adopted a cautious approach to lending at that time and the withdrawal of many overseas lenders together with the merger of Lloyds and HBOS resulted in lower levels of competition between lenders. It remains to be seen if EU competition laws may lead to a break-up of these merged and very large banks in future.

Larger development companies have more choice in terms of raising finance. Publicly quoted developers can look to shareholders for capital through a rights issue or may sell bonds or commercial paper. In all cases lenders or prospective equity partners will examine very carefully the proposals put to them. The importance of a robust business plan and of course the four Cs (i.e. cash stake, capability, collateral and character) are crucial in obtaining development finance. Borrowers may use a number of instruments to hedge against the risk of changes in interest rates; this may be by negotiating a cap and collar agreement, or by rolling up interest to assist with cash flow during the development period.

References

Bank of England (2009) *Trends in Lending* (London: Bank of England). Available in e-format at: www.bankofengland.co.uk/publications

Bowcock, P. and Bayfield, N. (2000) *Excel for Surveyors* (London: Estates Gazette).

Cheung, E., Chan, A. P. C. and Kajewski, S. (2009) 'Reasons for implementing public private partnerships projects: perspectives from Hong Kong, Australian and British practitioners', *Journal of Property Investment and Finance*, 27(1).

Dubben, N. and Williams, B. (2009) *Partnerships in Urban Property Development* (Chichester: Wiley-Blackwell).

Fawcett, S. (2003) *Designing Flexible Cashflows* (London: Estates Gazette).

Fraser, W. D. (2004) *Cash-Flow Appraisal for Property Investment* (Basingstoke: Palgrave).

Maxted, B. and Porter, T. (2007) *The UK Commercial Property Lending Market: Year End 2006 Research Findings* (Leicester: De Montfort University).

Morley, S. (2002) 'The financial appraisal of development projects', in Guy, S. and Henneberry, J. (eds), *Development and Developers: Perspectives on Property* (Oxford: Blackwell).

Ratcliffe, J., Stubbs, M. and Keeping, M. (2009) *Urban Planning and Real Estate Development*, 3rd edition (London: Routledge).

Savills (2009) *Commercial Development Activity* (London: Savills). Available in e-format at: www.savills.co.uk

Sayce, S., Smith, J., Cooper, R. and Venmore-Rowland, P. (2006) *Real Estate Appraisal: From Value to Worth* (Oxford: Blackwell).

Wilkinson, S. and Reed, R. (2008) *Property Development*, 5th edition (London: Routledge).

7

The classification of development finance

7.1 Introduction
7.2 Debt and equity
7.3 Categories of finance

7.4 Project-based funding
7.5 Corporate finance
7.6 Summary

Aims

Finance for development can be raised by companies in a number of ways. For example, major organisations may be able to go to the stock market for funds by issuing shares or selling bonds or commercial paper. More modest firms may have to rely on mortgage finance for simple schemes or perhaps enter into joint ventures for major projects, where greater equity is needed. The first part of the chapter examines the difference between debt and equity and between project and corporate funding. Later the role of indirect property investment is also discussed and the vocabulary of property finance is introduced.

Key terms

>> **Mortgage** – a loan normally for between two and 30 years to a borrower to finance the purchase or development of property. A mortgage is secured on the property to which the loan applies and this means that if the borrower defaults the lender can take possession of the property and dispose of it to clear the debt.

>> **Debt** – is borrowing by developers or investors from banks or other sources. For example a mortgage is a debt and would be shown as such on a company's balance sheet.

>> **Equity** – can be funds that a company uses from its own resources to finance a development or for purchasing a property. Equity may also be money raised in the markets, or it may be investment from a partner organisation who will take a share in the profits once a development is completed or let.

>> **Corporate funding** – is raised on the company itself and is divided into debt and equity. Companies may finance development projects by issuing

stock (usually long term) or commercial paper (usually short term). Equity finance can be arranged through share issues in which shareholders participate in the profits of the company by obtaining dividends.

>> **Project funding** – is raised on an individual development scheme and not on the company structure. It may have advantages to organisations in that if the scheme did not perform financially, then the project only and not the company itself is at risk.

7.1 Introduction

This chapter considers the difference between long-term debt and shareholders' equity in a firm and also the way that funding is secured. For example, a mortgage is a debt used to finance a development project or property purchase, but it is also possible in some circumstances to finance the project through investors who will take an equity stake or profit share in the project. Funding can be secured on a single project, the project being the bank's security in the event of default or monies can be raised on the back of a company itself. In the latter case, the company's financial strength is the security, rather than any property assets in isolation. An understanding of the difference between equity and debt is fundamental to an understanding of how finance works and this chapter will begin by exploring the distinctions. However this is not the only distinction as the funding of development can also be considered in terms of whether it is project based or corporate, a distinction which is also considered below.

7.2 Debt and equity

Debt finance basically consists of loans raised from banks and other sources against the project or non-project-specific loans raised in the market. Equity is money and resources provided by the developer, partners, investors and funds who participate in the risk and profit of the scheme. However sometimes the boundaries between the two categories become blurred as corporate funding, the raising of finance against the assets of a company, can be based on equity as well as debt.

Project and corporate finance

Generally, firms offer two basic types of securities to investors: debt securities are contractual obligations to repay corporate borrowing: equity securities are shares of common stock; and preferred stock that represent non-contractual claims on the residual cash flow of the firm. Issues of debt and equity that are publicly sold by the firm are then traded on the financial markets. These distinctions between equity and debt and between project and corporate finance are clarified in the following paragraphs.

Project finance is finance provided where the principal or only security for the finance is the property itself, although supporting guarantees and additional collateral may also be requested. As stated above, corporate finance is finance raised on the back of the corporate entity rather than the project. Traditionally, property and other companies provided funds for new projects from retained earnings, the issue of new shares and borrowing. In the 1950s

Funding matrix		
	Corporate funding	Project finance
Equity finance	Share issues	Partnership funds Single-asset unitisation
Debt finance	Loan stock Fixed interest debentures	Bank loans and overdrafts Short-term borrowing for development

Figure 7.1 Funding matrix

and 1960s fixed-interest mortgages and debentures were also used although by the 2000s a more complex package of different types of funds might be used to fund a major property development.

When trying to decide upon the best way to fund a venture it is sometimes helpful to think of the potential options in terms of a funding matrix as represented in Figure 7.1.

Capital structure

Financing arrangements determine how the value of a company is composed. The persons or institutions that buy debt from the firm are creditors. The holders of the equity shares are shareholders. The size of the company's balance sheet will determine how well the company has made its investment decisions. Ross *et al.* (2008) confirm that the size of the firm is its value in the financial markets which in simple terms is depicted by the formula:

$$V = D + E$$
Value of company = value of debt + value of equity

Corporate securities issued are a contingent claim on the value of the company. The shareholder's claim on the value of the company is a residual after payment to the debt holder, they get nothing if the value of the company is equal to or less than the amount promised to the debt holders. In Figure 7.2 below F is the promised pay-off to debt holders. X-F is the pay-off to equity shareholders when F is greater than zero; if it is not, then the pay-off to shareholders is zero.

Financial markets

The financial markets are composed of the money markets and the capital markets. Money markets deal with debt securities that pay off in the short term, usually less than one year. Capital markets deal with long-term debt and equity shares. Primary markets are used when governments or companies initially offer their shares to the public and this is discussed further later in this chapter. Secondary markets come into operation for the resale of securities. Debt and

Pay-off to debt holders   Pay-off to equity holders   Pay-off to both

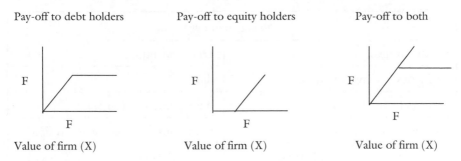

Value of firm (X)   Value of firm (X)   Value of firm (X)

Figure 7.2 Pay-offs to debt and equity (by Ross *et al.* (2007))

equity are traded in the security markets; there is a distinction between auction markets and dealer markets. Equity securities tend to be sold in auction markets (like the Stock Exchange) while debt securities are sold in dealer markets. Auction markets differ from dealer markets in two ways:

1 Trading in an auction exchange takes place at a single site on the floor of the exchange or with a centralised screen system.
2 The transaction prices of shares traded on the auction exchange are communicated almost immediately to the public by electronic media; this is not so in dealer markets (Ross *et al.* (2007)).

Direct investment versus property vehicles

The concept of project versus corporate finance can be looked at from a different perspective, i.e. that of direct investment in property as against investment through a property vehicle. Sayce *et al.* (2006: 217–49) has considered the advantages and disadvantages of investment by these two approaches. Key differences are summarised below in Figure 7.3 shown on page 160.

Two factors are working in opposite directions. These are correlation to other investments and liquidity. Correlation is important in obtaining a diversified portfolio of investments which helps to spread risk. Direct property has a relatively low correlation to equities but is more illiquid. Property vehicles are liquid but are more highly correlated to equities.

7.3 Categories of finance

Debt or equity

The distinction between debt and equity depends on whether the money is borrowed (debt) and here the borrower has no direct involvement in the project, or whether the money has been provided on the basis of sharing both the risk and the returns of the project (equity). Borrowed money needs to be repaid and interest will be paid on the outstanding amount until the debt is repaid. The equity return for the person who puts up the money is determined by the success of the enterprise. The person shares the profits and if there are none then no return is available.

Direct property	
Advantages	**Disadvantages**
low risk relative to equities	illiquid
diversification benefits	management intensive
hedge against inflation	minimum portfolio size required
good for matching inflation prone long-term liabilities	
Property vehicles	
Advantages	**Disadvantages**
liquidity	loss of control
divisibility	tax slippage
management expertise	short-term, relatively poor performance
specialisation of vehicle	high gearing
high correlation to stock market	
potential to shift weight/exposure	
income benefits from the discount to net asset value	

Figure 7.3 Direct property and property vehicles compared

The most obvious form of equity is cash subscribed as ordinary share capital. Equity shares can also exist in development situations where a financier is entitled to a share in profits of the scheme. There are also deferred forms of equity such as convertible loans, which start as debt paying a fixed rate of interest but can later be converted into equity shares.

Project finance or corporate finance

Project finance is the money borrowed for a specific project, usually a development project. The loan is based on the project itself and this becomes the main security. A larger company may be able to borrow on the strength of the assets of the company itself rather than its individual projects, and this will be corporate finance. Interest will generally be lower for corporate loans than for project loans because there will be more collateral available for security rather than relying on the single project.

Even some quite large companies may sometimes undertake developments of such a size that they exceed the company's own resources. The developer may then be concerned that if anything went wrong with the project, the lenders may have recourse to other assets of the company which may undermine its finances. In this case each development may need to be financed separately on a project basis and companies may try to make the project 'off-balance sheet' if possible.

Loan or traded security

Borrowed money may simply be a loan or it may be borrowed by inviting investors to subscribe for a bond, thus a piece of paper may then be available which is transferable. This is a form of IOU note and is called a security rather than a straight loan. This security can be traded onto other investors. In return the investors receive interest each year and also to have the original money repaid at the end of the agreed duration of the security. If they do not wish to wait for this repayment date, they can sell the rights to other investors, who then become entitled to receive the interest and the eventual repayment monies. Securities of this kind are bought and sold on the stock market.

Secured and unsecured

Lenders normally want security for the money they provide. The collateral for loans thus takes the form of a charge over the borrower's assets, either the specific assets of a business related to the project or the assets of a business as a whole. If the borrower fails to pay the interest when due or capital repayments as required, then the lender can put a receiver into the company and the receiver will repay the loans from proceeds from the sale of the company's assets or available revenues. A loan secured is safer than an unsecured loan but well-established companies may be able to raise unsecured loans because the safeguard for the lender is the company's established profit record out of which the interest can be paid. Most borrowings in the Euromarkets are unsecured, as are borrowings in the commercial paper market. The company's name, corporate credit rating and standing are the main guarantees.

Fixed-rate or variable-rate interest

Sometimes the rate of interest is agreed at the outset of the loan and remains unchanged over the life of the loan. With other loans, the interest rate will change according to movements in money market rates or other rates agreed. For large-scale floating rate borrowings, the most common yardstick of interest rates is the London Inter Bank Offered Rate (LIBOR). This is the rate of interest at which the banks themselves are prepared to lend to each other. The LIBOR market is often used to calculate charges on loans with variable interest rates. Buckle and Thompson (2004) confirm that the banks' lending rates move as LIBOR moves up or down.

Banks with excess funds can earn interest by making a deposit on the interbank market and conversely a bank which has demand for loans from customers can raise cash by borrowing from the market. The profit to the lender will be the margin they charge to their customers over and above LIBOR. For example, a company might pay a margin over the LIBOR rate, of say 2.5 percentage points (or 250 basis points). However, in practice, borrowers will try to reduce the risks of adverse changes in rates by seeking to fix rates where possible. The fixed rate that can be agreed is dependent upon the prospects for increases or decreases in rates in the future.

Long-term borrowings such as mortgage debentures are more likely to be at a fixed rate. The borrower can buy a cap for floating rate borrowing. This is a form of insurance policy which means that whatever happens to interest rates in general, a maximum limit is set to the interest rate that a borrower will have to pay.

Long term or short term

Loans are usually over a period up to 30 years. This range includes short and long-term loans but the intermediate area is not defined. Many people consider one to two years to be short term, equivalent to the development period for most projects, two to seven years as medium-term and more than seven years as long term. Overdrafts are technically payable on demand and thus are short-term borrowing but many companies have an overdraft outstanding almost indefinitely. With a multi-option facility (MOF), a company might technically be borrowing for three months at a time. At the end of three months it repays the original loans and takes out new ones for another three months. If the facility runs for five years, effectively it has the use of five-year money via 'rolling over'.

Recourse, non-recourse or limited-recourse loans

If the loan for a particular project or for a particular subsidiary company is guaranteed by the parent company, the lender has recourse to the assets of the parent. If the only security for the lender is the project itself, as in a pure form of project-based finance, and the parent company has given no guarantees, the loan is non-recourse. A non-recourse loan is very unlikely to be granted in practice, as banks generally require the loans to be limited recourse. The parent may have guaranteed interest payments but is under no obligation to repay the loan itself in these circumstances. A limited-recourse loan would still depend on the reputation of the borrower and the track record of the company as well as the quality of the project itself.

Domestic or Euromarkets loans

Loans can be raised in the UK or in the Euromarkets. Euromarket loans can be in sterling abroad (euro sterling) or other currencies (Eurodollar). A company may well raise monies in the Euromarkets in different currencies and then swap to sterling if sterling is not popular at the time of raising the funds. The terms and conditions of operation in the European market can be different, for instance euro loans are often unsecured.

7.4 Project-based funding

Project-based funding is where the funds are secured against the property being acquired or developed. Project finance is especially important for smaller unlisted property companies to whom stock market sources are unavailable. In these cases the existing assets may be fully charges against previous loans. The financial status of the companies may also not provide sufficient security for the financier.

Traditionally project finance was involved in two distinct operations:

1 *Short-term, interim or bridging finance.* This is the finance raised to pay the development costs over the development period covering site purchase, payments to the building contractor and professional fees.
2 *Long-term finance or funding.* This is required to repay the short-term finance on completion of the project. Long-term financing is not financing the development of the project but financing the retention of the project as a long-term investment. If the developer sells on completion, then long-term funding is unnecessary as short-term debt can be repaid with the sale proceeds. If the developer wishes to retain ownership or an interest in the completed development that requires funding, then long-term finance will have to be arranged.

Types of finance typically available for project funding are:

Equity arrangements
- equity partnerships
- forward sale
- sale and leaseback
- finance lease

Debt arrangements
- bridging finance
- mortgage
- project management fee
- general funding

General funding facilities are really based on the asset backing of the company or developer. The financing of projects has become quite sophisticated although a very brief excursion into the recent history of the topic reveals some of the attitudes which used to persist. For example Darlow (1988: 265–6) captured the attitudes of developers as summarised by the following rules for seeking finance.

Darlow's ten golden rules for developers seeking finance

1 Never use your own money in a development, try to arrange full external funding.
2 Never give a personal guarantee or personal collateral for any loan.
3 Roll up interest in the development period.

4 Keep as much equity as possible.
5 Fund in the local currency.
6 Avoid 50:50 ventures; someone has to be in control.
7 Avoid tax liabilities, exploit tax relief.
8 Larger projects are more uncertain, allow for contingencies.
9 Read the funding agreement, consider the consequences of a worse than expected outcome if conditions change.
10 Secure the funding commitment from the outset.

Most of the above rules still apply today and many large projects such as the Edinburgh Parliament Building and the Olympic Park in London's East End could learn a lot from the application of rule number 8: 'Larger projects are more uncertain, allow for contingencies'. Examples of various types of project finance arrangements are discussed below.

Equity partnerships

These relate more to a method of funding a development rather than true joint ventures and partnerships which are explored more fully by for example Havard (2008: 142–5). These may include arrangements such as participation lending and forward funding. In participation lending, the lender will take a share of the proceeds of a scheme and this may occur where a lender is taking a higher risk, by lending more or at more advantageous rates of interest.

Forward funding is where the purchaser of a development assists the funding of the development this provides security for the purchaser of having some control as the development proceeds. It may be that the forward funder will fund the development at a lower rate of interest. The subsidy of the interest rate and the reduction of risk to the developer will thus lead to a reduced developers profit payable and a higher yield on purchase of the completed development (because of reduced risk and reduced cost to the developer). Thus the purchaser purchases at a reduced price.

The problem with joint ventures and more general partnership arrangements is that the interests held by the parties are going to be difficult to resell until the development is complete, so the partners involved have no security to offer to lenders.

Forward sale

A contract for a future sale can encourage short-term funds, because the bank will know that it will get its money back within a period of time. Alternatively, the party providing the future sale contract may also provide bridging finance. If the investment yield for the scheme was 6%, then the forward sale might take place at 6½%. A forward sale with bridging finance might be 7%.

Pre-funded projects usually involve a forward commitment from the institution to purchase the development on completion. The arrangement would be that the institution advances interim finance at regular intervals at a lower-interest rate than the existing market rate. Once construction is completed or when the building has been let, completion of the sale takes place and the institution hands over the purchase price less the total development cost and rolled-up interest. Table 7.1 below illustrates the principles at work. Forward funding can be with or without rental guarantees. In the latter case the developer would not have to meet the rental income during a post-construction void period while tenants were sought. In the latter case the developer would have to pay the funder a rental income in the event of a void period.

There is a difference between a forward commitment where an end purchaser signs up now, but the funder's commitment is only absolute once conditions as to the building and its letting have been met, and forward funding, where the fund purchases the site, advances the capital and takes over the completed project with its share of excess profits.

There is no need for the disengagement of the developer from the funder in such an arrangement. By a joint venture or a side-by-side lease, where profits are shared, then ownership can also be shared. Securitisation offers an ideal way in which to enable the original developer to retain a percentage of income and future benefits. The fund may receive in such an arrangement a pre-agreed

Table 7.1 The principles of a forwards sale agreement without rental guarantee (adapted from Havard (2008: 129))

Project stage	Typical timescale	Activity/comments
Pre-development feasibility and planning	6 months	Forward funding deal signed with institutional investor, usually prior to commitment to develop.
Land purchase	3 months	Period of due diligence. Finalising of planning and design prior to start onsite. Considerable professional fees are consumed during this period
Construction period	12 months	Mainly negative cash flows to pay the construction contractor and consultants.
Letting period	Up to 12 months	Will depend on the market and the supply of similar properties relative to demand. Rent-free periods might have to be offered to secure tenants.
Investment life of the project	Commercial lease signed, the length and term of which will depend on a number of market factors. A typical lease length might be 15 years.	On letting, the sale completes and the ownership of the building passes to the fund. Cash flows will now be positive.

share of the overage. The latter being the additional return received over the previous maximum estimate in the calculation for cost, return and developer's profit. The share may be subject to the retention of all the overage if the capping of the development return is agreed.

Sale and leaseback

With a sale and leaseback, the developer sells a completed project to an investor and simultaneously takes back a long lease of the development at an agreed rent calculated on the basis of an appropriate rate of return applied to the purchase. The developer then sub-lets the project to occupying tenants and enjoys by way of a profit rent the difference between the rent paid to the institution/funder and that received from the tenants.

In the UK, one of the early major sale and leaseback arrangements was between the property developer Town & City and the funding institution the Prudential. Town and City would ask the Prudential to buy a site, pay the building costs and lease it to Town & City for a return of 6% plus 20% of income growth at rent reviews when the completed development was subsequently let. Thus a base rent was agreed beforehand, although arrangements could be complex as they are for equity partnership situations which involve slicing. So a freeholder takes a ground rent/base rent and participates in increases in income. Arrangements for payment of the base rent may include:

- *Lease guarantee*: if the development is not let in six months, the developer receives a profit from fund but takes a lease back guarantee at the base rent. The guarantee is extinguished on letting.
- *Profit erosion*: developer stakes a profit against voids and the guarantee is for two to four years. This is useful if the developer is unwilling to provide lease back.
- *Priority yield*: the fund sets the return at $6\frac{1}{2}$%, target is $7\frac{1}{2}$% (1% for developer) over target split 50:50.

Finance lease

A variation on sale and leaseback is the finance lease which is basically a sale and leaseback to a leasing company. The leasing company, due to the timing of tax payments and efficient use of capital allowances within a building, can reduce the interest element of the rental payment to below bank base rate. This structure only applies to the top 200 UK corporates and non-tax-paying bodies.

The structure of a finance lease requires a property to be sold to the leasing company who leases the building back to the vendor at a market rent. This rent is fixed for five years and is then increased at a predetermined level. At each fifth year, the vendor would have an option to repurchase the property at an amount which is equivalent to the original sale price plus any capitalised interest. The facility may be designed so that is off balance sheet, although the final arbiter of this will be the company auditors.

Types of debt

Debt for project financing can be divided up into three types depending on the duration of the loan:

1 short-term bridging finance;
2 medium-term loans and senior debt; and
3 long-term mortgages.

Bridging finance

This is a loan of up to three years. Interest is rolled up until the development is sold and thus the developer must be able to pay the interest and principal on completion of the development. The developer would do this by selling the scheme or refinancing the bridging finance with long-term loans.

Clearing banks would typically require security over and above the project such as other assets which are not charged. A clearing bank would also levy an interest rate of between 2% and 4% over LIBOR although would probably not be interested in an equity stake in the project. For larger and riskier projects a developer might have to do business with a merchant bank which would require the project as security and might levy a higher interest rate at possibly 4% to 6% above LIBOR and might want an equity share in the scheme.

Bridging finance can be provided as a complete funding package. The interim funding is replaced by a buyout. Interim funding is provided at a rate between the short-term borrowing rate and the investment yield. Bridging finance can also be used very short term, which is repayable in six months or less to cover the period between buying one property and selling another, or as an equity release pending refinance or sale. The market is dominated by clearing banks and the specialist lenders.

Syndicated loans

This is where a group of lenders combine on large loans which would be too expensive or too risky for one lender to take on. Thus the lenders diversify their loan books in respect of a number of loans on various assets to restrict the risk of being too heavily involved in any one. The loan is arranged and then syndicated by the lead banks. The syndicating bank may not contribute to the actual loan but may charge fees for underwriting the loan.

A typical 'syndicated loan' has the following characteristics:

- The bank with which the borrower has developed a relationship underwrites the loan and, in most cases, actually lends the monies.
- The loan agreement is drafted as an advance syndicated loan agreement, enabling the original lending bank to transfer to other banks tranches of the original loan.
- The asset teams of the original lending bank then sells off tranches of the loan in the banking market, the original lender acting as agent bank.

Mortgages

As far back as the 1960s, fixed-interest mortgages were used to finance the expansion of many of the large property companies. Interest rates were then low and repayments could be serviced from rents. Because of the difference between cost and value, projects could be 100% financed from a commercial mortgage. The following arrangement illustrates the principles:

New development:

Rent per annum:	£100,000
Yield @ 6.5%, YP therefore:	15.38
Gross development value:	£1,538,000
Maximum mortgage @ 60% of GDV:	£922,800
Cost of development	**£900,000**
Annual mortgage repayments @ 8½% over 25 years:	£88,000
Less annual rental income:	£100,000
Annual surplus income to developer:	£12,000

Note that in the above arrangement the developer (borrower) has 100% funding to cover costs and that there is an income surplus from day one and that the developer will receive *all* of the increase arising from rent reviews.

The position is very different now where developers indulge in deficit financing, where rents do not cover repayments until the first review. Mortgages are generally 10–25 years with an advance up to two-thirds valuation. The mortgage interest rate taken by the developer might be fixed or variable and there are interest-only, repayment and capital holiday options to choose from. Hoesli and MacGregor (2000: 241) suggest that the typical commercial mortgage is a balloon or interest-only loan with the capital repayable at the end of the term. Because of the added risk to the lender in this scenario the loan to value ratio might not exceed 60% and the lender will probably analyse the net income of the borrower to ensure that it is at least twice that necessary to service interest payments on the loan (discussed in chapter 6). Readers who are particularly interested in the mortgage approach to property funding could examine Brown and Matysiak (2000: 72–87) where the topic is discussed in more detail than is possible here.

7.5 Corporate finance

Two principal areas of corporate finance relate to debt capital (or loans) and equity capital (or shares). Equity finance is capital paid into or kept in the business by the shareholders, the owners of the business. It is long-term capital and carries the greatest risk and attracts the highest returns. Debt finance is money invested in the business by third parties usually for a shorter period of time than equity and carrying a lower risk and lower return.

Corporate finance is related to the financial structure of the company itself. Choosing the right mix of debt and equity capital that meets the investment requirement of a business is a key financial management decision. There are four strategic issues here:

1 *Risk*: There will always be some uncertainty in the business environment and the 2008–9 credit crunch and oil price increases which drove inflation at that time illustrate this fact of life. Firms always have to consider risk and how to act when there is a downturn in business activity and the economy.
2 *Ownership:* The ownership of the firm is critical, it is important to know who exercises control over the company. A desire to retain control will affect financing decisions and this may mean that borrowing is preferred to raising equity capital.
3 *Duration:* Finance should match the use to which it is put. Finance for investments with no returns in the early years, should be raised so there are no payments in these years. One should not raise long-term finance for a short-life programme, the firm will be overcapitalised and won't generate sufficient return to repay finance.
4 *Debt capacity:* The ability to borrow depends on the existing level of borrowing, the type of business and the sector of operation (Pike and Neale 2003).

The balance sheet model of the firm can be used to analyse the sources of cash available to the corporate structure. The basic sources of cash for the firm are discussed in the following paragraphs.

Shareholders' funds

The largest proportion of long-term finance is usually provided by shareholders and is termed equity capital. Share ownership lies at the heart of modern capitalism as by purchasing shares in a company, the shareholder has also purchased a degree of control over the company.

Ordinary share capital is the main source of new money from shareholders. They are entitled to participate in the business through voting in a general meeting of the shareholders and also to receive dividends out of the profits. As owners of the business, the ordinary shareholders bear the greatest risk but enjoy the main fruits of success in the form of higher dividends and capital gains.

Retained profits

For an established business, the main source of equity funds will be internally generated from successful trading. Any profits remaining after all operating costs, interest payments, taxation and dividends are reinvested in the business (i.e. ploughed back) and regarded as part of the equity capital.

Loan capital

Money lent to the businesses by third parties is debt finance or loan capital. Most companies borrow money on a long-term basis by issuing stocks or debentures. The supplier of the loan will specify the amount of loan, rate of interest, date of payment and method of repayment. The finance manager will monitor the long-term financial structure by examining the relationship between loan capital, where interest and loan repayment are contractually obligatory and ordinary share capital where dividend payment is at the discretion of the directors. This relationship between debt and equity is called gearing and is the proportion of debt capital to total capital in the firm.

The three sources of cash mentioned above are matched by three uses of cash in the firm:

1 Cash is used to service (pay returns to) the main sources of finance. Dividends are paid to shareholders and interest is paid to lenders along with repayment of the loan due. Tax is paid on the profits earned.
2 Cash is invested in long-term assets such as buildings and plant needed to produce goods or services. The investment decisions made in respect of these long-term assets are critical for the success of the company.
3 Cash is also used to pay for materials, labour, overheads and costs incurred in producing the goods or services offered to customers. It is also used to purchase stocks of raw materials, work in progress, finished goods and debtors. In a property-trading company these current assets would also include properties and developments in the process of completion held for trading. Current assets in a firm are offset by the current liabilities which are amounts owing to suppliers of goods and services (Pike and Neale 2003).

The main ways in which a property company could increase its capital include:

• the issue of debenture stock;
• the issue of loan stock;
• preference shares; and
• ordinary shares.

These instruments are described later in this chapter, but as a general introduction it is important first to look at issues relating to the difference between debt and equity. Equity investments in a company usually come in the form of share ownership and in this chapter, types of share including their issue arrangements are discussed in addition to a summary of debt approaches related to corporate finance. The use of different types of corporate finance can depend upon market conditions. Rights issues may be popular in times of economic uncertainty and when conventional forms of debt finance are in short supply. In the 2007–9 recession in the UK many large companies tried rights issues to raise capital but with varying degrees of success. In such circumstances a listed company will ask its shareholders for money by offering additional shares at a discount to the current listed price.

The problem with a rights issue in a poor market is that the share price may fall below the discounted price and put the buyer at a disadvantage. Much depends upon market perception of the reasons for the issue and this will influence the price of the shares immediately after the rights issue. A series of rights issues took place in the UK in early 2009 and the purpose of several of these was to reinforce balance sheets or reduce debt. For example, house builder Taylor Wimpey was able to raise £510 million to reduce its £1.57 billion debt burden at that time.

Equity finance

Equity finance in the form of direct investment and partnership will be discussed in chapter 8. The distinction between debt and equity is hazy when considered in the context of loans with conversion rights to shares and mezzanine finance, a halfway house between debt and equity. In this chapter when dealing with corporate finance, the distinction is:

Equity	Debt
ordinary shares	debentures
preference shares	loan stock
warrants	bonds
options	general facilities
convertible stock*	convertible stock *

* Stock can be converted from debt to equity.

Ordinary and preference shares

The equity of a company consists of ordinary shares, and shareholders participate in the profits of a company once prior demands have been met. These prior demands for payment will include creditors (trade creditors), holders of debt and preference shareholders. If a company finds that the total of accumulated and retained profits in the company's reserves have grown in relation to issued capital, then a script or capitalisation issue can be made.

Preference shares rank after debentures and loan stock but before ordinary shares in terms of a charge to the company. If profits are insufficient to pay the fixed-rate dividend then arrears can be carried forward if the preference share is a cumulative type. Conversion rights may be available to convert the shares to ordinary capital. This sort of share may be set up if the company is a new company and thus there may be a risk attached to the ordinary shares. If the company is a management buyout or start-up company then it may attract venture capital; that is, risk-taking capital used to finance new business opportunities. In this case the investor may wait some years for the company and its cash flow to stabilise before converting the fixed return preference share to an ordinary share. Preference shares are unsecured, so if no profits are made, no dividend will be paid. But if they are cumulative, they can carry forward the payment due as indicated above. The characteristics of preference shares are thus:

- more secure than ordinary shares;
- less secure than debentures or loan stock;
- return is from a fixed-rate dividend payable from profits;
- unsecured;
- can be cumulative or non-cumulative;
- can be voting or non-voting shares but rarely are voting; and
- can be convertible or not convertible into ordinary shares.

The priority of charge against the profits of the company are first to debentures and loan stock, then to preference shares and finally to ordinary shares.

Issues and options

Company shares together with other securities such as government bonds and stocks and the loan stock of public authorities are traded on the stock exchange. The stock exchange arose out of the need to deal in the shares of joint-stock companies which originated in the seventeenth century. By pooling of risk, combining resources and the development of limited liability, these companies expanded and created the requirement of transferability of capital. Owners of shares or loan capital in the companies required a market to sell their holdings, otherwise the original investment would not have been attractive. The stock market is thus a secondary market for investment in the sense of reselling shares and securities, but it is also a primary market as a source of new funds.

The primary market operates for new issues and where a company is seeking a listing on the stock exchange it will need to be represented by a broking firm. The broking firm will advise on the company's prospectus and the issue price. The Bank of England controls large issues to programme the timing of such issues. Underwriting is arranged so that if the stock is advertised but not fully taken up, the underwriters take up the under-subscription. This procedure is called a prospectus issue, but other methods exist such as an offer for sale, a placing and a rights issue.

For the investor, the advantages of property shares over direct investment relate primarily to issues of liquidity. It is possible to buy small volumes of shares and spread risk by buying into different property companies with different assets in different regional locations. Equity investments can also be traded easily in the stock market at low costs of transfer and where share prices are in the public domain. Thus buyers have ready access to information on prices and price movements. Other factors in the pricing of shares such as the fall and rise of the stock market also have a role to play as well as the overall economy.

'Shares in property companies trade at a discount to net asset value and perform like equities in the short term. They are relatively inefficient in tax terms, as investors are effectively taxed twice on the profits of the company' (www.reita.org (2007)). Thus there are advantages and disadvantages for the investor in buying shares in property companies. Developers looking to raise money will be aware of the attitudes adopted by the market. In 2007, the UK REIT was introduced and many companies converted to REIT status. The taxation advantages that are available for investors in REITS are clearly attractive to many investors since they avoid the double taxation on dividend income. This issue is discussed further in chapter 8.

Debt

As Isaac (2003: 118) confirms, debt can be applied to the corporate structure and can be seen simply in terms of the application of funds in a general funding situation where the criteria for the funding will be based on the status and assets of the borrower rather than for a specific project. The lender will look at the borrower's accounts and will want to see:

- good-quality property assets on modern leases;
- a realistic development programme;

- a good portfolio mix;
- not all the assets pledged; and
- a healthy proportion of equity.

A general funding facility may be negotiated where the agreed sum is secured on the developer's assets. This allows a developer to have access to predetermined amounts of money over a given period of time. These loans may be of ten to 15 years in duration with an option to exercise in a shorter period of say five years. This facility may be negotiated on the basis of an agreed interest rate. In a drop lock loan, the base interest rate is agreed and if the market rate of interest, which is assumed to be above at the commencement, falls to that level it is locked in as a fixed rate, otherwise it will vary with the market rate.

Overdrafts are also a common way for developers to finance short-term requirements such as the interim payments to builders in the construction phase of a development. Borrowing from a clearing bank is traditionally on a short-term basis with a variable interest rate tied to a margin over the LIBOR rate. Companies with a large amount of bank finance will be vulnerable to rising interest rates and short-term recall of the funds by the bank. Merchant banks and finance houses are normally willing to lend on specific terms for several years but such sources are more expensive.

7.6 Summary

The type of finance that a firm will raise depends upon the nature of the borrowing, whether long term or short term. The source may be clearing banks or for larger concerns the stock market. Funds are often secured on the project to be undertaken or may be secured on other assets. Large corporations may borrow by issuing bonds or by rights issues. There are different types of shares and bonds that can be used to raise finance. For example ordinary shares provide dividends once the obligations of the company to its creditors and preference shareholders, who have rights before ordinary shareholders. Thus if a company becomes insolvent, preference shareholders will have rights before ordinary shareholders if there is any cash remaining in the business once all debts have been settled.

In some cases transactions are agreed whereby a partner to a development project will lend money and obtain shares in or retain dividends in the completed scheme.

Developers with limited resources may seek to enter sale and leaseback arrangements where an investor will purchase the site and lease it back to the developer in return for a pre-agreed share of the profits. The latter will be based on the investor's required rate of return.

References

Brown, G. R. and Matysiak, G. A. (2000) *Real Estate Investment: A Capital Market Approach* (Harlow: FT Prentice Hall).

Buckle, M. and Thompson, J. (2004) *The UK Financial System* (Manchester: Manchester University Press).

Darlow, C. (1988) 'Direct project funding', in Darlow, C. (ed.), *Valuation and Development Appraisal*, 2nd edition (London: Estates Gazette).

Havard, T. (2008) *Contemporary Property Development*, 2nd edition (London: RIBA Publishing).

Hoesli, M. and MacGregor, B. D. (2000) *Property Investment: Principles and Practice of Portfolio Management* (Harlow: Longman).

Isaac, D. (2003) *Property Finance* (Basingstoke: Palgrave Macmillan).

Pike, R. and Neale, B. (2003) *Corporate Finance and Investment*, 4th edition (London: FT Prentice Hall).

Ross, S. A., Westerfield, R. W. and Jaffe, J. F. (2007) *Corporate Finance Essentials*, 5th edition (Boston and London: McGraw-Hill Irwin).

Ross, S. A., Westerfield, R. W. and Jordan, B. D. (2008) *Corporate Finance Fundamentals*, 8th edition (New York and London: McGraw-Hill Higher Education).

Sayce, S., Smith, J., Cooper, R. and Venmore-Rowland, P. (2006) *Real Estate Appraisal: From Value to Worth* (Oxford: Blackwell).

www.rieta.org (2007) Website providing information on Real Estate Investment Trusts and administered by the British Property Federation, London.

8

The structure of property finance

Aims

This chapter aims to explore in a little more depth than has been possible in earlier chapters some of the key organisations and structures which serve to provide funds for commercial property development. The chapter will therefore investigate the importance of institutional investors such as pension funds and insurance companies. The chapter also compares and contrasts the merits of ordinary shares in property companies with other investment media such as Real Estate Investment Trusts (REITs), unitisation and securitisation. The chapter also explores how joint ventures can be a way of supporting property development in certain situations.

Key terms

>> **Indirect investment** – relates to investments created out of pooled assets such as REITs, bonds and units trusts. These investment vehicles are designed to be more liquid than traditional methods of investing in property and they enable diversification, as a modest portfolio can be spread over different assets groups.

>> **Property companies** – may develop and retain completed properties which are then let and the income retained in-house, thus becoming an investment. Property companies may also be traders in that they find sites, complete the development, obtain tenants and then sell the completed development on the investment market.

>> **Joint ventures** – involve linking together funders, landowners and developers on the principle that the pooled resources can create synergy for a development to become viable where it otherwise would not. Joint ventures

can for example enable a landowner without development expertise to participate in the ultimate profits arising from a completed development.

8.1 Introduction

This chapter examines the involvement of institutional investors in property and how their exposure to property has varied in recent decades depending upon economic conditions and the returns available from other investment opportunities. While many institutions were active in funding and direct development to create investments in the 1980s, the increase in bank lending up until 2007 created opportunities for smaller developers and investors as well. The role of property companies is of course central to property development and listed property companies can raise money for projects through share issues. However there has been some resistance by investors to purchasing property company shares because of the taxation disadvantages, especially to tax exempt investors such as charities and pension funds.

The introduction of the UK REIT (Real Estate Investment Trust) in 2007 is an important factor in this context because it gave stock market-listed companies the opportunity to convert into a REIT. This conversion provides a more favourable tax position and should enable a REIT to attract a wider variety of investors. The impact of REITS is discussed below but of course the difficult market conditions that began towards the end of 2007 and extended into 2010 had the effect of suppressing the market, and a clearer perspective on the performance of REITS will only be possible when more stable market conditions return.

Joint ventures are also considered towards the end of the chapter as they are also an important way of combining resources and sharing risk in the context of funding property development, particularly in challenging circumstances such as recessions.

8.2 Trends in institutional investment

In the UK the principle financial institutions consist of the insurance companies and pension funds which together comprise one of the major channels for the nation's savings. As far back as the 1950s these financial institutions began to dominate the funding of commercial property development and this continued into the 1980s when passive lending to developers had largely been replaced by direct involvement by institutions.

One form that more direct involvement took was that an institution would fund a sale and leaseback. This involved the sale of a freehold site by a developer to an institution with the developer taking back a long lease in order to complete the development and then let it to occupying tenants on conventional business leases for anything up to 25 years. Early deals had no provision for rent reviews but by the late 1960s and early 1970s rent reviews every five years began to become the norm. In this way the financial institutions achieved interests in what were effectively inflation-proofed equity investments while at the same time (in most cases) avoiding the property management responsibilities which were taken on by the developer.

By the 1980s it had become common practice for a number of established developers to obtain short-term finance to complete a major development and then arrange a buy-out by an institutional investor. However Evans (1992) has explained that from 1985 until the early 1990s, the new money that supported commercial property development was increasingly provided by banks, property companies and overseas investors. Thus the dominance of the financial institutions in funding property development and investment began to be challenged by money from new sources such as the banks.

The increase in indirect investment in property companies by banks was reflected by the increase in outstanding bank loans to property companies from £5 billion in 1985 to just over £40 billion in 1991. However it fell back to £32.5 billion in 1994 (Central Statistical Office 1994). Over the 1986–92 period institutions purchases were generally exceeding their sales but their net property investment had been a declining share of their total investments.

By 1999 net institutional investment in property had risen to over £1.5 billion but fell back in 2001 at a time when international instability following 9/11 and the 'dot com boom–bust' had affected confidence. As Figure 8.1 below indicates, there have been fluctuations with a peak in 2006 when net investment reached over £2 billion before declining as the credit crunch triggered a recession from 2007 resulting in divestment in 2008.

Net commercial property investment over a ten-year period by the financial institutions has therefore exhibited erratic behaviour as funds have responded to wider economic circumstances by switching in and out of property in the relentless search for better returns. Some forecasters at the beginning of 2010 were predicting a 'wall of money' which the financial institutions would deploy by purchasing prime property in anticipation of an economic recovery. In that scenario Figure 8.1 could be expected to show an upturn beyond its cut-off point in 2009.

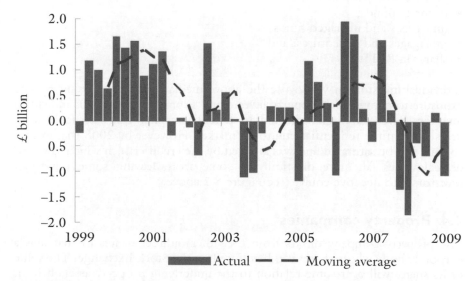

Figure 8.1 Institutional net property investment £billions, 1999–2009 (Fletcher King 2009)

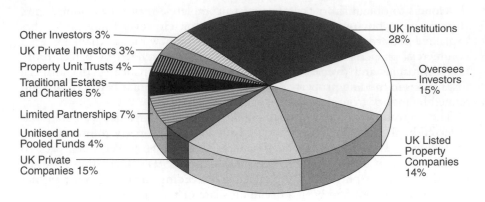

Other Investors 3%
UK Private Investors 3%
Property Unit Trusts 4%
Traditional Estates and Charities 5%
Limited Partnerships 7%
Unitised and Pooled Funds 4%
UK Private Companies 15%
UK Institutions 28%
Oversees Investors 15%
UK Listed Property Companies 14%

Figure 8.2 Investors in UK property (reita.org 2009: 3)

8.3 Direct versus indirect property investment

The major insurance companies and pension funds not only have substantial funds to invest but they also have extensive property departments which are capable of actually carrying out development as well as advising on the purchase and management of completed investment properties. However not all funds are of the same scale and capability, and because of the various risks that confront investors in the direct property market as well as the larger lot size, smaller funds face inevitable barriers to entry in this investment market. The smaller fund may therefore choose more liquid indirect investment media such as:

- property company shares;
- property bonds;
- unit trusts and managed funds;
- mortgages and debentures; and
- shares in REITs.

Individual investors may also use the above media as a way of gaining some exposure to commercial property investment. From the mid-1990s individual investors have also been attracted to potential capital gains available from investment in the residential buy-to-let market. However by 2008 that market appeared to be saturated and was affected by the credit crunch which saw residential values fall quite drastically in some areas, leaving some buy-to-let investors with negative equity (see Figure 8.2 above).

8.4 Property companies

The property company differs from the other indirect routes in that it is a corporate body whose shares can be quoted on the Stock Exchange. The value of its shares will bear some relation to the underlying property assets held in the portfolio of the company but the link is not a direct one. Property bonds and unit trusts work on a different principle. The value of the unit is directly determined by the value of the properties in the fund. Funds which operate on the unit principle may be 'open-ended' in the sense that the number of units can increase or decrease with the purchase or sale of assets, whereas the share capital of a company is fixed apart from new issues of shares or capital reductions requiring legal permission.

The property business could be defined as the extraction of value from land and buildings such that the landlord takes a creditor's view rather than an equity holder's view of the occupiers. In 1988 the total quoted property company sector-owned property valued at £17 billion with a market capitalisation of shares worth £13 billion. This could have been compared at the time with the market capitalisation of BP (£15 billion) and the commercial banking sector (£16 billion)). Seventy per cent of the shares at that time were owned by institutions (Millman 1988). The total book assets of the sector increased up to 1990 when it peaked at nearly £30 billion but subsequently decreased in 1992 to £25 billion (S G Warburg Securities 1993). By 2009 the total market capitalisation of all non-REIT-quoted property companies was £4.186 billion and companies with REIT status had a total market capitalisation of £22.191 billion (Reita 2009).

Table 8.1 Major quoted non-REIT UK property companies (adapted from reita.org (2009))

Company	Share price pence	Market capitalisation £m
Unite Group	272.25	434.5
Terrance Hill Group	22	46.6
Stewart Wright	570	8.9
J Smart and Co	472.5	47.6
Savills	293.3	386.7
St Modwen	212.3	425.4
Safeland	14	2.4
Quintain Estates	68.25	355.2
Panther Securities	333	56.2
Minerva	54	87
Balfour Group	44	31.8
Mapley	200	59.2
London and Associated Properties	43.5	35.6
Helical Bar	332	335.5
Grainger plc	253.4	351.2
Fletcher King	34	3.1
DTZ Holdings	73	188.3
Development Securities	298.5	245.5
Dajean Holdings	2698	439.6
Cardiff Property	638.8	10.1
CLS Holdings	450.25	216.2

Property companies from an investor's perspective

It is clear from Table 8.1 that listed property companies in the UK represent considerable repositories of valuable assets which may be an attractive option for investors both large and small. However as with any share dealings, prudent investors would at least undertake some basic research into company prospectuses to determine the underlying financial health of the companies in which they are investing. The main features of a property company which should be evaluated by the potential investor include the following:

- *The quality of assets in the portfolio*: the age, location and tenure of individual properties will be important as well as the investment's relative importance in the portfolio. The different types of property and the proportion of overseas investment in the portfolio should also be considered.
- *The perceived quality of company management:* this perception is very subjective and is often restricted to the market's view about individuals who occupy management positions in a particular company.
- *The sources of income of the company*: these will vary between well established property investment companies relying on rents for income and property trading companies whose income arises from disposing of completed developments.
- *The capital structure and gearing of the company*: a highly geared financial structure is more appropriate for established companies deriving a large proportion of revenue from rental income rather than for trading companies dependent on less secure trading profits. The nature of a company's debt is also important.

Property shares

Property companies hold all or most of their assets in property shares, which are thus a surrogate for the properties owned. There should in theory be a close correlation between share prices and property values, but the vagaries of the stock market can also affect the share price. Shares have traditionally been more favoured than direct property because of greater liquidity and the ability to diversify exposure to different companies and sectors simultaneously. The drawback of share ownership against direct property investment is the incidence of tax, this affects the returns compared to direct property investment as the shareholder is in effect double taxed. However, property company shares offer the investor four main features.

Management

Share ownership removes the direct problems of management, as the property company will possess staff with the requisite skills to manage investment properties.

Gearing

The gearing of the larger quoted companies has varied over time quite dramatically. For example in 1993 the property company Speyhawk (before its demise) had a negative equity of £105m, Stanhope had a gearing of 600% while Land

Securities had a gearing of 54% (S G Warburg Securities 1993). As well as the level of debt, the type of debt is important as to whether it is fixed or variable rate, short or long term. Gearing can increase the equity return but can lead to problems of insolvency if overall returns fall. Since the 2007–9 recession many of the major property companies have been reducing their gearing and LTV ratios. For example SEGRO (the Slough Estates Group) reduced its gearing ratio from 119.1% in December 2008 to 98% in August 2009 (SEGRO 2009).

Liquidity

The market in shares has a central price and there is speed of entry and exit in and out of the market. As Scarrett (2008: 25) points out, this is far more convenient than the actual buying and selling of investment properties which is an uncertain process involving delay, periods of due diligence to check property titles and the credentials of purchasers and costs such as stamp duty and solicitors' fees.

Other participants

Liquidity exists because there are other participants in the share market, institutional investors hold a high percentage of share. Usually the shares are held as part of an equity rather than a property portfolio and thus are managed in the more market-led style of equity shares rather than the more asset-led style of direct property (Mallinson 1988).

Discount on net asset value

As Isaac (2003: 175–6) points out, property investment companies as opposed to property trading companies are valued on the basis of their net assets rather than the income produced. A feature of property shares is that they are traded at a discount to the net assets held. This may not be in cases of a very bullish market and over longer periods for exceptional performers, but generally this discount appears to be around 20%. The average discounts on net asset value for property investment companies between 1990 and 2009, are shown below in Figure 8.3.

The discount depicted above is measured as:

$$\frac{\text{Net asset value per share (NAV/share)} - \text{Share price} \times 100\%}{\text{NAV/share}}$$

This means that the underlying assets were undervalued because of this discount and three reasons are commonly given for the phenomenon:

1 Concerns regarding the possible losses if a forced sale of a company's assets is required.
2 The capital gains tax liability on disposal of the properties in a company's portfolio and the tax inefficiencies of holding shares as opposed to direct investment.
3 Recognition that the valuations carried out by surveyors on large commercial investment properties are as much an art as a science, given that

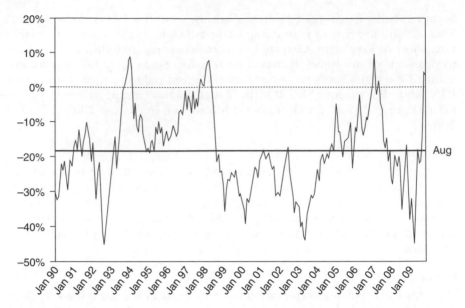

Figure 8.3 Average discount on net asset value, 1990–2009 (www.reita.org)

assumptions and judgements have to be made by individual valuers against the rise and fall of the market. There may therefore be a tolerance of perhaps +/–10% on the capital values indentified.

The presence of this discount has an effect on financing and activity in the sector. Assets are undervalued because of the discount and this discourages the growth of property companies through equity expansion and forces them into borrowing to expand. This leads to companies being highly geared and in turn this discourages takeovers within the sector.

Corporate capital structure

The question of an optimal capital structure is an issue for property companies because, as the discussion above confirms, they typically have high levels of debt. The problem is the choice of the best mix of debt (loans, debentures) and equity (ordinary shares, reserves and retained profits). The following factors ought to be considered, but assessing the weight to be given to each one is a matter of judgement and constant review for property company boards.

Cost

The current and future costs of each potential source of capital should be estimated and compared, but the costs of each source are not independent of one another. It is generally desirable to minimise the average overall cost of capital to the company.

Risk

It is unwise to place a company in a position where it may be unable, if profits fall, to pay interest when required or to meet redemptions. It is equally undesirable to be forced to cut or omit the ordinary dividend to shareholders.

Control

Except where there is no alternative, a company should not make any issue of shares which would have the effect of removing or diluting control by the existing shareholders.

Acceptability

A company can only borrow if investors are willing to lend to it. Few listed companies can afford the luxury of a capital structure which is unacceptable to the main institutional investors. A company with readily mortgageable assets will find it easier to raise debt.

Transferability

Shares may be listed or unlisted. Many private companies have made issues to the public so as to obtain a listing on the Stock Exchange and improve the transferability of their shares.

8.5 Securitisation and unitisation

Securitisation is the creation of tradable securities from a property asset while *unitisation* is also the creation of a tradable security but the aim in this case is to produce a return comparable to direct ownership.

This distinction may sound confusing, but an analysis of the difference between debt and equity should clarify this. To begin with one must consider a single property rather than a portfolio. For a single property, if we divide the interest into a number of holdings, then we divide the equity and this is unitisation. If we divide the interest and add debt securities, in the way a company may have shares and loan stock, this is securitisation. In fact securitisation is rather like imposing a corporate finance structure on a property so that it becomes a single-asset property company. However this approach simplifies matters because it is important to understand the objectives of securitisation and unitisation which will differ from the objectives of operation of a property company.

From the above, securitisation thus includes unitisation and can be used as a general term in this chapter except when discussing securitisation historically or when the securitisation of the equity alone is considered. The distinction between securitisation and unitisation is shown in Figure 8.4

The distinction of a single property is important to this analysis, if a portfolio of properties is considered, then unitisation is basically akin to property units as in a property unit trust, while securitisation of a portfolio would be a property company's shares and loan stock/debentures. A matrix of options is shown in Figure 8.5 below.

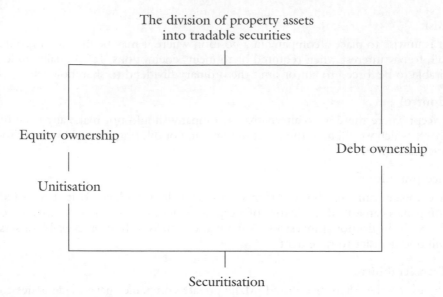

Figure 8.4 Securitisation and unitisation

Securitisation		
	Equity	Debt
One property asset	Unitisation Securitisation	 Securitisation
Portfolio of assets	Unit trusts Shares in a property company	Mortgage-backed securities Loan stock/debentures in a property company

Figure 8.5 Securitisation matrix

History of the development of securitisation

The drive towards securitisation and unitisation arose because of problems with the ownership of large property investments, which gave rise to a lack of liquidity in the market. There are difficulties in transferability of these ownerships as extended negotiations may be necessary to achieve deals. Problems with illiquidity are also encountered because of the significant size and value of some of the individual investments which become available. Many contemporary commercial developments have market values which are many hundreds of millions of pounds sterling and this raises implications regarding the levels of risk to the vast sums of capital tied up in a single asset.

Regarding the risk and difficulties of disposal of property mega-projects, Monaghan (2009) reports that Lend Lease, an Australian property developer and investor, had to write down the value of its 30% share in the Bluewater shopping centre on the eastern edge of London. The value of Lend Lease's share of the shopping centre fell by £76.8 million over the 12-month period up to June 2008 leaving the 30% share valued at £570.6 million. Lend Lease had considered disposing of its holding in Bluewater several years earlier in a more buoyant market but could find no buyers willing to meet their valuation of the asset at that time.

There are therefore challenges associated with the disposal of major developments as potential purchasers are effectively restricted to an elite group of international property investors who operate on a global stage. For example the Swiss Reinsurance Company (known as Swiss Re) which had funded and developed the Norman Foster-designed office development popularly known as the Gherkin (shown on the cover of this book) in the City of London disposed of the building in early 2007.

As Inman (2007) explains, the sale of the Gherkin was to joint purchasers: German property company IVG Immobilien and UK private investment group Evans Randall. The sale, which took place prior to the onset of the recession, netted £630 million for Swiss Re at a reported yield of 4.5% and thus the annual rental income stream must have been in the order of £28.35 million at that time. If Swiss Re had postponed their sale by a year, it is doubtful whether it would have achieved £630 million. The timing of the disposal of these large assets relative to the economic cycle is crucial to determining the value of the sale.

On the theme of liquidity and timing, Montia (2009) reports on HSBC bank's decision to undertake a sale and leaseback on its London headquarters building in Canary Wharf in 2007 when it sold the office tower to Spanish investors Metrovacesa for £1.08 billion. At the time the sale represented the single biggest property deal in the UK. HSBC leased back the building on a 20-year lease at an annual rent of £46 million. With the onset of the recession, HSBC were able to buy back the building one year later for £838 million but sold it again in 2009 on a sale and leaseback arrangement for £772.5 million to a Korean pension fund.

Certain property developments may simply be too large to fit neatly within the portfolio of an existing institution or the capital tied up in a major building may represent a significant opportunity cost for an organisation, preventing it from redeploying the capital in other business ventures. Some institutions are therefore wary of committing a large proportion of their available funds to a single property investment and indeed this may be contrary to corporate policy in many cases. Over-commitment to one property may also increase risk within a portfolio by upsetting the balance between investments.

Objectives of securitisation

One of the alleged benefits of securitisation is that it can overcome some of the problems highlighted above by providing additional liquidity in the commercial property investment market and this can sustain the level of values, increase the size of the market and speed up transactions. It is also thought that securitisation assists in the diversification of risk as it provides opportunities for investors to mix their portfolios by investing in different developments, thus matching more precisely to the investor's risk–reward profile. Securitisation offers the ability to invest in debt and equity securities which, in themselves, have different risk profiles.

Securitisation is yet another method of freeing an investor from the responsibilities of managing a property and which would occur with direct ownership. The management function can thus be left to those who are more skilled and experienced in these matters. Securitisation also avoids the double taxation which exists with property company shares and it provides a more flexible financial structure to encourage the sale of debt instruments and thus develop gearing situations. Securitisation is also thought to allow more flexibility for the sale of interests or part interests in properties and thus providing better opportunities for refinancing short-term development finance with long-term investment funds.

Given that there are undoubted benefits associated with securitisation, it is not surprising that a number of leading UK companies with interests in land are beginning to use it as a way of creating liquidity, while retaining long-term and operation interests in property. Chesters (2009) for example, reports on Tesco's completion of a £559.1 million securitisation through its own property finance vehicle. The securitisation was achieved with the sale of 30-year bonds secured on the income from 17 properties comprising supermarkets and a distribution warehouse. This was the second securitisation of specific property assets by Tesco following an earlier sale of bonds which secured £458 million for the company.

However despite the theoretical arguments in favour of securitisation and unitisation the concept remains something of a delicate specialist area within property investment markets and Havard (2008: 140) confirms that experimentation with unitisation vehicles has not always met with success.

To summarise, securitisation is the conversion of an asset into tradable securities which are certificates of ownership and rights to income. In a commercial property context, securitisation is the conversion of properties into tradable securities which may be debt or equity based. Unitisation is included in securitisation but specifically refers to the securitisation of the equity interest. In its simplest form unitisation will provide a share of the rental and capital growth with no management obligations. This approach contrasts to property share ownership in the sense that with unitisation, the investor selects specific property assets in which ownership is held rather than having to accept an existing managed portfolio.

8.6 Real Estate Investment Trusts (REITs)

The problems associated with large lot size, lack of liquidity and the costs of acquisition and disposal for major properties as described above, was acknowledged in a report by the UK government in 2004 which explored the potential of Real Estate Investment Trusts (REITs) as a way of widening participation in the real estate investment market.

Other problems with large investments may relate to situations where a developer or investor wishes to organise a partial disposal, for instance, or where developers may wish to retain the investment but recoup some of the project cost. There is also a lack of opportunity to spread the risk of investment portfolios because the incorporation of larger buildings in the portfolio, which may be attractive assets because of location and prestige, will mean that they dominate the portfolio in terms of value. There are also problems associated with the valuation of large properties by traditional methods of valuation where comparable evidence is often lacking. Valuers may also apply a bulk discount relating to size or a discount reflecting the lack of ease of transferability which becomes an issue in the event of a forced sale.

Indirect investment in property shares and unit trusts has been available to investors for many years and to some extent address some of the problems of illiquidity discussed above. Unauthorised unit trusts are available to substantial tax-exempt investors such as charities and pension funds, but are specialist and not available to the private investor.

Property bonds also suffer from illiquidity problems and some funds contain provisions which may delay repayment of investments. This became an issue in the 2007–9 recession when investors sought to move out of some funds that were performing badly. There were cases where certain funds placed a temporary moratorium on withdrawals. This happened where there were insufficient reserves held to cover all requests for withdrawals or where assets would need to be sold quickly at discount to meet the demand of the investors for their cash.

A major issue with property shares is that there is no purity of investment in the sense that the portfolio of properties can be large, varied and changing and it is therefore difficult for the investor to identify the asset ownership and relate it to share value. Finally, net asset values of property investment companies are discounted on the stock market relative to share price as discussed earlier, while property trading companies are valued on the assessment of future profitability which may not be related to existing asset values.

In addition, company share ownership suffers from major tax difficulties. There is the problem of double taxation of income (the shares are not tax transparent). The company shares are subject to corporation tax on their earnings and then the investor pays tax on the income received and any capital gains.

The UK REIT was launched in January 2007 as an attempt to counter some of the above problems after much negotiation with the Treasury concerning the issue of double taxation. Many property companies converted into REITs although others retained their existing status if it suited their business model. The new rules for REITs abolished double taxation, and so the income is now taxed at the investor level only. This was of course subject to specific rules concerning the operation of a REIT and which include the following:

- A UK REIT must distribute at least 90% of its profits to shareholders.
- Investors will pay tax at their normal rate which is either 25% or 40%.
- A REIT must be a fully listed company, resident in the UK for tax purposes.
- The primary business of a REIT must be property investment rather than property development.

A REIT can include rights to interest on debt as well as income from a property business. There are different types of UK REITs covering storage and secondary commercial property as well as those that offer a spread of prime investments. While there are established REIT markets in the USA, Hong Kong and a variety of other countries, progress in the UK has been stymied by the 2007–9 recession which has affected capital growth and reduced dividends. There remain challenges ahead for the UK version of the REIT and authors such as Baum (2008) discuss the potential impact of depreciation on the distribution of income from UK REITs, which may reduce the potential for high returns.

8.7 Joint ventures

Joint ventures or partnerships which enable equity sharing of the rental income from property developments have been discussed in chapter 4 where slicing arrangements and ground rents were considered. It is apparent from that discussion that joint ventures for property development can be very complex and relate to the balance of risk and return sought by the parties involved. The focus on joint ventures in chapter 4 was primarily on the different ways that the value arising from a development project might be distributed between the parties at the completion of a scheme and subsequently at rent reviews. Here the focus on joint ventures extends beyond that discussion by considering the structure of the joint ventures, funding and how these partnerships share risks and responsibilities.

There are a number of different types of joint venture arrangements but basically as confirmed in chapter 4 they involve the joining together of two or more parties to undertake a project. The parties may include financial institutions, developers, banks, contractors, overseas investors, local authorities and public sector bodies such as regenerations agencies.

As Havard points out (2008: 142–8) the reasons for forming a joint venture are varied but particular issues which stand out in major commercial development projects are funding, access to land, development expertise and risk sharing. With regards to funding, a property development company may not have sufficient finance to enable it to complete a development because the costs involved exceed the company's resources or prudent borrowing limits. In these cases financial advisers may market the scheme to attract an investor.

Developers may also form joint ventures with a landowner to carry out a development where the landowner does not have the expertise to develop but wishes to remain involved in a project. Joint ventures could thus be viewed as a pragmatic response to particular circumstances encountered by the entrepreneurial developer, but as Wilkinson and Reed (2008: 146) point out:

> Developers are typically reluctant to share profits with third parties, unless it is the only way of securing a particular site or finance for a development scheme. Partnerships with landowners may be required if the landowner wishes to participate in the profits of the development scheme or wishes to retain a longer term legal interest in the property, preferring income to a one-off capital receipt.

The pooling of resources so that no single party is overexposed to project debt is also another motive for forming joint ventures. This is particularly important during recessionary periods when risks for especially speculative projects increase and the availability of development loans might be limited.

An example of a complex joint venture arrangement is that put in place for the Shard of Glass development at London Bridge on London's South Bank. The Shard of Glass is an 80-storey mixed-use tower designed by Renzo Piano, containing offices, retail and residential space and a hotel. The Shard will contain over 130,000 m² of floorspace and a secondary tower which will be phase 2 of what will become London Bridge Quarter, will add a further 56,000 m² of floorspace.

Although some of the space in the Shard has been pre-let, a venture of this magnitude with construction costs estimated at £400 million remains very risky. This is especially the case as the project's ground works began in 2009 during what was a recessionary period in the UK. A scheme of this scale is beyond the resources of most developers and this is one reason why the developer LBQ Ltd is as Russell (2009) explains, an equal partnership of three Qatari banks, a Qatari real estate company and the Sellar Property Group (the lead developer). Thus the risk in the project is effectively split five ways but so are the rewards which are expected to flow from a scheme whose ultimate capital value is expected to reach £2 billion.

Resource pooling, risk sharing and equity participation therefore lie at the heart of joint ventures such as the one described above. Isaac (2003: 190) confirms that some of the key reasons why joint ventures have become an option for commercial property development could be summarised as:

- A practical way of reducing development risks.
- A solution to periodic scarcities of equity in the finance market which creates problems for property companies who are unable to raise new funds on their own accord.
- A response to pressure to reduce debt in the property sector by the Bank of England and lenders.
- As a way of responding to the demands of overseas investors who may require joint ventures in their property development projects.

Structuring a joint venture agreement

The main types of joint venture structure are the partnership and the joint venture company (JVC). The choice between the two will rest on a number of criteria including the tax status of the parties, the desire to limit liability, the need for control mechanisms and the number of participants. The timescale for the development, its method of funding and whether it will be sold or retained on completion will also have a bearing upon the form of joint venture adopted by the parties.

In a property context, joint ventures tend to be formed for trading purposes enabling a development to be completed, let and then sold as an investment to a third party. At the point of disposal the parties will realise a share of the capital profit (depending on the specific terms and conditions of the joint venture agreement).

Table 8.2 Joint ventures: a summary

Forms of joint venture	Purpose of joint venture	Joint venture agreement	Clients for joint ventures
Limited liability companies. Partnership. Partnership for profit sharing.	One-off, or for a number of projects. To realise tax advantages. To attract project funding. To incorporate development expertise. To share debt and therefore risk. To buy into an existing development programme. To incorporate a landowner.	Should contain details of: funding; development period; management and control; profit distribution; dissolution; and dispute resolution mechanisms.	Landowners without development expertise or finance. Developers without finance or land. Owner-occupiers with land but limited capital and development experience. Banks and other funding institutions seeking equity involvement in developments.

The participants in a joint venture need to ensure that there is proper documentation setting out the rights and responsibilities arising for each party. The nature of the agreement needs to look at the overall control of the project, the day-to-day operation and the final exit or separation of the parties. The detailed agreement governing the activities of a joint company will be embodied in its articles of association. In the joint venture arrangement it is important to distinguish between the overall control and day-to-day management. The important point is to avoid destructive disputes and it is not surprising therefore that specialist law firms are often engaged to structure clauses in joint venture agreements in order to remove uncertainty and ambiguity.

If things go wrong, then the dissolution of a joint venture may be the only option. This could be done by one party buying out the other parties at an agreed valuation. The formula for the valuation could be previously agreed. However it could be that triggering the dissolution of a joint venture might come at a difficult time for one or other of the joint venture partners especially in respect of the valuation of any work in progress. One solution to such a deadlock as Dubben and Williams (2009: 222) describe is the 'Texas option' which would see one of the parties offering to purchase the other's interest within a given timescale and at a figure quoted by the offeror. The offeree then has the option of either accepting the offer or buying the offeror's interest at the same price. If interests are not equal, then this will need to be done on a pro-rata basis.

8.8 Summary

The role of finance in property development changes depending upon macro-economic conditions and degree of financial regulation, especially from the mid-1980s onwards. Banks have regularly increased their exposure to property development in strong markets and retreated when the economy goes into recession. This was evident in the early 1990s as well as between 2007 and 2009 when the credit crunch disrupted the financial system.

The introduction of the UK REIT market has enabled a variety of investors to enter the market primarily because unit costs are now lower and it is possible to diversify risk more easily by investing in companies that have converted to REIT status. However the full potential of UK REITs as a solution to some of the barriers to property investment particularly for small investors have not so far been fully realised due to challenging economic circumstances under which no property investment vehicles have functioned particularly well.

References

Baum, A. (2008) 'Depreciation, income distribution and the UK REIT', *Journal of Property Investment and Finance*, 26(3).

Central Statistical Office (1994) *Financial Statistics*, CSO, London.

Chesters, L. (2009) 'Tesco to complete £559m property securitisation', *Property Week*, 15 September.

Dubben, N. and Williams, B. (2009) *Partnerships in Property Development* (London: Wiley-Blackwell).

Evans, P. H. (1992) 'Statistical review', *Journal of Property Finance*, 3(1): 115–20.

Farrow, P. (2007) *Guide to Commercial Property Investments and REITs* (London: Sunday Telegraph and Reita).

Fletcher King (2009) *Investment Bulletin* (London: Fletcher King). Available in e-format at: www.fletcherking.co.uk

Havard, T. (2008) *Contemporary Property Development*, 2nd edition (London: RIBA Publishing).

Inman, P. (2007) 'Gherkin's £600m sale sets London property record', *Guardian*, 6 February.

Isaac, D. (2003) *Property Finance* (Basingstoke: Palgrave Macmillan).

Isaac, D. and Woodroffe, N. (1995) *Property Companies: Share Price and Net Asset Value* (London: Greenwich University Press).

Mallinson, M. (1988) 'Equity finance', in Barter, S. L. (ed.), *Real Estate Finance* (London: Butterworths).

Millman, S. (1988) 'Property, property companies and public securities', in Barter, S. L. (ed.), *Real Estate Finance* (London: Butterworths).

Monaghan, A. (2008) 'Bluewater plunges in value as credit crisis bites', *Telegraph*, 4 August.

Montia, G. (2009) 'HSBC sells Canary Wharf headquarters', *Banking Times*, 15 November.

Reita (2009) 'Understanding commercial property investment', available in e-format at: ww.reita.org

Russell, J. (2009) 'Work to start on £2bn Shard of Glass', *Telegraph*, 24 February.

Scarrett, D. (2008) *Property Valuation: the Five Methods*, 2nd edition (Abingdon: Routledge).

Segro plc (2009) *Half yearly results to August 2009.* Available in e-format at: www.segro.com

SG Warburg Research (1993) *UK Property: Monthly (November) Review* (London: S G Warburg).

Wilkinson, S. and Reed, R. (2008) *Property Development*, 5th edition (Abingdon: Routledge).

9

Design and construction

Aims

This chapter explores the related topics of building design and construction and begins by examining the various facets of design which arise in the context of development. Design embraces the aesthetic appearance of buildings in the townscape, the efficient use of a site and the cost-effectiveness and sustainability of a building. The second part of the chapter discusses construction and the main procurement routes and types of contract that a developer might use. The extent to which sustainability, partnering and modern methods of construction feature in the construction process are also explored.

Key terms

>> **Procurement route** – the decision by a developer on the best way to get a building built when using the services of a building contractor. The three main procurement routes are: traditional, management oriented, and design and build.

>> **Partnering** – an agreement between the developer, main contractor and members of the supply chain to work together in a trusting and cooperative manner, to avoid disputes and to aim to deliver excellent buildings on time and within budget for the client. Partnering would normally extend beyond one project and is more a philosophy than a procurement method.

>> **Design and build** – a method for procuring a building where the client's requirements are put out to tender for contractors to bid to complete the design and build the development for a fixed price. The method integrates design with construction and is most appropriate where time and cost are important and where standard types of building are required.

>> **JCT standard form** – the Joint Contracts Tribunal suite of standard forms of contract from which clients requiring the services of a building contractor may choose the appropriate contract for the project having decided upon their preferred procurement method.

9.1 Introduction

This chapter explores two related topics which are critical to the success of a development project: (a) the design of the building; and (b) the realisation of the building through the construction process. These are both vast topics and so the emphasis in this chapter for practical purposes is upon the key issues which relate to the main purpose of this book, which is the appraisal and finance of development.

9.2 Design and development

There have in recent years been raised expectations on developers to procure good quality, sustainable buildings which respect their townscape setting. In the UK local authorities have a policy obligation placed on them by central government to reject at the planning stage schemes which do not meet these expectations. The result is that developers have to think much harder about design issues by engaging with their professional teams and other stakeholders in order to work up schemes which will attract planning consent. The stakes have effectively been raised as illustrated by the following extract from a refusal of consent issued in 2009 by the London Borough of Greenwich to a developer proposing to redevelop part of Greenwich Market to provide a hotel, shops, offices and studio space:

> The proposed development by reason of its overall height, scale, bulk, massing and siting would result in the overdevelopment of the site and would adversely affect the existing patterns of development in the West Greenwich Conservation Area and Maritime Greenwich World Heritage site in which it is located. The proposed development is considered to lead to 'town cramming' and would have an adverse impact on the character of the area and fails to safeguard the interests of adjoining properties.

The above is an extract from one of seven reasons for refusal cited by the local authority against the scheme. While the proposal was in a particularly sensitive location and therefore faced a particularly tough test, the general principle is that local authorities are likely to reject a developer's scheme if it does not meet design expectations. A developer does have a right of appeal within six months of such a rejection, but the cost, delay and effort of going to appeal where an inspector might agree with the local authority's decision makes this an option of last resort. A developer's professional team would normally try to work up a scheme that was 'right first time' or, if there were a refusal, to revise the scheme so that it could be resubmitted for approval.

The following discusses some of the design hurdles that a developer's professional team now faces when trying to navigate a scheme to planning consent. This partly explains why more time is now consumed in the pre-construction stage of the development process.

Design policy

In the UK, the quality of 'townscape' has become an important issue because many towns and cities are felt to lack the quality that can be found in continental European cities such as Barcelona, Paris, Lisbon, Frankfurt and Prague which are seen as exemplars of sophisticated 'place-making'. In the UK the devolved governments in England, Scotland and Wales have been engaged in a campaign aimed at developers, their architects and local authorities to encourage them to be more 'quality conscious' when producing buildings and urban spaces. This is the reason why the government in England established the Commission for Architecture and the Built Environment (CABE) in 1999 to champion the cause of urban design. The respective design champion in Scotland is Architecture and Design Scotland and in Wales it is the Design Commission for Wales.

Ministers in the UK have been keen to associate themselves with promoting good design and this has fed through into government policy. In England government level design policy is contained in Planning Policy Statement 1: Delivering Sustainable Development which states that:

> High quality and inclusive design should be the aim of all those involved in the development process...It means ensuring a place will function well and add to the overall character and quality of the area, not just in the short term but over the lifetime of the development. (Office of the Deputy Prime Minister 2005: para. 35)

There are similar policies in devolved administrations in the UK with the effect that the design and appearance of buildings are considered to be matters of proper public interest. Local planning authorities in the UK therefore have a responsibility to ensure that the schemes which are approved are well designed and that poor designs are rejected. This policy framework provides local authorities with leverage over developers and their architects, and while some would say that this is excessive others would suggest that it provides architects with the headroom to produce better work.

Judgements relating to the design of a building involve a degree of subjectivity as the extract from the refusal letter above from the London Borough of Greenwich indicates by its use of phrases such as 'overdevelopment', 'town cramming' and 'adverse impact on the character of the area'. In that case the planning officer supported the developer's proposals and it was the councillors on the planning committee (who have the ultimate power in these matters) refused the scheme primarily on design grounds. The developer felt that the design had taken sufficient account of the context and was supported by the majority of third party consultees.

Occasionally the building design debate becomes very high-profile particularly when Prince Charles becomes involved. In 2009 the Prince courted controversy by publicly criticising bold redevelopment proposals for the Chelsea barracks site in London. The result was that the developer abandoned the plans and replaced the architect with a practice which had a reputation for more classical designs. These cases illustrate some of the difficulties that developers and their professional teams face in producing a design which satisfies all stakeholders and is still financially viable. Recognising the dilemma, the government in England feels that the way forward is as follows:

> The overall objective of good design is to ensure that buildings, infrastructure, public spaces and places are buildable, fit for purpose, resource efficient, sustainable, resilient, adaptable and attractive. Good design is synonymous with sustainable construction. Our aim is to achieve greater use of design quality assessment tools relevant to buildings, infrastructure, public space and places. (HM Government 2008: 7)

Design tools

The quote above makes reference to 'design quality assessment tools' and these are essentially guidelines and criteria which local authorities put in place so that developers and their professional teams are given some indication on the types of buildings which would meet with approval.

As far back as the 1970s local authorities such as Essex County Council recognised that the design of places and buildings is crucial in sustaining local identity and character. That authority's reaction against what it saw as an invasion of 'anywhere housing' led to the production of the *Essex Design Guide* in 1973. That document which is now in its 3rd edition (Essex Planning Officers' Association 2005) led other authorities to produce similar guidelines and to raise awareness and expectations around the quality of development.

A site specific variant of the design guide is the *design code* one of the first of which to be used in the UK was produced by urban designer Leon Krier acting for Prince Charles in the late 1980s. The latter was bringing forward development on part of his Duchy of Cornwall Estate at Poundbury in Dorset and wanted to set an example for the development industry by producing a high quality scheme. Krier's design code established the scale of development, street dimensions, styles of façades, facing materials, density, building heights and the layout of public spaces at Poundbury. The resulting development achieved instant 'buy-in' on the part of house purchasers and businesses who took space in the development, suggesting that design codes could add value in a UK context.

Further successful experimentation with design codes was undertaken by Northampton Borough Council and English Partnerships (2005) in the development of Upton in Northamptonshire and this led the government in England to adopt the principle (Communities and Local Government 2006a). If a developer's professional team produces a design code, the scheme should have a better chance of overcoming third party objections and winning the support of the local authority. Design codes can be linked to a Local Development Order which grants express planning consent for development which accords with the code. There should therefore be significant time savings for developers who use design codes. However this particular tool is most applicable to large-scale town extensions containing predominantly housing.

For smaller brownfield sites where housing or commercial development is anticipated, it is more likely that a local authority will have prepared a *development brief*, which sets out some basic design parameters within which a developer's team is expected to work up a scheme. A development brief might therefore set limits on the height of a development, specify the uses applicable for a site, establish floorspace limits and identify particularly sensitive parts of the site which warrant special attention. For example one side of a site might overlook existing residential development and the local authority will therefore expect an architect's detailed design to preserve the privacy of residents by preventing overlooking. The scale of development on that part of the site might be reduced or set back so that daylight is not obscured by the proposed development. Given the ambitions to foster sustainable development, a development brief for an urban site which is close to public transport may limit onsite parking spaces, in effect car-capping a development.

In England since 2008 design and access statements must accompany planning applications and this means that a developer must commit to some design principles even at the outline planning stage. While a developer can make matters such as layout, scale, landscaping, appearance and access 'reserved matters' to be determined at the detailed planning stage, a design and access statement must still provide information about the design envisaged. As mentioned earlier, the Commission for Architecture and the Built Environment (CABE) is the government agency in England whose remit is to champion good design and it has provided guidance on how developers might respond to this new regulatory requirement. As CABE (2006) confirms the information in the design and access statement will frame the discussions at the detailed planning stage.

CABE and Building for Life

CABE carries out its duties as a design champion in a number of ways including:

- Conducting design reviews for all important developments while they are still at the drawing-board stage.
- Providing practical design advice to local authorities and those procuring buildings.
- Publishing good-practice guides for developers, communities and practitioners.

A design review by CABE involves a panel of experienced architects, urban designers and planners who consider major projects which developers are promoting in a city or region. The panel's advice is passed back to the developer and the local authority, and this might necessitate changes to a scheme before it received planning consent.

Where a developer remains unresponsive to a design review panel's advice and tries to push a scheme through planning, it is likely that the local authority would refuse the scheme. For example, in 2006 a George Wimpey proposal for 570 dwellings in Thurrock was refused by the borough council following design advice from CABE. The ensuing appeal by the developer was dismissed by the Secretary of State who noted CABE's advice regarding the prominence of the site in the Thames Gateway. The rationale for the decision was that if this uninspiring scheme were permitted, it would confirm low expectations for subsequent development in the Thames Gateway when what was required was high design quality (reported in *Planning*, 6.10.06).

Design review panels are not predisposed to find fault with development proposals and they may lend their support to well-designed projects helping them to make progress through the planning process. An example was Ralph Erskine's *Greenwich Millennium Village*, a high-density urban housing development on a brownfield site which attracted CABE's support (readers may wish to view the images and design principles employed on that scheme at: www.urbandesigncompendium.co.uk/greenwichmillenniumvillage2).

CABE has occasionally used the media to lambast the standards of design in new development. One such occasion followed a survey of housing quality in England undertaken jointly with the Home Builders Federation (HBF). The survey (CABE 2007) found that when assessed against design criteria 18% of new housing was either 'good' or 'very good', 53% was 'average' and 29% was 'poor' and should not have been given planning consent.

In order to encourage local authorities to reject poor designs but reward well-designed schemes, CABE (2008) has produced a simple design appraisal tool for housing development entitled: Building for Life: Twenty Questions. If a scheme generates a positive response from 14 of the 20 questions (reproduced below in Figure 9.1) it is eligible for a silver standard award and 16 positive responses or above would generate a gold award. If a development proposal achieves these types of scores, it should have no difficulty obtaining planning consent on design grounds.

The quality of design and development value

CABE are keen not to be seen as negative and bureaucratic and part of their research effort is focused upon trying to establish a link between good design and increased development value. One of CABE's web site statements tries to articulate this:

> The way we plan and design a place has a significant impact on…social and economic fortunes. This is true in the regeneration of existing neighbourhoods and the development of new communities. Good urban design can help increase property values, reduce crime, contribute to public health and ease transport problems. (CABE 2008)

Research by CABE (2001) has assessed whether the additional cost of 'better design' can be recovered through increased capital and rental values in commercial developments. The methodology involved an appraisal of pairs of commercial developments in Birmingham, Manchester and Nottingham. Stakeholders (architects, developers, owners, occupiers and local authorities) were asked to rank each development against seven urban design criteria which were: character; continuity and enclosure; quality of the public realm; ease of movement; legibility; adaptability and diversity. Each of the criteria attracted up to five points and so an outstanding scheme would score 35 out of 35. The subjective ranking of stakeholders against the criteria was then compared with each development's market performance in terms of yields (capital values) rental values and vacancy rates/occupier demand.

Although the sample size in the research was modest and there was a degree of subjectivity involved in the methodology, there did appear to be a positive correlation between the market performance of the developments and their

Character	Does the scheme feel like a place with a distinctive character?
	Do buildings exhibit architectural quality?
	Are streets defined by a well-structured building layout?
	Do the buildings and layout make it easy to find your way around?
	Does the scheme exploit existing buildings, landscape and topography?
Roads, parking and pedestrianisation	Does the building layout take priority over the roads and car parking, so that the highways do not dominate?
	Are the streets, pedestrian, cycle and vehicle friendly?
	Is the car parking well integrated and situated so that it supports the street scene?
	Does the scheme integrate with existing roads, paths and surrounding development?
	Are public spaces and pedestrian routes overlooked and do they feel safe?
Design and construction	Is the design specific to the scheme?
	Is public space well designed and does it have suitable management arrangements in place?
	Do buildings or spaces outperform statutory minima, such as the building regulations?
	Has the scheme made use of advances in construction or technology that enhance its performance, quality and attractiveness?
	Do internal spaces and layout allow for adaptation, conversion or extension?
Environment and community	Does the development have easy access to public transport?
	Does the development have any features that reduce its environmental impact?
	Is there a tenure mix that reflects the needs of the local community?
	Is there an accommodation mix that reflects the needs and aspirations of the local community?
	Does the development provide for (or is it close to) community facilities, such as a school, parks, play areas, shops, pubs or cafés?

Figure 9.1 Building for Life: Delivering Great Places to Live – the 20 questions

urban design score. Thus there was some tentative evidence that developers would be rewarded financially by investing a little more in the design process.

CABE (2003a) have also researched the effects on development value when more design effort is made on housing schemes. Pairs of housing developments were assessed in four localities where a 'conventional' scheme was compared to an 'exemplary' scheme in design terms to gauge the effect on the financial values achieved. Although the sample size was small, it did appear that there was some correlation between the additional design effort made on exemplary schemes and increased market value. The results seemed to suggest that a developer would be more than compensated for the additional design costs involved in producing an exemplary housing scheme. CABE found that where little attempt was made to design a distinctive scheme the effect on development value was negative.

CABE has also published helpful advice (2003b) for those organisations which do not ordinarily procure buildings in order that they might get the best out of their design team and building contractor by framing a deliverable brief.

The creation of a special agency to champion good design in the built environment reflects the fact that in many ways local authorities are placed in a reactive position in that they do not drive the design process but can only respond to what developers and their designers submit. In countries such as Sweden there is a stronger role for the municipality in the design process from the outset as illustrated by the development of Hammarby Sjöstad which is an urban extension to Stockholm. At Hammarby, as reported by Mulhall (2009) the municipality was both landowner and planning authority and in that position it was able to master-plan the site before disposing of plots on a phased basis to private sector developers. Land disposal was tied to legal agreements requiring that the developers producing buildings in accordance with the municipality's master plan and so the design control acts directly rather than indirectly. The results at Hammarby are impressive and it has become an exemplary scheme which is providing inspiration for many developers and urban designers in Europe.

9.3 Design and sustainability

In chapter 1 of the book it was noted that there is growing awareness of sustainability among companies seeking commercial buildings from which to operate their businesses. While this phenomenon is at a delicate early stage in its development, it is likely that companies which have a policy on corporate social responsibility will begin to specify sustainability criteria when searching for or procuring new buildings. At present the 'badge' which indicates that a commercial building is sustainable in the UK is provided by a BREEAM good, very good or excellent rating. Even where companies do not have a corporate social responsibility policy they may become more interested in whole lifecycle costing and energy performance certificates, i.e. they might begin to think about the longer-term costs to the business of using and maintaining a building. It is very likely that a building which is economically efficient to use and maintain will be also be a sustainable building, so ultimately market forces will begin to harmonise with sustainability.

However that perhaps idealistic position has not yet been reached and most professionals, contractors and clients are on a learning curve when it comes to specifying and producing sustainable buildings. There is also a bewildering array of regulation and policy with complex interrelationships as well as confusing acronyms which is creating 'information overload' and possibly a degree of regulatory overreach. As the sustainable buildings agenda develops it will benefit from some consolidation which will improve clarity and help more clients, professionals and contractors sign up to the principles.

To illustrate the different approaches to sustainable development within the built environment, housing development is assessed for its sustainability under an entirely different system (the Code for Sustainable Homes) from commercial buildings (BREEAM) while statutory minima are set out in the building regulations and requirements for renewable energy are set out in local authority policy such as the Merton Rule. Perhaps this divergent approach reflects both the early stages of a sustainability 'movement' and the practical differences which exist between these broad categories of building types. However, given time, the regulatory apparatus in this field will benefit from evolution and rationalisation.

Code for Sustainable Homes

This Code was first introduced by the English government in 2006 (Communities and Local Government 2006b) and subsequently updated in 2008 (Communities and Local Government 2008a). The Code, which is an evolution of the Building Research Establishment's Eco Homes standards, requires all new housing built from 2008 to record a score against the levels in the Code even if that score is zero. The government intends that mandatory recording begins a process of gradual improvement so that by 2016 all new housing must achieve Code level 6, which is an exemplary sustainable home. The aim of the Code is to steer housebuilders towards more sustainable building practices, by measuring the 'whole home' against nine design categories which are shown in the left-hand column of Table 9.1 below.

The Code's Level 1 represents entry standard which is set just above the requirements of the building regulations and subsequent levels move progressively towards level 6. The Code is being promoted on the grounds that it has a number of benefits for different stakeholders and of course the environment in terms of reduced greenhouse gas emissions. As awareness in the housing market develops there may be a marketing advantage for developers who produce dwellings which achieve higher Code levels than their competitors. This of course assumes that there are or will be more discerning and environmentally aware customers and/or more house purchasers will become interested in lower running costs.

Apart from meeting minimum scores for materials, surface water run-off and waste at entry level the Code is flexible, allowing users to accumulate points against any of the nine categories in the Code. Following consultation with the construction industry and other stakeholders, the categories in the Code have been weighted as shown in Table 9.1.

Code assessors compare a development's characteristics against the above categories and award an overall score which generates the Code level for the development as shown in Table 9.2.

Table 9.1 Code for Sustainable Homes: nine design categories – credits, weighting factor and points

Categories of environmental impact	Credits in each category		Weighting factor (% points contribution)	Approximate weighted value of each credit
Category 1: Energy and CO_2 emissions	Dwelling emission rate	15		1.26
	Building fabric	2		
	Internal lighting	2		
	Drying space	1		
	Energy-labelled white goods	2		
	External lighting	2		
	Low or zero carbon energy technologies	2		
	Cycle storage	2		
	Home office	1		
	Total	29	36.4%	
Category 2: Water	Indoor potable water use	5		1.5
	External water use	1		
	Total	6	9.0%	
Category 3: Materials	Environmental impact of materials	15		0.30
	Responsible sourcing of materials – basic building elements	6		
	Responsible sourcing of materials – finishing elements	3		
	Total	24	7.2%	
Category 4: Surface water run-off	Management of surface water run-off from developments	2		0.55
	Flood risk	2		
	Total	4	2.2%	

Category	Item	Count	%	Value
Category 5: Waste	Storage of non-recyclable waste and recyclable household waste	4		0.91
	Construction site waste management	2		
	Composting	1		
	Total	7	6.4%	
Category 6: Pollution	Global warming potential of insulants	1		0.70
	NOx emissions	3		
	Total	4	2.8%	
Category 7: Health and well-being	Daylighting	3		1.17
	Sound insulation	4		
	Private space	1		
	Lifetime homes	4		
	Total	12	14.0%	
Category 8: Management	Home user guide	3		1.11
	Considerate constructors scheme	2		
	Construction site impacts	2		
	Security	2		
	Total	9	10.0%	
Category 9: Ecology	Ecological value of the site	1		1.33
	Ecological enhancement	1		
	Protection of ecological features	1		
	Change in ecological value of the site	4		
	Building footprint	2		
	Total	9	12.0%	
Total	–		100%	–

Table 9.2 Relationship between a development's total percentage score and Code level

Code levels	Total percentage score (equal to or greater than)
1 *	36 Points
2 * *	48 Points
3 * * *	57 Points
4 * * * *	68 Points
5 * * * * *	84 Points
6 * * * * * *	90 Points

In the public sector the Homes and Communities Agency (HCA) has set a minimum standard of procuring homes at Code level 3 in its National Affordable Housing Programme 2008–11. From 2012, the HCA will require a minimum of Code level 4 for the housing schemes which it supports and then from 2015 the ambition is Code level 6.

To achieve even Code level 3 requires that the energy and water consumption of a home must be at least 25% better than current building regulations. To achieve this, a home would need to be designed so that the thermal efficiency of the walls, windows and roof was significantly improved, that air permeability be reduced, that a high-efficiency condensing boiler be installed and that thermal bridging be reduced. In terms of water efficiency, dual-flush WCs would be required, flow-reducing taps be installed and smaller baths and flow-reduced showers would need to be specified. Level 3 would also require that surface water be removed by soak-away or other porous areas, that sustainable building materials were used in construction and that there was a waste management plan in place during construction.

To achieve Code level 3, an assessor would need to be able to find additional points to achieve the total of 57 points required by the Code. This could be done in any number of ways and so, for example additional points could be earned by specifying sound insulation which outperformed the building regulations, further points could be awarded if full onsite recycling facilities were provided in a development and more points could be earned if there was an additional internal space which could be adapted as a home office. With each incremental improvement a few additional points is gained so that designers would have to think across a range of improvements to move schemes up the levels in the Code. There are therefore no 'quick fixes' which can catapult a scheme from Level 1 to higher levels and the assessments are undertaken by trained independent assessors using a technical guide produced by the Department for Communities (2009). The Code is therefore not a cosmetic marketing exercise which a developer could manipulate or self-award.

From the perspective of a regulation-shy and cost-sensitive housing developer, the government's ambition of reaching Code level 6 by 2016 presents a challenge. However those in favour of a regulatory approach would claim that the housebuilding industry has not on the whole shown itself to be particularly innovative and without regulation it is unlikely that very much headway would be made in terms of reducing carbon emissions.

9.4 Design and cost

The design of a building has a number of facets which have implications for its aesthetic appearance, its cost to build, its capital value and economic performance over its lifecycle and the degree to which it serves its purpose, i.e. its functionality. From an economic perspective, a well-designed high-quality building should be both more efficient and more valuable. An efficient building may be economic relative to the cost of construction but also economic in terms of minimising costs in use over the life of the building. To achieve these goals the designer at the outset has to juggle some key constraints which are:

- the site and its surroundings;
- the client's budget which sets economic limits on the quality of construction achievable;
- compliance with building regulations and limits in a planning consent;
- the end user's requirements.

The architect's role is to produce a design which satisfies the client and the local authority. The client has to be satisfied in respect of the budget, the space and layout, finishes, services, appearance and access. The local authority will have to be satisfied as to planning, highways, public health and building regulations. The architect may also have to convince other consultants within the development team that the design is appropriate as well as the financier who is providing funding for the scheme. Some of the aspects relating to these constraints are now considered.

The site

The design team will need to know the load bearing capacity of the subsoil to determine the substructure. The team will also need to know if there are any restrictions on the legal title of the site such as easements and restrictive covenants which might affect the design. Planning authorities are sensitive to the effect of height, mass and materials on the street scene, particularly in areas of historic character.

Economic limitations

The architect should aim to increase the value of the completed development by reducing the costs in the design. The value on completion can be increased by enlarging the floorspace but this obviously adds to cost as well. The capital value of the completed development can also be improved by a more economic layout defined by the efficiency ratio between gross and net floorspace and also by specifying high-quality finishes which are durable and easy to maintain.

The shape of a building is an important consideration and the shape closest to a cube gives the greatest economy in terms of the relationship between external surface and internal floorspace. However this type of geometric solution is not always achievable simply because sites are not always rectangular and even when they are aesthetic considerations might require a different design solution. The geometry of cube-shaped buildings produces deep-plan floor plates which rely more heavily on artificial lighting and air conditioning. An atrium is often inserted into the centre of such buildings in order to prevent the core of the building becoming gloomy and this in turn reduces the net lettable floor-space.

The efficiency ratio is the relationship between gross internal floor area and net usable space. The difference between the two is the space used for internal access and which is used in common such as stairs, lifts, fire escapes, toilets, showers and storage space. Open-plan offices reduce the space used by internal divisions and in that respect are more efficient than cellular arrangements. A fairly optimum efficiency ratio for an office is about 80% but shops typically give around 90%. In covered shopping centres, non-retail space will need to be allowed for in malls and arcades and for servicing, plant rooms, offices for the manager and communal toilets.

The type of construction specified will also affect the budget and for example there are different cost considerations regarding the structural frame which could be a steel frame and precast concrete floors or a reinforced concrete frame cast *in situ*. Column spacing varies according to the use to which the property is put. For shops a 6 metre grid is conventional; offices are normally designed using a 1.5 metre planning grid with typical depths of between 12 and 18 metres. Column spacing might be 6 or 9 metres to maximise unencumbered space although large clear spans can have knock-on cost implications in terms of loadings on the columns and foundation pads.

External cladding can also have a dramatic affect on the costs of construction depending on the specification and where glass-curtain walling predominates there arises the potential problem of heat gain and how that is handled throughout the building. In terms of internal finishes, suspended ceilings and floors are now frequently used to conceal service runs leaving floor to ceiling heights in offices at between 2.7 and 3.0 metres. Often commercial space is let in a shell form enabling the tenants to fit-out the space for their particular requirements.

The users' requirements

Users' requirements relate to the future tenants' requirements but sight should not be lost of the need to accord with the requirements of future owners, investors and financiers. If institutional investors are going to buy the development, they will have certain criteria for design, including floor loadings, ceiling or eaves heights and size of units. For industrial and warehousing premises, the location may need to be close to transport infrastructure. Manufacturing premises will need to be convenient for a workforce including transport and community facilities.

A developer will usually provide various sizes of buildings in a typical commercial estate to cater for different demands. The site layout of industrial and warehouse estates is also important. The units can be terraced or semi-detached to achieve economies in cost and maintenance. Adequate turning spaces need to be provided for the manoeuvring of heavy goods vehicles. Car parking requirements may vary considerably depending on the numbers of staff employed and the customers and visitors calling at the premises. In terms of eaves height, for warehousing, an economic height is around 10 metres, although this can be much higher for the high-bay warehouses which use computerised storage systems. For standard manufacturing units the eaves height is generally 4 metres. Ancillary offices for industrial and warehouse premises are generally provided at no more than 10% of total space but with high-tech premises this proportion could be much higher. Offices should have some form of central heating and be insulated from noise from the manufacturing areas.

In terms of construction costs there will be variations regarding the standard required by the client and indeed how high the building will be. The average construction cost per m^2 for offices in the second quarter of 2009 produced by BCIS was £1,167 per m^2 for blocks containing three to five storeys while for blocks of six storeys and above the cost was £1,554 per m^2. Of course the average figure disguises a range of actual costs which vary upon whether the building has air conditioning, has a BREEAM rating and the general quality of build.

For business parks and science parks the location is very important with good access to road, rail and air transport and this is illustrated by the success of business parks such as Stockley Park to the West of London which has convenient access to the M4 and M25 motorways and Heathrow airport. Crossways Business Park in north Kent is marketed on the basis of convenient access to the M25 and M2 and fast rail links to London and Paris via Ebbsfleet International Station.

Business parks are generally low density developments with building footprints consuming only around 25% of the site area with the remainder set aside for landscaping, circulation and car parking. Developers will typically build out business parks in phases and may well dispose of plots with planning consent to other developers to stimulate cash flow and spread risk. Another way of spreading risk is to vary the unit sizes on business parks in order to appeal to the widest range of businesses. Thus smaller units of around 160 m^2 over two storeys might be produced on a speculative basis in short terraces. Much larger detached units might offer 13,000 m^2 on four storeys. These large units could either attract one corporate tenant (or owner-occupier) looking for a headquarters building or the building could be subdivided and let to several tenants.

Regarding science parks, the use of the unit should include research and development and exclude conventional production uses. A dynamic relationship between the entrepreneurs on the site and researchers and staff of an academic institution is useful. There are few differences between business parks and science parks as both would contain buildings whose use is classified as B1 under the Town and Country Planning Use Classes Order and which enables them to be used for offices, R&D and light industry. A business park however might have a higher representation of B2 units (general industry) and B8 units (storage and warehousing) than would be found on a science park.

Car-parking standards for business and science parks tend to vary within a range of between 1 space per 20m^2 of floorspace up to 1 space per 38m^2 of floorspace. The differences will reflect the proximity of the business park to public transport nodes and the parking standards applied by the particular local authority. Local authorities are attaching more importance to transport planning than was once the case and it is now common for a scheme to be assessed in terms of its Public Transport Accessibility Level (PTAL) which ranks accessibility of a site on a scale of 1 to 6. A site which has a PTAL score of 6 will typically have excellent access to public transport and will therefore probably be in the centre of a city where car use and onsite parking spaces would be restricted. Sites with a very low PTAL score of, say, 1 would be very remote and probably not prospects for development anyway. Edge-of-town and suburban sites which are poorly connected might have a PTAL score of 2 or 3 and there might be an argument for higher parking provision onsite.

Given the ambition to foster more sustainable developments there could be expected to be downward pressure on the number of parking spaces provided in business park developments in future. Employees are increasingly being encouraged to car-share or cycle to work or use public transport as part of green travel plans which developers will have to enter into at the behest of local authorities.

Specific types of property

In shopping centres the chief design criteria is to achieve concentrated pedestrian flows in the malls and arcades. The selection of key tenants and the overall tenant mix is the second most important ingredient of success. To attract shoppers, the magnet or anchor stores should be located where they will draw people along the malls. Careful siting and management of car parks is essential. Tenant mix should include a balance of uses to meet shoppers' requirements. Restaurants, play space and seating help towards the attractiveness of the shopping centre. Malls and arcades should be wide enough for pedestrian traffic, but not too wide to lose window shoppers' attention (15 metres for the mall but 6 metres for the arcades with a height of 4.5 metres).

Shopping units will vary in size from the department store with up to 25,000 m^2 of floor-space to specialist stores or around 6,000 m^2 with smaller standard units at between 100 to 400 m^2. The large car-orientated edge of town supermarkets operated by the large chains such as Sainsbury, Asda and Safeways have increased in size in recent years with average new developments at around 5,000 m^2 with a few very large units nearing 10,000m^2. The traditional town centre supermarket would typically be much smaller at around 2,000m^2. These are gross internal floor areas.

Retail warehouse parks can be located on the ring road around a town centre or edge of town so long as they are accessible to centres of population and major road networks. In many cases, in order to provide economic buildings, developers deliberately avoid high specifications. A range of units within a retail park may be from 500m^2 to 5,000 m^2. The frontage to depth ratio is at least 1:2. Surface parking is essential for a non-food store, ideally at a ratio of one space to 20 m^2 of floor-space.

British Council for Offices

Every four years the British Council for Offices (2009) updates its Guide to Specification for office development. The guide does not have statutory status but does attempt to capture best practice in office development which has surfaced over the previous four years and it tries to predict what office occupiers, investors and regulators will expect from new office developments.

Contributors to the Guide are industry practitioners and experts and so the guide is very influential in the UK in terms of spreading best practice in office development.

Given that heightened concern with reducing carbon footprints to tackle climate change was the dominant theme leading up to the publication of the 2009 Guide it was perhaps inevitable that the topic of how to build more sustainable office developments featured prominently in the 2009 edition.

The Guide acknowledges that the BREEAM rating method has become the established benchmark by which clients, occupiers and regulators in the UK are judging the degree to which an office development is sustainable. Indeed as the Guide points out the BREEAM benchmark has already been unofficially adopted by a number of local authorities as the standard they are seeking for office developments. As well as acknowledging the inevitable direction of travel towards higher minimum regulatory standards for sustainability, the Guide identifies strengthening corporate social responsibility policies. It is likely that the latter will see office users and investors increasingly requesting evidence that the buildings which they occupy or procure have a recognised sustainability rating.

The Guide recognises the fundamental dilemma faced by office developers in that as they strive to increase the degree to which a building is sustainable by raising the specification from, say, BREEAM 'good' to 'very good' or even 'excellent' they will almost certainly be increasing development costs. As market awareness on sustainability is still in its infancy it is difficult for developers and their sales and/or letting agents to be able to achieve a rental or sales premium to compensate for the additional development costs. Thus at 2009 the Guide points out that there remains a risk particularly for a speculative developer that while the added investment in the building fabric to make a building more sustainable will result in lower-running costs for an occupier, the developer may be unable to share in those longer-term savings. However as the mandatory energy performance certificates and energy display certificates begin to capture more attention in the lettings and occupier markets it could be expected that ultimately higher sustainability ratings will begin to command a premium in the office market. Research on the American office market by Eichholtz *et al.* (2009) has revealed that a green certification of a building does lead to a marginal market premium in terms of increased rental and capital values.

The early 2000s saw a spate of speculative iconic glass clad tower buildings proposed in the London office market, some of which have been put on hold pending an economic recovery after the credit crunch. The Guide suggests that these buildings may have marked a watershed in development extravagance and that henceforth buildings will rely less upon glazing in the building envelope given its propensity to generate heat gain which then becomes an energy consuming problem in the summer months. Building envelopes might therefore be expected to adopt more conventional, solid construction technology which helps to reduce solar impact and enable the adoption of passive ventilation solutions rather than air conditioning.

The Guide also explores space configuration for office floor plans and suggests that the optimum solution adopts a 1.5 metre planning grid and which has become standard practice in the UK. For a deep-plan building this modulus enables optimal window to core depths of between 6 and 12 metres, window to window or window to atrium depths of between 15 and 21 metres and column spacing at 7.5, 9 or 12 metres. For shallow-plan buildings the Guide suggest that window to widow or window to atrium depths should be between 12 and 15 metres and that window to core depths should be between 6 to 7.5 metres. The ensuing floor plates generate efficient floor to wall ratios and enable reasonably convenient subdivision for multiple tenancies. The Guide also suggests that those designing offices should aim at between 80% and 85% net to gross floor space relationship which will maximise rental income for clients.

The Guide notes that in recent years companies are working their office space much harder and that the average floorspace occupancy per employee has been falling and in the UK is now in the range of between $8m^2$ and $13m^2$ per employee. This is simply because companies are seeking more value from their premises and are more likely to accept flexible working practices such as hot-desking so that firms simply need less office space. The trend towards smaller workspaces is also a consequence of smaller desktop PCs and screens and a general trend towards the paperless office where filing cabinets are less in demand.

9.5 Construction and procurement

The objectives for a commercial developer are to maximise the value or income from the development project. When the construction phase of the project has been reached these objectives translate into ensuring that the project is completed on time, within the budgeted cost and to the required quality, as shown in Figure 9.2

A rational developer would therefore want to see the construction stage completed in the least time, to the highest quality at the lowest cost. Of course in reality this is seldom possible and one or other of the criteria would assume priority. Hackett *et al.* (2007: 24) discuss how the cost, quality and time

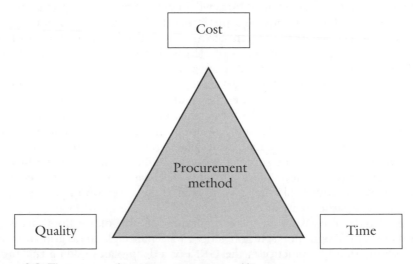

Figure 9.2 The cost–quality–time procurement dilemma

procurement triangle in Figure 9.3 can be distorted to suit a client's particular priorities.

For example, if time were of the essence and there was a tight budget, then a system building method might be adopted to complete the project as quickly as possible within the budget. However there would be trade-offs between the cost and time saved against the quality of the building, which would reflect that it was built rapidly within a limited budget. This might be perfectly acceptable if the building is a retail warehouse which only required a basic specification and did not need to achieve any great aesthetic standards. However if the building needed to be a piece of statement architecture for a one-off purpose, such as Zaha Hadid's design for the swimming pool in the Olympic village at Stratford in London, then the emphasis would be on time (to be ready for the commencement of the games) and quality (to meet the Olympic committee's expectations on landmark architecture). Cost would not entirely disappear from the equation but it would be in the bronze medal position in this particular case.

Procurement options

There is understandably some confusion between the terms 'procurement method' and 'construction contract' and indeed they are sometimes used by authors in this field in an interchangeable manner because there is a large degree of overlap between the two concepts. Strictly speaking, procurement comes first and contract selection comes second, one should therefore dictate the other. Thus the chosen procurement route is a strategic decision taken by a client on how best to get a project built. The client may take advice from professional advisers but this strategic decision is essentially the client's.

Once a procurement route has been decided upon, there follows a choice about which construction contract to use. It is the contract which engages a contractor and sets up the detailed rights and responsibilities for the parties to the contract. Thus the contract and its implementation constitute one part of what might be a longer procurement process. That of course is the theoretical position but it is probable that most employers of building contractors will not tend to draw such a fine distinction between the procurement route and the contract used as the two are thought of as being synonymous. However this chapter will persevere with the idea that there is a subtle but meaningful distinction to be drawn between procurement and contract.

The traditional form of procurement involves the client appointing consultants to design the building and provide costings. The consultants are independent but contractually responsible to the client to produce the best design solution given project constraints. The client then enters into a contract with a building contractor following advice from the professional team. This procurement route is very sequential as it separates the process of designing the building from engaging a contractor who is expected to build precisely to the design.

Other procurement routes are more integrated in that they deliberately combine design, management and contractor input such as when a management contractor takes on the role of selecting works contractors on behalf of the client. This route provides some interaction between the management contractor, the client, the client's professional team and the chosen contractor.

Table 9.3 Types of procurement: characteristics and examples

Procurement route	Traditional	Management orientated	Design and build
Key characteristics	Separation of the design and construction processes. The building contractor is chosen on the lowest tender price after the design and specification has been completed.	A management contractor acts as an intermediary and progress chaser between the client, the design team and package subcontractors.	The client's requirements are framed in general terms and the contract to finalise the design and build the scheme is awarded to a contractor for a lump sum.
Examples of the implied type of construction contract	Standard building contract with (or without) quantities. Standard building contract with approximate quantities.	Management building contract. Construction management.	Design and build contract. Package deal (also known as a turnkey project).

This procurement route therefore has three dimensions: design, management and contract.

It is very likely that a new procurement route related to partnering (discussed later in this chapter) and emphasising sustainability will become recognised in the near future. This new approach, which the Joint Contracts Tribunal (JCT) (2009a) terms 'integrated procurement' currently has two contract options under the title Constructing Excellence. The reason that this option has yet to be widely acknowledged as a fully-fledged procurement route is because it is new and few projects have so far followed this route.

One of the first building completions which has followed this route is the Vehicle Operating Services Agency goods vehicle testing centre at Bristol. The JCT reports (www.jctltd.co.uk) that the client was very happy with the simplicity of the contract and that it helped in delivering a sustainable building on time and under budget. It is likely that this option will therefore become popular with at least some clients who are looking for more integration and collaboration between the client, the design team and various providers in the supply chain including building contractors.

At present however a summary of the three main types of procurement route being used by developers is shown in Table 9.3.

Traditional procurement

Research by Morledge (2008) reveals that the traditional procurement route is still the most popular method followed by design and build (13% of projects) and only a minority (1%) following a management route. Hackett *et al.* (2007) suggest that there is growing popularity with the design and build route although given the significant reduction in the number of building contracts awarded in the UK during 2008 and 2009 it is difficult to be definitive on this issue. However when a normal volume of construction activity is resumed readers who are particularly interested in this topic could consult the periodically updated *Contracts in Use* survey published by the RICS.

Morledge suggests that the durability of the traditional procurement method reflects the fact that most clients do not regularly procure buildings and as such prefer to pass on the risks associated with price and time to the contractor. Murdoch and Hughes (2008) add that the enduring use of the traditional method is more to do with inertia as the method may be arrived at in default of ambition or advice to clients to use an alternative procurement route. Havard (2008: 264) suggests that despite its lack of integration and relatively slow staged process, the traditional method (illustrated in Figure 9.3) holds attractions for property investment clients because it provides them with the control that they need which can be articulated in fully worked up designs and specifications.

Despite the benefits of certainty that the traditional procurement route promises, there are some consequences for clients when choosing this route. The traditional route separates the process of design and specification by the client's professional team, from the process of building. This can cause resentment on the part of the building contractor who, as Havard (2008: 255) states, effectively becomes an outsider and is unable to contribute what is probably a considerable body of knowledge and experience. The latter is a resource which is not exploited in this procurement method and therefore valuable advice on ways to improve the buildability of the project and/or achieve efficiencies and savings (sometimes referred to as value engineering) are lost.

Traditional procurement follows a sequence so that the design has to be largely completed and ideally the bill of quantities produced so that they provide the basis for the tender documents against which contractors bid to carry out the project. Thus in this method there is little scope for overlap between the design stage and the construction stage as the former has to be complete before contractor can be chosen to complete the project, usually on the basis of the lowest price tendered. Thus while the traditional route can generate a lump sum price for the client the whole process can be lengthy and once the design has been frozen for tender purposes subsequent variations by the client are not advisable as they are likely to be very disruptive and costly.

Management-orientated procurement

As Ramus *et al.* (2006: 34) point out, the increasing complexity of buildings, the need for efficient financial planning, the need to reduce design and construction periods and more complex contract administration have combined to encourage experimentation with different forms of building procurement. One such method is known as management procurement.

There are a number of variations in this route, one of which is illustrated in Figure 9.4 and which sees a management contractor employed by a developer/client to undertake the management of the construction process for a fee. The management contractor takes in the relationship that consultants have with the client in the traditional system. The management contractor

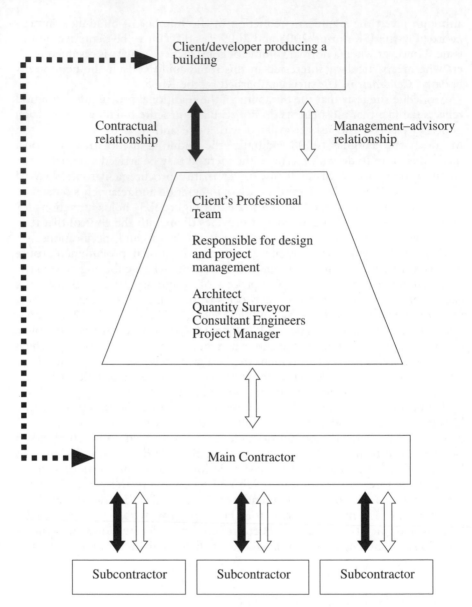

Figure 9.3 Traditional procurement route

then lets discrete contracts to specialist contractors who build specific aspects of the project.

The management contractor is involved in the project at an early stage and so can contribute to the design process before it is completed. Indeed as parts of the design are finalised (such as the foundations and structure) the management contractor can award contracts to specialist contractors who can start work on those elements of the building while remaining design work on other elements of the building may still be ongoing. Thus a contact might be awarded to a specialist contractor for ground works and piling and then later a separate contract may be awarded to a specialist steel contractor. The design and building process can therefore overlap and there is some room for adjustment and changes in parts of the design which have yet to be finalised and tendered.

The problem associated with this approach is that the contractor does not take the risk if things go wrong but is only liable to the extent of the percentage fee which may reduce under these circumstances. This form of procurement, which is illustrated in Figure 9.4 below, is generally good for

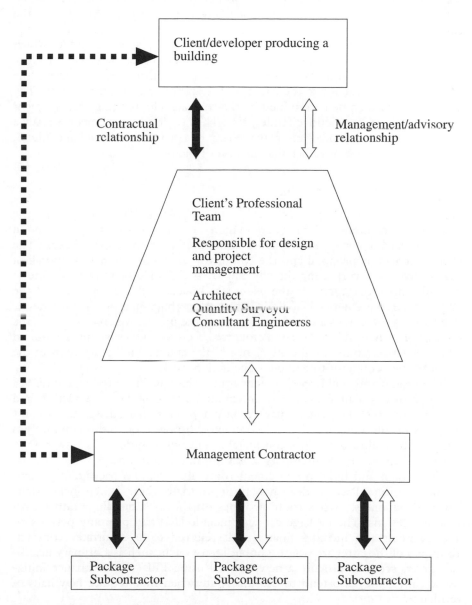

Figure 9.4 Management-orientated procurement route

performance but poor on cost certainty, as the construction packages are awarded at different times and the client can only really see the total cost when all the packages have finally been awarded.

A variation in management procurement is *construction management*, where the contractual relationship is directly between the client and all subcontractors. All parties in a construction management arrangement have a direct relationship with the client who provides overall management. The client employs a construction manager who takes responsibility for running the project. The construction manager thus provides a service of management for a fee but all contractors deliver the project and each enter into a direct contract with the client.

Another option for a client is a project management approach under which a project manager is engaged to coordinate a team of consultants who produce alternative schemes and advise the client. If the client decides to proceed, the project manager will advise the client on the appropriate contract system. The procedure will then be determined by the contract adopted (e.g. management fee or traditional competitive tender, etc). Thus project management is really a system of planning, control and management of a project to be used in conjunction with other systems rather than instead of them.

Design and build procurement

Design and build involves the client engaging an architect to set out the 'employer's requirements' which are tendered to a number of design and build contractors who prepare a design and submit their time and cost proposals. The client accepts one proposal and the contractor completes the design and all of the construction work using directly employed staff or subcontractors. One of the subcontractors might be the client's architect who originally devised the employer's requirements. The logic is that the architectural practice has developed some momentum and knowledge about the project which can benefit the contractor. Where this approach is followed a novation agreement is required which effectively transfers the allegiance of the architectural practice from the client to the contractor to complete the design work.

The design and build procurement route which is illustrated in Figure 9.5 below, provides a high degree of integration between the construction and design processes. The client may employ a professional adviser to monitor progress by the design and build contractor, however once the contract has been let the contractor enjoys considerable autonomy in deciding how best to meet the 'employers requirements' as set out in the contract.

The design and build procurement route also includes package deals and turnkey projects. Package deals may be appropriate where a client needs standardised buildings, as this route provides off-the-shelf buildings rather than bespoke designs. The package can also include land and planning permission and where it also includes finance it is referred to as a turnkey contract. Examples of the latter are where a public sector client such as a primary healthcare trusts seeks to procure a new hospital using PFI (private finance initiative). Universities also tend to use this route when they require new halls of residence.

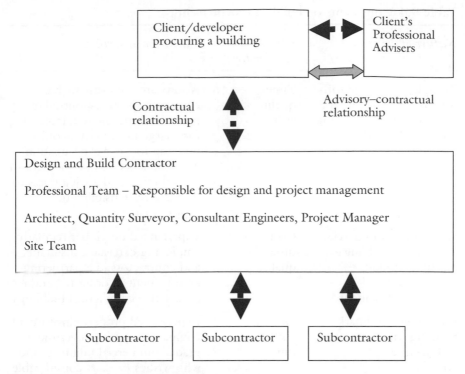

Figure 9.5 Design and build procurement route

Constraints on the procurement choice

Given that there are alternative procurement routes, it is important for a client to have some criteria by which to judge which route is most appropriate for a particular project. The nature of the building work, the size and complexity of the contract and the purpose of the building are obvious considerations as are the client's priorities with regards to cost, quality and time. There is therefore a unique interplay of variables for each project and it is not possible to map all of the possible permutations. However by way of illustration, even in the short three by three matrix below shown in Table 9.4, 27 permutations could arise, although some are perhaps more obvious combinations than others.

When developers are considering which procurement route to adopt, an awareness of key variables which can lead to the success or failure of a project is obviously helpful. Essentially, these relate to the:

- degree of integration of the client with the project team;
- organisation of the design team; and
- degree of involvement of the construction contractor in the design and management process.

It is important to differentiate between a client who has no construction expertise and an organisation where there are in-house staff who can liaise with the project team. The term 'client' is sometimes used interchangeably with the term

Table 9.4 Constraints on building procurement

Nature of the project	Client's order of priorities	Client characteristics
Complex, large one-off bespoke building with a high-sustainability rating such as BREEAM excellent.	Time quality cost	A software company with a corporate social responsibility policy and specific requirements for a large headquarters office building for owner-occupation. No experience of development or construction and a willingness to delegate responsibility to a project manager.
Speculative commercial investment building reaching modest architectural and sustainability standards.	Cost time quality	Experienced developer regularly employing external consultants and contractors in a partnering arrangement in order to produce speculative commercial buildings.
Prestigious landmark building with statement architecture.	Quality cost time	Experienced property investment company requiring investment-grade commercial buildings and who wishes to exert considerable control over the design, specification and selection of a contractor.

'employer' when procurement is being discussed and this is because the client who procures a building subsequently 'employs' the services of a building contractor using a construction contract. Those contracts tend to use the word 'employer' when referring to the client and 'supplier' when referring to the contractor, although in the leading-edge Constructing Excellence contracts, the terms used are 'purchaser' and 'supplier' to reflect different parties and their relationships in the supply chain.

The organisation of the design team is important because the attitude toward construction management will differ depending on whether there is a project manager overseeing the project or whether the architect acts as head of the design team and project manager. Walker (2007: 243) suggests that in trying to fulfil the two roles of *design* and *management* the architect could be overstretched and might lose objectivity when the two roles come into conflict, as they occasionally will on a project.

Where a project manager is to be employed the client has a choice on whether the project manager should play an executive or non-executive role. Walker (2007: 246) explains that the executive project manager is entirely independent from the design team and exerts control over it on behalf of the client. The executive project manager holds a powerful position and acts as the sole point of contact with the client. In that respect the project manager carries a lot of the risk for progressing the project and this could easily lead to an aggressive and authoritarian approach which could cause resentment among the professional team, but as Walker states:

> However, in practice, the project manager should work in a collaborative manner with the contributors and a major role would be one of facilitating the work of all of the contributors so that the project is developed by a team approach. The project manager's primary concern would be that appropriate decisions are taken by both the client and the project team at the right time. (2007: 247)

The alternative is that the project manager plays a non-executive role in parallel with other members of the professional team. In this role the project manager is not empowered to make decisions on the client's behalf and plays more of a team coordinating role. Given that the project manager in this role has limited authority any added value will largely be dependent on the project manager's interpersonal skills and persuasive abilities.

The integration of the contractor into the design and management process is facilitated by systems which allow management and design functions to be provided by a contractor, as these more closely involve the expertise of the building contractor in the design process.

Tendering

Building contracts may be tendered for in competition or by individual negotiation, the choice between these options will depend on a number of factors including:

- Whether a framework agreement is in place promoting longer-term partnering between a contractor and a developer client.
- The size and complexity of a project.
- The building type, i.e. offices, industrial, leisure or housing.
- The likely method of construction (e.g. traditional or modern methods of construction).
- The time available before a start onsite is required.
- The likely involvement of the contractor in the design process.

Cost

Cost will always place constraints on a client when procuring a building and the need to control this factor may in the end be the deciding priority for many clients when choosing a procurement route. It is worth therefore at this point looking at some of the factors which influence construction costs and which the client's professional team will have to factor into their project planning work.

Construction cost estimates are normally produced by the client's quantity surveyor prior to the preparation of detailed drawings and specification. As previously discussed in chapter 3, building costs can be estimated on the basis of a price per square metre multiplied by the gross internal floor area of the building. The initial estimates of cost are based on average costs arising from comparable contracts awarded in the recent past, although adjustments would need to be made for site location, site characteristics and the design and specification required by the client.

Location will affect the cost of building because the price of labour, materials and plant will differ according to the locality in which they are sourced and employed. Labour is to some extent mobile but there is a regional effect on wage rates. Materials are also to some degree mobile but where there are abundant local supplies, the costs of delivery of large loads and quantities to sites can obviously be reduced. Local scarcity can occur in the supply and therefore price of materials and labour where there is significant construction activity, thus market conditions can affect costs. For example the Building Cost Information Service (BCIS) index for regional variations in building cost for the second quarter of 2009 provided the following variations benchmarked against a UK mean value of 1.00.

Northern Region: 0.94
Yorkshire and Humberside: 0.93
East Anglia: 0.95
South East Region excluding Greater London: 1.08
Greater London: 1.22
South West: 0.93
North West: 0.90
Wales: 0.97
Scotland: 1.04
Northern Ireland: 0.67

The cost of construction will be affected by the soil conditions, water table and access to a site, which will be unique each time. For example, the cost of piling in situations where subsoil conditions are difficult can add 10% or more to the cost of works. Basement construction is also expensive especially if there is a high water table. Underground car parking for instance can be expensive and not economical unless there are severe restrictions on accommodating parking elsewhere onsite. Demolition costs can be partially offset where there is the ability to recycle materials in the construction work or by obtaining income from salvageable items. Conversely where the building to be demolished contains asbestos this can add significantly to costs through the extra care and time needed to remove safely and dispose of the hazardous material.

The form, height and width of the building will affect the cost. The lower the height of the property, the lower will be the construction costs generally. The quality of build specified by the client will obviously affect cost. A marble-clad office development with air conditioning and high-quality internal fixtures and fittings will obviously incur a higher build costs than a standard speculative business park unit which uses standard materials and leaves the cost of fit-out to the end user. Clients will be advised by their quantity surveyor on what is possible within specified budgets.

9.6 Selecting a procurement route

As discussed earlier in this chapter, the choice of a building procurement route is shaped by an interplay of factors which includes the client's brief for the project, the nature of the project and the constraints on procurement such as the requirement to remain within a specific budget or to meet a particular deadline. The following example considers procurement options against a set of client objectives.

Client's brief

In this example the client is procuring a new supermarket in England, which is a relatively large contract of straightforward design but which contains expensive services and finishes. There needs to be some flexibility in the procurement method chosen to allow for some variations in design which will probably arise because of the rapidly changing business environment for retail food sales.

The development involves the construction of the supermarket plus two upper floors of car parking. The construction method specified by the client's team is a reinforced *in situ* concrete frame with brick cladding. The building requires high-quality internal finishes and some complex services such as air conditioning, refrigeration and a lift which will require strict management control. The construction period is estimated to be 18 months. The sum available for the building contract excluding profit but including preliminaries and subcontractor payments is £8 million. A substantial amount of the work is associated with service installations and fittings carried out by subcontractors.

Assessing alternative options

The choice of procurement is influenced by the nature of the project and its implied management and contractual relationships stemming from the client's objectives.

At first sight, the complexity of the subcontract work, where a number of variations may occur and where the programme of work would need to be closely followed, does not appear suitable for the traditional procurement route. The purpose of the building and the need for a high standard on the finishes suggests close liaison between the client, the design team and the contractor. This would also appear to count against the adoption of the traditional method of procurement. The complexity and high quality of finishes required may also rule out a design and build solution.

Cost is obviously an important factor but it must be weighed against other objectives. While management contracting, along with other management approaches, offers a degree of flexibility and integration, it may also be a more expensive than the traditional method.

A design and build method may be cheaper, but provides a solution using standardised products which may be of lesser quality. Quality is important in this case as the supermarket requires good-quality finishes and service provision. A supermarket is essentially based on a high functional and technical standard rather than an aesthetic one. The traditional method of building procurement scores well on quality but most other systems, including design and build, could also provide a quality building in most circumstances. The design team may be under greater pressure in management contracts than in the traditional ones and this might reduce the quality of the finished product.

Time is also important in this situation, not only because of financial impli-cations, but also because of the client's desire to establish a business in an area in advance of a competitor supermarket chain. The client's corporate ambition to maximise the market share of food sales in the town might be damaged if a competitor completed a store during the building contract. In relation to the criterion of time, the traditional system fares badly and thus has none of the advantages of other procurement methods where fast-tracking techniques of running design and construction processes in parallel exist.

The type of client is important in this case, as the client may be able to provide in-house expertise to monitor the various management approaches to contracting. The existence of in-house expertise means that management contracting could be a more favourable option whereas a form of executive project management may be less applicable. In terms of decision making, it is assumed that the company has a flexible approach to contracts and can proceed with alternatives to a fixed price contract.

Risk is not considered an important factor in this case as the uncertainty of a contract sum is unlikely to affect the building decision given that the market research has been carried out and a site acquired. However, systems like management contracting put more risk on the client than the contractually 'safe' methods of competitive tender or design and build. Flexibility is a key variable in this project and traditional systems have less flexibility than some management systems. Package deals, in providing a set format for buildings are also less flexible but management contracting, construction management and separate contracts score well on this variable.

Weighted criteria

In order to assess the alternatives and assist in the decision-making process, Franks (1998: 39–45) suggests the use of a matrix which relates the require-ments of the project to the different procurement methods. To begin with a score of 1 to 5 could be attributed to the core client requirements as shown below in Table 9.5. This approach is subjective but it does make the client's priorities explicit and may help to screen out those procurement methods which are least applicable.

Table 9.5

Requirement	Score 1 to 5, where 1 = unimportant and 5 = important
Time	4
Quality	5
Cost	3
Risk	0
Flexibility	5
Complexity	3

Table 9.6 Procurement method

Performance requirements	Traditional	Management fee	Package deal	Design and build	Project management
Time	1	4	4	4	4
Cost	3	4	4	4	5
Quality	4	3	1	3	3
Complexity	3	3	3	4	4
Flexibility	2	5	2	4	4

The matrix approach can be developed further as shown above in Table 9.6 where 1 is poor performance and 5 excellent performance. 'Risk' has been omitted because it was identified in the first stage above (Table 9.5) as being relatively unimportant in this case.

The key requirements for flexibility and quality are best met by a system other than the package deal system and the traditional method. The traditional method also scores badly on the time requirement. If the requirement of size of contract is now examined, a separate contracts system could lead to a complex system of contracts and perhaps conflicts. Because of the importance of the design of the interior finishes and services, a specialist design team may need to be appointed. It may be that this form of design work could not easily be dealt with by the in-house staff of a design and build contractor or management contractor.

The above assessment may leave two options, project management and management contracting using a separate design team. Because of the expertise of the client, a project management solution might by unwieldy. The process could be better integrated using an in-house non-executive project manager with a management contractor and a separate design team. It is important to monitor progress and costs through the project management appointment. This solution integrates both client and contractor into the design process and allows for flexibility and the quality required.

The outcome

Management contracting would appear to be most appropriate system in this case. A design team would be separate and an in-house non-executive project manager could represent the client. This solution deals with the major objectives of flexibility, quality and time but its weakness lies in cost as it is unlikely to be cheaper than the traditional method. The project manager would therefore need to monitor closely the costs and progress of the project.

9.7 Types of contract

The contract arrangements are very important in determining the degree of certainty around building costs. To safeguard the developer in any particular building contract, the project manager where appointed should set objectives encouraging the selection of a competitive contract and the completion of the development within the programme time. A project manager can also advise the client on the most appropriate time to introduce a contractor into the particular project. A project manager can also ensure that tender documents are framed with sufficient clarity so as to create genuine competition between contractors who submit bids.

With regards to contract selection these are grouped in categories and relate to the chosen procurement route. Where a traditional procurement route is preferred by a client it is most likely that a standard building contract will be the most appropriate contract choice. That type of contract can be with or without bills of quantities or with approximate bills of quantities.

The general principle embodied in these contracts is that the client is looking to fix the price by attracting a lump sum bid from contractors who then bear the risk in the event that construction costs are more than was envisaged when the bid was submitted. The lump sum approach is also thought to encourage competition between contractors and so in theory the client attracts the most advantageous bid. There are variations in the principle in that the fixed lump sum relies upon firm bills of quantities while remeasurement contracts are associated with approximate bills of quantities at the tender stage. As construction proceeds, the work is remeasured and priced using the rate in the approximate bill of quantities. The remeasurement contracts have an advantage in the sense that not all the design information needs to be available at the time of tendering.

Another way that some certainty can be created around cost in these contracts is on a reimbursement basis, so that the payments to the contractor are made on the basis of the reimbursement of the actual costs of materials, plant and labour with the addition of a fee for profit and overheads. Traditionally, fees have been around 8% for these contracts.

Where management procurement is preferred then a construction management or management building contract could be used. Essentially management contracts involve the execution of work by subcontractors under the supervision and coordination of the management contractor who does not carry out the building work.

Where design and build is the preferred procurement route there is a corresponding contract which again attracts lump sum bids from contractors.

There is therefore some choice in contract selection even when a client has taken a strategic view on the procurement route. Table 9.7 below shows a

Table 9.7 Comparison of contract arrangements

Criteria	Standard building contract with bill of quantities	Management contract	Design and build contract
Time economy	1	4	4
Cost economy	4	2	3
Cost certainty for the client	4	2	4
Build quality	4	3	3
Degree of control exerted by the client	4	3	2
Post-contract cost control	4	2	2

comparison of just three contract options which reflect their relative suitability against some key criteria which have been weighted on a scale of 1–4 with 1 denoting the least suitable fit and 4 the most suitable fit.

JCT standard forms of contract

The type of contract normally entered into by a developer and a contractor will normally be a standard form of contract provided by the Joint Contracts Tribunal (JCT). These contracts have evolved over a number of years within the construction industry and one of the roles of the JCT is to update regularly and add to the range of contracts offered. For example in 2009 a number of revisions were made to the main JCT contracts (2009b) so that they now contain specific clauses which promote sustainable building practices. This reflects a growing expectation in the industry that it is the client's responsibility to take a lead by setting out clear sustainability expectations in projects and ideally embedding key performance indicators (KPIs) to benchmark progress against sustainability criteria. Occasionally a new form of contract is introduced such as the Constructing Excellence contract (JCT 2009a) to take account of the growing trend towards partnering in the construction industry.

As discussed above, the traditional procurement route is still a popular form of realising a construction project and there is a corresponding *traditional* form of JCT contract which engages a main contractor to carry out the construction in accordance with the design and specification prepared by the developer's professional team. While it is not possible in this chapter to consider all of the JCT contractual forms (readers can consult JCT 2009a), by way of example the traditional form of contract will now be considered.

The traditional form of contract

Traditional building procurement has been referred to by authors such as Morledge *et al.* (2006: 108) as 'design–bid–build' as those are broadly the three steps taken in sequence. The client briefs an architect who provides outline schemes for costing by a quantity surveyor and the client selects a proposal. The architect then consults other specialists (structural and services engineers, etc.) and detailed drawings and specifications are prepared. The quantity surveyor prepares a bill of quantities and other tender documents are sent to selected contractors who submit tenders. The building contractor estimates the costs involved in the project and calculates the duration of the project, if not already determined by the client. A profit and overheads figure is added to the costs.

If a tender is accepted, then the builder concerned enters into a contract. The contractor establishes the site management and building programme and subcontractor's work where required, for both subcontractors engaged directly by the contractor and those nominated by the architect.

In the suite of contracts provided by JCT (2009b) this traditional approach is encapsulated in the *Standard Building Contract* (SBC) and it has three variants: with quantities, without quantities and with approximate quantities.

The SBC with quantities contract would require the developer's team to produce full drawings and a bill of quantities which together would provide contractors with the information needed to submit a lump sum bid. The successful contractor would normally be chosen on the lowest price submitted. Once construction had started the contractor would receive monthly payments based on the work completed as agreed by the client's architect and costed by the quantity surveyor. Usually, a small percentage of these interim payments to the contractor are retained by the developer until the end of the defects liability period under the contract. When any defective work is remedied, retained monies are released to the contractor.

The SBC places most of the risk on the contractor who is not able to influence the design process. This type of contract is thought to be most appropriate where the client wants to control the specification and quality and wants a degree of certainty around the costs and timing. However while it does provide a high degree of control and reduces risk for the client it is a lengthy staged process as construction cannot begin until all details have been finalised by the client's professional team.

The SBC without quantities will require contractors to use their own quantity surveyor to estimate the amount of work involved in order to submit a lump sum bid. Thus the risk still remains with the contractor who will have to work within the costs which have been committed to. Morledge *et al.* (2006: 110) explain that the SBC with approximate quantities contract is seldom used, as it is mainly applicable where there is some uncertainty regarding the design at the outset but which does not prevent construction from starting. The full extent of construction costs can only be ascertained when work has been completed and when it is re-measured to clarify the costs involved. Thus there are risks in this contractual route that parties to the contract will disagree on the final cost and while the benefits are that work can start before the design work has been completed there is financial risk for the client.

A developer adopting a SBC will have employed a team of professionals who are responsible for the design of the building and for administering the contract. The architect or project manager leads the project team and calls in specialist advisers as necessary. For instance there will be structural, mechanical and electrical engineers required. Quantity surveyors are appointed at the outset so that the full benefit of their cost control services are available. The architect is responsible for obtaining planning permission unless a planning consultant is used. The architect is responsible for the design of the building in terms of aesthetics and functionality and the team would normally consult a valuer to advise on economic viability. The architect is also principally responsible for the management of the contract although supervised by the project manager, if one is appointed.

The quantity surveyor is responsible for preparing estimates of building costs, preparing tender documentation and, during construction, for preparing the valuations of completed construction work upon which the architect issues the interim and final certificates. The quantity surveyor should be appointed early to advise on cost and alternative forms of construction. The quantity surveyor reports on the cost of construction and monitors payments against the estimated cash flow over the construction period. The quantity surveyor is also responsible for estimating the cost of variations in design so that the development team can decide on whether or not to agree these variations.

Provided that the contractor executes the building work in a good and workmanlike manner in accordance with the architect's drawings and any the specification in the bill of quantities and with any subsequent instructions from the architect, the contractor will not normally be responsible if the building is not suitable for the purpose it was designed. Developers must turn to their architect and other professional advisers for any remedy if the contractor has fulfilled the terms of the contract but the building is not fit for purpose.

Developers will normally require the design team to enter into deeds of collateral warranty which extend the benefit of the developer's contract with the team to investors, financiers and subsequent users of the building. These deeds require the professional advisers to warrant that all reasonable skill, care and attention has been exercised in their professional responsibilities.

The length of the building contract may be subject to extension for a number of reasons. Some extensions also entitle contractors to recover additional expenses. Thus the developer might not only find that the completion of works is delayed, but also that increased costs are involved. Reasons for the extension of contract time, which entitle the contractor to recover additional expenses include inadequacy of the contract documents, delay by the architect in issuing drawings and instructions or delays caused by tradesmen directly employed by the developer. In addition, there are reasons which may entitle the contractor to an extension of time but not additional expense and these would include failure of subcontractors nominated by the architect. Other reasons would include bad weather, strikes and lockouts, shortage of labour or materials, damage by fire and force majeure (acts out of the control of those involved in the contracts – acts of God).

Because of the financial risk involved with high value projects, contractors may be asked to take out a performance bond with an insurance company which guarantees to reimburse the developer for any loss incurred up to an agreed amount as a result of the contractor failing to complete the contract.

The choice of contractor when using a SBC is usually by means of an invitation to a selected list of perhaps six to eight reliable and financially stable contractors. Contractors usually submit bids on either a firm price or a fluctuation basis. The firm price means that the contract price will not vary even though in reality the market cost of labour and materials may fluctuate over the contract period. On the fluctuation contract the contract may adjust for an increase or decrease in the costs of labour and materials.

Monitoring construction progress

The project manager, where appointed, will report to the developer on the construction progress and cost. Any delays in completion will probably affect the profitability of the development. The developer will need to update the cash flow appraisal. Every project manager will have an individual way of reporting, but the best methods use charts and graphs to compare actual progress and cost against the original forecasts. As Broomfield and Drury (2009: 85) point out, a useful reporting method is a bar chart known as a Gantt chart, which is essentially a calendar of the development programme. The programme is divided into various tasks and the period during which each of these is to be carried out is shown on the chart. Relationships between activities can be recorded so that it is clear that process X cannot begin on site until process Y has been completed. The bar chart can be used to indicate when information or decisions are required by the architect/project manager from the developer and contractor.

The contractor's bar chart identifies the timescale for each trade involved on site and is usually accompanied by a method statement showing the way in which the work will be carried out. Cash flows, tables and graphs would normally be prepared and updated by the project manager who would probably use a project management software package. The cash flow fulfils a number of management functions including the monitoring of the draw down of any loan facility that is being relied upon to make interim payments to the contractor. The cash flows also provide an audit trail for post project evaluation and possibly to assess any outstanding tax liabilities. The project manager will normally use cash flow data and the quantity surveyor's cost reports to prepare financial reports enabling the developer to identify variations in costs throughout the contract.

9.8 Partnering

The UK construction industry is capable of delivering world class buildings on time and within budget. However it unfortunately also has a perhaps unfair reputation for delays, cost overruns, variable quality of work and a propensity for legal disputes between clients, professional consultants, main contractors and subcontractors.

Media coverage of the construction industry often focuses on high profile projects which have experienced difficulties and this tends to reinforce negative stereotypes. For example, costs on the Bath Spa project in England spiralled and legal disputes caused the project to overrun by ten years. Although arguably an architectural masterpiece, the new Edinburgh Parliament building in Scotland experienced significant delays and cost overruns and the media is currently speculating on the extent of cost escalation for the 2012 Olympic Park in London's East End. It is not surprising therefore, that pundits seldom refer to construction as a leading industry when discussing performance, capital investment, methods of working and staff training.

Of course, not all construction companies conform to the negative stereotype. Some companies in the sector have first class training and capital investment programmes and have reputations for their professionalism and the ability to deliver high quality projects on time. Where construction projects experience delay there are sometimes mitigating factors in that construction companies operate in volatile market conditions in which many of the small and medium-sized companies exist on a contract to contract basis. It is difficult for particularly smaller firms to plan ahead, invest in staff development or capital equipment when they are facing peaks and troughs of demand for their services. Construction (for the most part) also takes place outside in variable weather conditions and each site and project is different, creating challenges for productivity, project learning and technology transfer between projects.

To deal with the risks involved, subcontracting has evolved, enabling specialist teams to be engaged for particular stages of a project and then released when that stage is completed. This has obvious benefits in keeping the main contractor's fixed overheads to a minimum and in terms of bringing in the right specialists at the right time. However subcontracting has also led to fragmentation in the construction supply chain. The latter is thought to be one of the factors which fosters a contractual mentality and 'blame culture' which exists in parts of the industry.

Conscious that the industry had become litigious and was losing sight of the quality of delivery to the client, the Latham report (1994) *Constructing the Team* made recommendations on how to resolve disputes by creating a more cooperative team culture between the client, the professional team, the main contractor, subcontractors and suppliers. Proposals were also made by the government commissioned Construction Task Force chaired by Sir John Egan, whose report: *Rethinking Construction* was published back in 1998. That report suggested that productivity gains could be made if the culture of awarding contracts to the lowest bidder could be tempered by more of a focus on timeliness and quality. Egan was effectively promoting ways that construction could add more value to the client's core business.

Egan proposed that the construction industry could learn from the supply chains of motor companies and major retailers, where Egan saw a 'process of continuous improvement' which he did not see in the construction industry. Egan recommended that performance and quality indicators be embedded in the construction supply chain. In order to meet these new challenges, contractors would have to cooperate much more and show improvement from contract to contract. Egan felt that the key to unlocking improvements lay in 'partnering' which was defined in the Task Force Report as follows:

> Partnering involves two or more organisations working together to improve performance through agreeing mutual objectives, devising a way of resolving any disputes and committing themselves to continuous improvement, measuring progress and sharing gains. (Report of the Construction Task Force 1998: 9)

The Egan definition has subsequently given rise to more complex and subtle definitions of partnering which include words like: 'synergy', 'transparency', 'trust' and 'mutual competitive advantage'. Whatever the precise definition, Egan argued that if partnering was to have any benefit in a construction context, then the clients who procure buildings had a critical role in setting clear objectives from the outset of a project.

Authors such as Morledge *et al.* (2006: 91) note that one of the principle causes of delay, cost increase and sometimes litigation is the multi-headed client which is prone to make changes (known as variations) at critical stages of a construction project. The Commission for Architecture and the Built Environment (2003) has produced advice for clients to help them clearly frame a brief for a building with the design team so that the need for variations is significantly reduced once construction has started. In terms of inducing positive change in the supply chain, clients should also be clear about the degree of leverage that they have over their contractors in terms of the volume and continuity of business that they are awarding.

Egan's proposals were welcomed by government and it was not long before government departments and agencies responsible for procuring buildings had become Egan compliant. For example, the Scottish Government is an Egan agency and so is the Homes and Communities Agency in England. The latter organisation ensures that Housing Quality Indicators and Key Performance Indicators are achieved by investment partner housing associations (also known as registered providers) who bid for public grant to support housing developments. Garnett and Perry (2005) report that this selective partnering approach favours larger housing associations who have a track record of delivering good quality projects on time and who will have probably achieved organisational efficiencies. Investment partners will normally have shown an ability to work cooperatively with local authorities and private developers.

Partnering has also been adopted on private commercial projects and there is a JCT *Partnering Charter* (2005) which although non-binding commits the signatories to act in an open and trusting manner and to avoid disputes by adopting a no-blame culture. As Ramus *et al.* (2006: 47) confirm, partnering in this context is about trying to engender a win–win philosophy throughout the client's delivery team. However where more formal arrangements are preferred the JCT has a Framework Agreement which provides the basis for working relationships to extend from project to project. JCT has also produced a Constructing Excellence contract which binds parties more formally to partnering at a detailed project level.

There are dilemmas which could arise because of on-going partnering relationships between developers, professional consultants and construction contractors. Relationships could become anti-competitive and less cost effective than might arise through an unrestrained competitive tendering approach. It is beyond the scope of this book to evaluate these dilemmas although readers could consult Jones and O'Brien (2003) who have considered the benefits of partnering in the affordable housing sector and Hackett *et al.* (2007: 113–19) who discuss the advantages and disadvantages of partnering more widely. The latter authors suggest that the partnering ethos recognises that the cheapest price does not necessarily provide the best value for money and that individuals are entitled to receive a reasonable return for their efforts and that partnering is consistent with good professional and commercial practice.

9.9 Modern methods of construction (MMC)

Given that construction costs will normally account for the largest outgoing in a developer's budget there has always been interest in potential ways to control or reduce construction costs. The discussion elsewhere in this chapter has considered contractual ways that greater predictability and certainty can be created around construction costs but that leaves the fundamental issue of whether technology can achieve efficiencies and thereby reduce costs in the building process.

Unlike factory based production lines which lend themselves to automation or the use of robots to carry out repetitive tasks, construction has to take place on specific sites and often in difficult circumstances. The latter may be due to adverse weather or limited space in which personnel can operate plant, store materials or carry out complex processes. Despite the widespread use of prefabricated components, construction still remains labour intensive and involves many in-situ processes.

In recent years there has been interest in how to fully exploit Modern Methods of Construction (MMC) so that suppliers of factory produced components such as pods, panels and frames are given continuity of production. In theory this could reduce construction times, remove difficulties around on-site materials storage, achieve economies of scale though greater standardisation and reduce wastage. There is also potential to achieve greater quality control given factory standard finishes and tolerances and this has positive implications for ongoing maintenance costs.

These ideas are of course not new and date back to the 1940s and 1950s when prefabs were seen as temporary solution to a housing shortage. System built high rise housing and schools were also widely used in the UK during the 1960s. Unfortunately some of the on site assembly practices in those times resulted in poor build quality and ever since has stigmatised the concept of prefabrication as a cheap and poor quality alternative to traditional building techniques.

To try to overcome the stigma, raise the profile of MMC and to explore whether genuine cost reductions could be achieved in the construction process the former Deputy Prime Minister in England: John Prescott laid down a challenge in 2004 to housebuilders to produce a house for £60,000 or less, excluding the land value. The competition was launched under the banner: *Designed for Manufacture* (Department for Communities and Local Government, 2006c).

The context for the competition was that housebuilders had reported that the average housing plot accounted for approximately 20% of the total costs to produce an average dwelling and therefore it was within the 80% of the costs devoted to building the dwelling where cost reduction initiatives might best focus. The 80% proportion includes labour, materials, professional fees, developer's profits and overheads such as interest on loans. These costs were causing concern, as they were rising faster than inflation. There were also concerns regarding a shortage of skilled construction workers, which threatened to reduce output from the industry, just when the government wanted to move in the opposite direction.

The target of £60,000 could be met by building small and cheaply and so the competition criteria specified a two bedroom home with at least 76.5m^2 internal floor area and which should meet the then Eco Homes 'very good' standard (equivalent to level 2 in the current Code for Sustainable Homes).

There were a number of encouraging outcomes from the competition, not the least of which were the number of entries, proving that cost reduction could be achieved while simultaneously maintaining quality. Participants included some leading developers, such as Barratts and George Wimpey as well as large housing associations, so the exercise was not a fringe publicity stunt.

The competition revealed that those competitors who worked closely with their supply chains were the most successful in both cost management and quality enhancement. The use of MMC by winning competitors confirmed rapid construction times, good on-site health and safety performance and reliable quality. The use of off-site manufactured timber and steel frames and panels together with standardised pods for bathrooms and kitchens confirmed their build-ability and quality.

It is probable therefore that *part* of the solution to reducing construction costs in housing development does lie in the innovative use of MMC. Similar principles probably apply in the commercial property sector although because of the wider range of building types generalisation is not possible and specific studies should be consulted.

9.10 Summary

The raised ambitions regarding the sustainability and design quality of new development has created more challenges at the front end of the development process for developers. For a large scheme these challenges could well include Environmental Impact Assessment, a design review, a green travel plan, a design and access statement, a possible section 106 agreement and various expectations around sustainability. In themselves these are desirable requirements aimed at raising the standards of development. However the result is that developers have to spend more time and money honing development proposals so that the regulatory apparatus and various stakeholders are satisfied. The next few years might therefore see some consolidations and streamlining of procedures so that credible schemes can progress to construction in a shorter timeframe. The government in England is aware of this issue and has set up expert reviews such as the Killian Pretty Review (Communities, 2008b) to advise on how best to rationalise procedures without compromising on quality.

While developers and their professional teams are being pushed harder regarding the design of housing and commercial schemes, there is some evidence that extra design costs can be recovered in enhanced development values.

During the construction phase of a development, developers become the clients of the construction industry as they will normally need the services of a building contractor in order to get their projects built. The choice on which construction procurement route to take is contingent on the interplay of a number of variables not the least of which are the priorities placed on cost, time and quality by the developer.

Once a commitment has been made to a procurement route, specific contractual arrangements can be considered and again there are key choices to be made by the client in consultation with the professional team. The contract selected will normally be chosen from the suite of standard forms of contract offered by and regularly updated by the JCT. It is within the chosen contract that the client can make explicit the degree of commitment to sustainability and partnering in a project.

References

British Council for Offices (2009) *2009 Guide to Specification* (London: British Council for Offices).

Broomfield, R. and Drury, A. (2009) *Developing Affordable Housing: A Guide to Development and Regeneration*, 2nd edition (London: National Housing Federation).

Commission for Architecture and the Built Environment (2001) *The Value of Urban Design* (Tonbridge: Thomas Telford). Available in e-format at: www.cabe.org.uk

Commission for Architecture and the Built Environment (2003a) *The Value of Housing Design and Layout* (Tonbridge: Thomas Telford). Available in e-format at: www.cabe.org.uk

Commission for Architecture and the Built Environment (2003b) *Creating Excellent Buildings: A Guide for Clients* (London: CABE). Available in e-format at: www.cabe.org.uk

Commission for Architecture and the Built Environment (2006) *Design and Access Statements: How to Write, Read and Use Them* (London: CABE). Available in e-format at: www.cabe.org.uk

Commission for Architecture and the Built Environment (2007) *Housing Audit: Assessing the Design Quality of New Housing in the East Midlands, West Midlands and South West* (London: CABE). Available in e-format at: www.cabe.org.uk

Commission for Architecture and the Built Environment (2008) *Building for Life* (London: CABE). Available in e-format at: www.cabe.org.uk

Communities and Local Government (2006a) *Preparing Design Codes: A Practice Manual* (London: Department for Communities and Local Government). Available in e-format at: www.communities.gov.uk

Communities and Local Government (2006b) *Code for Sustainable Homes: A Step-Change in Sustainable Home Building Practice* (London: Department for Communities and Local Government). Available in e-format at: www.planningportal.gov.uk

Communities and Local Government (2006c) *Designed for Manufacture – The Challenge to Build a Quality Home for £60K: Lessons Learnt* (London: Department for Communities and Local Government). Available in e-format at: www.designfor manufacture.info

Communities and Local Government (2008a) *The Code for Sustainable Homes: Setting the standard in sustainability for new homes* (London: Department for Communities and Local Government). Available in e-format at: www.communities.gov.uk

Communities and Local Government (2008b) *The Killian Pretty Review Planning applications: A Faster and More Responsive System – Final Report* (London: Department for Communities and Local Government). Available in e-format at: www.communities.gov.uk

Communities and Local Government (2009) *Code for Sustainable Homes: Technical Guide Version 2* (London: Department for Communities and Local Government). Available in e-format at: www.communities.gov.uk

Eichholtz, P., Kok, N. and Quigley, J. (2009) *Doing Well by Doing Good? An Analysis of the Financial Performance of Green Office Buildings in the USA* (London: RICS Research Report). Available in e-format at: www.rics.org

Essex Planning Officers' Association (2005) *The Essex Design Guide*, 3rd edition (Chelmsford: Essex County Council). Available in e-format at: www.the edi.co.uk

Franks, J. (1998) *Building Procurement Systems: A Client's Guide*, 3rd edition (London: Longman).

Garnett, G. and Perry, J. (2005) *Housing Finance* (Coventry: Chartered Institute of Housing).

Havard, T. (2008) *Contemporary Property Development*, 2nd edition (London: RIBA Publishing).

Hackett, M., Robinson, I. and Statham, G. (eds) (2007) *The Aqua Group Guide to Procurement, Tendering and Contract Administration* (Oxford: Blackwell).

HM Government (2008) *Strategy for Sustainable Construction* (London: Department for Business, Enterprise and Regulatory Reform). Available in e-format at: www.berr.gov.uk

Joint Contracts Tribunal Limited (2005) *Partnering Charter (Non-binding)* (London: Sweet & Maxwell Limited). Available in e-format at: www.jctltd.co.uk

Joint Contracts Tribunal Limited (2009a) *Building a Sustainable Future* (London: Sweet & Maxwell Limited). Available in e-format at: www.jctltd.co.uk

Joint Contracts Tribunal Limited (2009b) *Deciding on the Appropriate JCT Contract* (London: Sweet & Maxwell Limited). Available in e-format at: www.jctltd.co.uk

Jones, M. and O'Brien, V. (2003) *Best Practice Partnering in Social Housing Development* (London: Thomas Telford).

Latham, M. (1994) *Constructing the Team: The Latham Report* (London: Department of the Environment).

London Borough of Greenwich (2009) 'Decision notice on the planning application for Greenwich Market reference 09/0829/F issued on 28.8.09' (London Borough of Greenwich). Available in e-format at: www.greenwich.gov.uk

Morledge, R. (2008) *A Review of the Value of the Main Contractor*, Construction and Building Research Conference (London: RICS). Available in e-format at: www.rics.org

Morledge, R., Smith, A. and Kashiwagi, D. (2006) *Building Procurement* (Oxford: Blackwell).

Mulhall, T. 'Sweden's showpiece', in *RICS Land Journal*, November–December 2009. (London: RICS).

Murdoch, J. and Hughes, W. (2008) *Construction Contracts: Law and management*, 4th edition (Abingdon: Taylor & Francis).

Northampton Borough Council and English Partnerships (2005) *Upton Design Code* (Northampton Borough Council). Available in e-format at: www.northampton. gov.uk

Office of the Deputy Prime Minister (2005) *Planning Policy Statement 1: Delivering Sustainable Development* (London: ODPM). Available in e-format at: www. communities.gov.uk

Ramus, J., Birchall, S. and Griffiths, P. (2006) *Contract Practice for Surveyors*, 4th edition (Oxford: Butterworth-Heinemann).

Report of the Construction Task Force, The (1998) *Rethinking Construction* (London: Department of the Environment, Transport and Regions).

Roger Evans Associates (2007) *Delivering Quality Places: Urban Design Compendium 2* (London: English Partnerships and the Housing Corporation). Available in e-format at: www.urbandesigncompendium.co.uk

Walker, A. (2007) *Project Management in Construction*, 5th edition (Oxford: Blackwell).

10

Market research, marketing and disposal

Aims

This chapter explores three topics: *market research*, *marketing* and *disposal* which should in theory have a linear relationship in the context of property development. However theory is seldom applied in such a pristine manner in practice and this is certainly the case in property development. However the chapter begins by exploring the application of market research to property in terms of identifying market demand so that developers have an opportunity to respond with appropriate supply. The chapter then looks at marketing approaches which could be used to attract business tenants to take leases in properties or to attract investment purchasers.

Much of the theory in this field was derived from the 1980s and 1990s, although advances in information technology have had an impact upon the role of property agents. Both the conventional and modern approaches to marketing and selling are considered. Finally the chapter investigates some of the issues which have to be resolved when a development is to be disposed of following a successful marketing campaign.

Key terms

>> **Marketing strategy** – this arises from the interpretation of initial market research and information gathering. Decisions can then be made on how to promote and price the product while engaging in public relations activity to increase awareness of the firm and its developments.

>> **Selling** – involves using various methods of persuasion or inducement to assist with the closure of a transaction. A salesperson in the property field is perhaps primarily a facilitator who brings buyers and sellers together. The success of the salesperson depends upon some factors which can be

controlled such as marketing budgets and the strategy adopted to reach the target audience. Other factors cannot be controlled, such as the price of the product and the market conditions at the time of the sale or letting.

>> **Methods of promotion** – include advertising, mail shots to target groups, promotional events, sponsorship and the use of Internet sites. Their purpose is to disseminate information and increase awareness. The success of such methods depends upon the ability of a sales team to interact with buyers to stimulate and maintain consumer interest. Promotional methods cannot be used passively if they are to succeed.

10.1 Introduction

Theoretically a prudent developer would commission market research before embarking on a scheme in order to discover what the market required, where it was required and in what quantity and quality. Where there was no pre-sale or pre-let, the prudent developer would then market the development to potential occupiers or end purchasers as the scheme was being built in order that it could be disposed of for a profit on completion.

Of course this pure application of theory is seldom possible in the real world of property development where developers will often be presented with windfall sites of not quite the right size in not quite ideal locations relative to what the market actually wants. In those circumstances, experience, ways of doing things, gut instinct and 'hunch' will tend to cut across the theoretical purity of the model described above. However this is not to say that market research and marketing have no place in the world of the property developer, as Syms (2002: 216) points out:

> The ultimate objective of property development is to find tenants or purchasers for newly constructed or converted buildings and one of the most important aspects of that process is good marketing of the product.

This chapter will therefore begin by looking at aspects of the market research process which are relevant to the property development process before considering selected principles of marketing. Traditionally developers and their agents have relied on paper-based marketing media such as brochures and advertisements to promote their schemes. However the Internet has created new opportunities to improve presentation, market penetration and also 'traffic counting' to assess interest in a scheme as reflected in hits on a website. The use of digital photography and computer-generated imagery (CGI) for yet to be completed developments have also become important tools for the property marketing agency, especially where pre-lets and off-plan sales are sought.

Finally the chapter looks at some of the important considerations for a developer which arise when a marketing campaign has been successful and a development can be disposed of.

10.2 Market research

Market research is an important subject for the property developer as it aims to establish the current demand and supply of different types of property within an area, enabling the developer to model a scheme so that it has a good chance of attracting a sale or letting.

Perhaps the most important aspect of market research is to establish what an actual or notional client's needs are. For example the development of a new shopping centre would require detailed research to establish whether there was sufficient demand in the retail catchment for more retail space. Some towns and cities in the UK are simply 'over-shopped' and it would be highly risky for developers to try to add more retail floorspace unless they were able to distinguish it in qualitative terms, perhaps by identifying a niche market which was undersupplied.

Assuming that some form of demand was identified, then a developer would also need to ascertain realistic rental levels, the lease lengths which retail tenants would find acceptable and whether inducements might be needed to attract retail tenants to a scheme.

Barkham (2002: 53) notes that market research in the commercial property sector has developed primarily because of the vast sums of money committed to projects and the growing sophistication of the decision-making process on whether a project should be funded or not. However development opportunities are first identified by a developer who, in many ways, is like the classic entrepreneur who acts on instinct and intuition. Leading on from this Barkham (2002: 54) comments:

> In some ways, therefore, market research for property development is a sort of informal hypothesis testing exercise. The developer provides the hypothesis and the research organisation tests it. This is a relatively efficient way to proceed, since the hypothesis provides structure and direction for the research.

By way of an example, Barkham (2002: 55–72) has described the stages that would be involved in the market research for a proposed office development – and these are discussed below.

Market research for an office development

This would involve an analysis of macro-economic data such as interest rates, inflation, employment rates and gross domestic product as these factors all contribute to the degree of business confidence held by firms and individuals. As well as this macro-economic data, the RICS Quarterly Commercial Market Surveys are particularly good at assimilating key data which a property developer would be interested in.

For example in the second quarter of 2009 the RICS market survey identified weakening tenant demand for office space, falling office rents, shorter lease lengths, more available space and the need for more inducements (longer rent-free periods) to attract tenants to take leases in office developments. The hard data are supplemented with the opinion of property agents working on the ground, enabling a general picture of a particular market to be built up. For example the RICS survey for the second quarter of 2009 commented that:

> Inducements are rising at the fastest pace in the office sector followed by retail and then industrial. Inducements are rising at the fastest pace in the

Central London office market indicating that bargaining power remains firmly in the hands of tenants. (RICS 2009: 3)

The demand for office space, like the demand for any commercial floorspace, is derived from the plans of businesses to provide goods and service. If economic indicators are negative and business confidence is low then that will ultimately have a knock-on effect for the property sector. However, if business confidence is high and forecasts indicate that the economy is entering a strong phase, then that is obviously a positive sign for a developer.

Overview of the local office market

Although the demarcation lines are not absolute, it appears that office markets tend to fall into one of four categories: international, national, regional and local. This distinction therefore predisposes these markets to different sets of occupational and investment clients. This categorisation can be combined with market information regarding rents, yields, capital values, vacancy and take-up rates which can be compared with regional and national averages. The availability of sites and thus potential competitor developments is also a factor to consider under this heading. Co-star's online *Focus* service is very useful in this respect as it not only provides data on deals and how long properties were on the market before they were let or sold, it also provides reports on broader issues affecting development in a particular town or city. For example a Focus 'town report' will provide a synopsis of the demographic of an area, its employment profile by industrial sector, unemployment rates, main employers, development plan status, communications and an overview of each property sector in the particular town or city.

Demand analysis

For office development the attention will be on the growth or contraction of the service sector which is the user segment of that market. Other factors are the 'churn rate' which is the rate at which existing occupiers relocate to new buildings. Information regarding company expansions and the in-movements of service sector companies to an area will also help to build up the demand side picture.

Research undertaken by the Oxford Institute for Sustainable Development (2009), which was discussed in chapter 1, identified that companies seeking office premises do have an order of priorities, which at present is dominated by location and cost (and not *location, location and location* as some pundits have suggested). However the research did detect that sustainability was creeping up the rank order of search criteria for companies and particularly for those which had an established policy on corporate social responsibility. It is likely that those companies will have developed some awareness around the green labelling of buildings which in the UK are identified by a BREEAM rating.

As the green buildings issue moves up the agenda, it will ultimately have implications for the quality of schemes brought forward by developers and there is scope for developers to associate with the green brand which potentially provides a developer with a marketing edge. The Gherkin shown on the cover of this book represents a modern synthesis of a successful iconic commercial office building which is also a sustainable building.

Qualitative analysis

As well as identifying *quantitative* issues, property market research should also investigate the *quality* of the available office stock. For example, if it were discovered that the existing second-hand office stock was not meeting occupiers expectations, then that would be a positive signal for a developer. This type of information does not readily surface from data analysis and thus Syms (2002: 44) recommends carefully facilitated focus groups or telephone interviews to garner opinion and views from market experts.

Supply pipeline

Because the supply response is said to be inelastic in property development, market research for office development should ideally assess the volume and stage reached by competitor office developments in the four stages of the 'development pipeline' which encompass:

1 Sites where planning permission has been sought for offices but upon which a decision was awaited.
2 Sites with existing planning permissions for offices but where construction had not started.
3 Office space under construction.
4 Completed developments which were available but unlet.

If a large supply of office space was identified at all stages of the pipeline and other data such as the length of voids was extending and the length of inducements was also increasing, then this obviously places doubt on proposals for more offices. The best market research may be that which is objective and dissuades a developer from embarking on a foolhardy scheme which would in all probability lead to receivership.

Faced with the realities of difficult market trends, developers must show a degree of pragmatism and flexibility by exploring other development options. For example the challenging conditions described above manifested themselves in 2009 in Croydon which is a major office centre to the south of London. Developers there began a dialogue with the local authority to seek changes of use for empty office towers to residential and to seek land use reallocations in the local plan so that undeveloped office sites could instead be considered for other uses.

Provision required

Where market research suggests that there is un-met demand, it is important that the segments of the demand are analysed so that the right type of product is provided in terms of affordability, location and size. Thus it is pointless providing very high-specification prime property at high rents in high volumes when research reveals that the demand is from smaller companies with tight operating margins who can successfully operate in secondary locations. Cleaveley (1984) adds that having gone through a rigorous research methodology it is important that the conclusions and recommendations are clearly set out in a comprehensive report so that they can be translated into action by the developer/client.

10.3 Property marketing

Commercial property is produced for a market where buyers and sellers interact. There is an investment market for new and second-hand property and there is also a market populated by companies and businesses who simply want to lease property from which to operate their businesses rather than own premises. Commercial property has a use value and an investment value which is subject to supply and demand in the marketplace.

Given the sizeable asset value of most commercial properties, it is not surprising that marketing is an important activity, as it has the power to convert a customer's purchasing power into effective demand. In property, as in any other market, marketing is the skill of matching the needs of a buyer with the product of a seller for profit.

Successful property marketing requires specialist marketing agents and to be effective they require a strategy which is ideally research led (as discussed above) and the use of promotional tools such as adverts, exhibitions and public relations events.

A marketing strategy theoretically incorporates a number of steps as follows:

1 Market research (identify unmet demand in a market)
↓
2 Identify the market segment (shops, offices, leisure, mixed use, etc.)
↓
3 Marketing strategy (identify the right message and get the message across)
↓
4 Decide upon the best sales method (private treaty, auction, formal tender, etc.)
↓
5 Decide upon the selling techniques (brochures, mail shots, press advertising, site boards, Internet sites, demonstrations or a combination of these)

Ratcliffe *et al.* (2009: 478–81) broadly agree with these steps although add that it is important to select the right team (agency) to market the product and that there should ideally be a marketing representative embedded in the development team from the outset. In that way the 'messages from the market' can be absorbed by the client's design and construction team so that a marketable development ultimately emerges. Emphasis is also placed upon ensuring adequate follow-up activity and being realistic about a marketing budget, as to be too parsimonious may lead to financially damaging delays in letting or selling a development.

The marketing of a development property is usually undertaken by the marketing departments of the leading surveying firms or specialist companies or who have established a reputation for providing this type of service. In a

marketing context it is sometimes possible to stimulate demand for new products, but certainly in the property market and generally in other markets, most
profitable ventures arise from the identification of a need or market gap. Thus
it is better and less risky to start from the basis of solid market research; however
in practice a lot of property ventures are much more speculative and therefore
risky in nature.

An example of a rather shallow attempt to exploit a concept without any real
linkage to market research was the rapid development of so called 'high-tech'
industrial units built on business parks in the UK in the 1980s. Most of these
ventures did not have any clear market requirement identified. In most situations the developers were providing traditional premises differing only in terms
of headroom, finishes and landscaping from traditional types of property which
would have been provided. High-tech became associated with high rents and
did not provide any technological or qualitative advantages in terms of the space
provided.

Some cynics say that contemporary claims that developments offer carbon
offsetting or are eco-friendly amount to 'green-wash' and that most speculative
developments are not particularly sustainable. This is an example of a weak
marketing strategy and would not be sufficient to convince funding institutions
or professionally advised clients. Marketing now has to be more firmly
grounded in fact, particularly given that regulation now requires Energy
Performance Certificates and Energy Display Certificates which provide a basis
for credible benchmarking. Independent verification is also required for a building to attract a BREEAM rating. In any case the Property Misdescriptions Act
1991 quite properly prevents 'artistic licence' from being stretched too far
when a property is described in marketing material.

Logically, the presentation of a marketing proposal for a development should
include:

- *Market research findings:* showing evidence of end-user requirements, the
  balance of supply and demand and the presence or otherwise of competitor
  schemes.
- *Marketing strategy:* which should have clear objectives, an identified target
  group, a promotional plan and a timescale.
- *Pricing strategy:* rental values must be realistic, inducements such as rent free
  periods or capital discounts must be logical and the overall package must
  make the development competitive.
- *Monitoring and management:* mechanisms must be put in place in order to
  monitor the effectiveness of marketing and allow action to be taken to adapt
  the strategy if it is not working.

Marketing differentiated from sales

Sales are an outcome of a successful marketing campaign, which may have
included advertising. In other product areas, salespersons are usually employed
as the most important means of obtaining information on products and services
and these are regarded as being much more important than advertising or mail
shots. However, mail shots and advertising in journals such as *Estates Gazette* and
Property Week are the commonly used approaches in the property industry.

There are of course a number of other channels of persuasion which will encourage a potential consumer to purchase the product and Syms (2002: 219–25) includes radio, video, advertising signboards, show suites, exhibitions, conferences, seminars and subliminal promotion such as references in literature or the press. Millington (2000: 212) adds that a good agent will know what combination of these media will be most appropriate in a particular geographical context relative to the type of scheme being promoted.

The development of a marketing campaign for a development property needs to be planned effectively. The stages that may be passed through might include:

- The definition of the objectives of the campaign.
- The examination of the property to see how it fits within these objectives.
- The search in the overall market for the specific niche market for the property.
- The segmentation of the market into different user groups.
- The establishment of the competitive edge in the promotional campaign.
- The design of marketing systems appropriate for the promotion which is going to be carried out.
- The development of a marketing plan.
- The implementation of the plan at which stage there is a review and evaluation which may take the procedure back to the definition of objectives and the examination of the property itself. These are set out in Figure 10.1 below.

Market segmentation

Segmentation describes groups of consumers inside a market who share a common need. Segmentation identifies those variables which are used in the purchase decision and which can be ranked in order of importance by a market researcher. A term commonly used in the segmentation activity is 'gap analysis' which describes the gap in the market which potential products can fill. Most markets break down into what is termed preference segments. There are three of these and, although fairly wide, they represent the first step in segmentation analysis.

1 *Homogenous preferences:* where all consumers in the market have roughly the same preferences. Most companies will position their product in the middle.
2 *Defused preferences:* consumer preferences here are scattered, with each requiring something different from the product. Companies often decide to position in the middle to minimise consumer dissatisfaction.
3 *Cluster preferences:* distinct clusters are evident suggesting further segmentation. A company must decide which course of action to follow. For instance, to position in the centre to appeal to most groups, position in the biggest cluster to try to become market leader or develop several brands to cover each cluster.

Ratcliffe *et al.* (2009: 483–7) make the perhaps obvious point that the commercial property market is highly segmented in terms of the business community

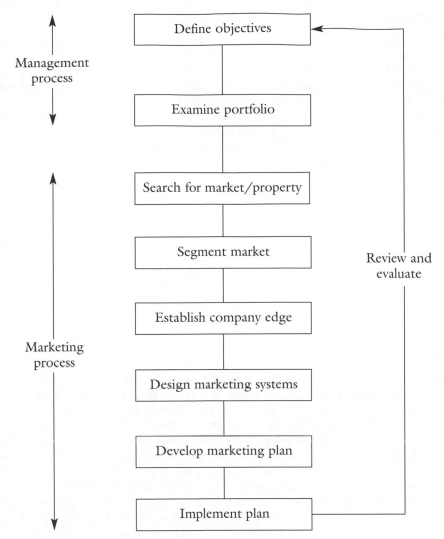

Figure 10.1 The management and marketing process

that it seeks to provide for. Not only are there the obvious divisions between retail, offices, industry, warehousing and leisure, but that even within these categories there are a whole host of different client groups with different attitudes towards their business premises.

For some businesses, operating from a secondary location in a low-cost 'no-frills' property meets their business needs. However, other companies may have very specific requirements in terms of building specification and location. As Havard (2008: 281) points out institutional property investors will have different attitudes to risk and different assessment criteria in terms of the types of properties they wish to invest in. Property developers thus have to be very clear about which market segment they are aiming their product at.

Promotion

Promotion is the art of communicating with prospective customers. It is a vital component of the marketing mix used to sell a product. The purpose of promotion is to bring a product or service to the attention of a buyer or group of buyers in the target market. Promotion includes selling as one of its constituent parts, but it is an activity under the marketing umbrella.

The need, as indicated earlier, is to ensure that the target market has been assessed early in the development process when evaluating the scheme and developing the design. There is a need to brand the building by naming it and providing an appropriate logo or concept so that this theme can be recognised by the market and perhaps reflect the strategy of the advertising campaign. The target market, it should be remembered, is not just the potential occupier but the potential purchaser and financiers. The property should promote the space but also the amenities and location of the area.

Promotional communication will normally focus upon the satisfaction element that will be achieved by presenting the product to the marketplace. In terms of a speculative property development, different promotional activities can be planned to relate to the stage reached by the development and the degree of interest and commitment likely to be shown by the target group at each stage. This is summarised in Table 10.1 below.

Selling

Marketing is obviously an essential tool in letting and selling a development and it is assisted by the public relations exercise to promote, communicate and reinforce the corporate image of the development company. Developers need to realise that their image plays an important part in the success of their developments. Initially property developers did not employ professional advisers in the advertising world, but this practice has developed over time. The agent's role is to persuade the purchaser or tenant to purchase or rent a property at the right price and terms. It is obviously important, as discussed earlier, for the developer to identify the target market which is referred to as the market segment.

The property agent's role is particularly important with regards to selling completed developments. Agents have advantages because of their better location in a market where they will have local contacts, and also their detailed knowledge of the local market. Agent's fees for successfully letting floorspace may amount to 10% of the annual rental value or when facilitating a disposal perhaps 2% of the value for sale. However, joint agents may be instructed to let

Table 10.1 Promotional activity

Buyer stage	Promotional activity
Awareness	Advertising and press editorial
Comprehension	Literature, exhibitions and special events
Conviction	Direct selling, signboards, advertising and site visits
Purchase	Direct selling, public relations

or dispose of a property and in those situations a developer will pay a larger fee, of say 15% of the annual rental value for letting or 3% of the capital value on a sale. Joint agents will share the fee on an agreed basis.

As mentioned earlier in the chapter, agents should ideally contribute to the planning, design and evaluation of the project and should be brought in at an early stage. As well as helping to shape the scheme the additional benefit of early involvement is that the agent will become familiar with the product that they are selling. It is important however not to get too many agents involved. In some cases, agents may be retained by clients and therefore will not seek a fee. When agents refer applicants to a client, they will expect a commission if a sale results from one of their introductions.

Advertising

Advertising can be aimed at potential occupiers or agents in national or local newspapers or in the property journals. The advertisement should contain the design and layout of the property but it also needs to create an appropriate impression according to how the property has been targeted. The cost of a one-off advertisement needs to be set against a programme of smaller advertisements over a period of time. The information should be readily available in the advertisement as to the type of property, the approximate size, the location and whether the premises are for sale or to let.

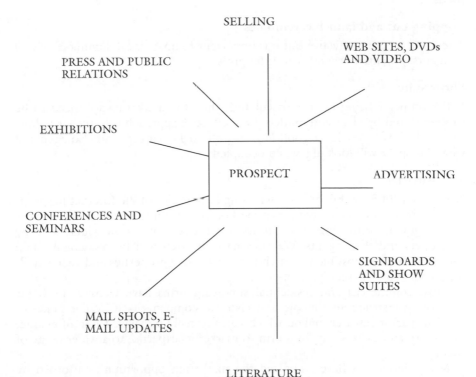

Figure 10.2 Components of promotion

Mail shots

These can be very effective especially from a cost point of view. A selected list of potential occupiers would need to be used. These can be provided by specialist direct mail order firms. The mail shots need a short sharp message. Given the professional target, market gimmicks are not advisable with mail shots which can be either conventional mail or e-mail.

Particulars and brochures

Particulars and brochures can be sent to potential occupiers and agents and lodged on Internet sites in PDF format. They describe the location of the premises, the accommodation, the dimension, specification, services, parking ratio and whether the interest is to be let or sold. In most cases these brochures require graphic designers to ensure effective use of colour, shape, corporate style and layout. The tenant's guide to the building could be drawn up which details the building, construction and specification and can also provide information on maintenance and energy-saving data.

Site boards and hoardings

The use of site boards and site hoardings can be very effective for advertising purposes. They can also provide good public relations for the company involved as well as concealing what might be ugly construction works from adjoining roads.

Topping out and launch ceremonies

These can be quite effective but it is important to invite local dignitaries as well as agents, potential occupiers and the press.

Show suites

If the property being built is speculative, then the marketing will need to be supplemented by plans and models. One effective approach is to fit out a show suite, which will provide a good idea to potential occupiers and also agents of what the space will look like when occupied.

The Internet

Norwood (2005) highlights the increasing importance of the Internet for property marketing in recent years. As a method of providing information, conveying images and providing virtual tours of a property it is now widely used by developers and their agents. Websites have been created by residential estate agents where it is possible to search for the suitable properties and view details that meet browsers requirements.

Most commercial and residential surveying firms have websites both for promoting instructions for sale and also the company itself. Major practices publish market research online which can normally be viewed free of charge, this is also an obvious way for a firm to market its expertise to a wider range of clients.

Many developers have embraced the marketing opportunities afforded by websites to include quality visual images of elevations, floor plans, perspectives, maps and other images together with appointment and feedback options for potential customers to use. Norwood (2005) explains that the effectiveness of an Internet site will depend upon the careful selection of keywords used by the website designer to ensure that search engines are able to find and prioritise the site for browsers.

Summing up on marketing and promotion

Ensuring that a completed building is let or disposed of could be regarded as one of the last responsibilities of a project manager, although for a major project that task will almost certainly be delegated to property marketing experts. A project manager will however want to know that the advertising and marketing campaign around a project is well thought out, properly coordinated and phased in such a way that the property is placed before the target audience in an ordered and consistent manner. It is important that, as well as some initial launches of the proposal, there is follow-up activity during the development period to ensure that potential users and funders are kept aware of what is happening. It is important to agree the budget for the marketing campaign and to monitor the work of the marketing team.

10.4 Disposal and warranties

Warranties

The JCT forms of contract were discussed in the last chapter where it was noted that provided a contractor executes the building work in good and workman-like manner in accordance with the architect's drawings and the specification in the bill of quantities and with any subsequent instruction given to the contractor by the architect then the contractor would not normally have any responsibility if the building is not suited for the purpose for which it has been designed. This therefore takes care of the legal rights and responsibilities between the procuring developer and the contractor and professional team which produced the building.

However as Havard (2008: 245) points out, those rights and responsibilities need to be extended to successors in title after the developer has sold or let the building to third parties. Those third parties will need legal redress if the building is found not to be fit for purpose. New buildings do sometimes experience defects of one kind or another which are expensive and time-consuming to remedy. For example it may be discovered that a building is not entirely weather tight or that the energy performance does not accord with claims on the Energy Performance Certificate or that particular electro-mechanical service is not functioning properly.

Wilkinson and Reed explain (2009: 208) that the extension of rights of redress is achieved by the developer through a requirement on the design team and contractor (and any subcontractors) to enter into deeds of collateral warranty for the benefit of successors in title. The deeds will require the professional practices and contractor(s) to warrant that all reasonable skill, care and attention have been exercised in their professional responsibilities thus creating a duty of care. In addition the professionals will need to demonstrate that they are covered by adequate professional indemnity insurance.

These specialist legal issues have to be resolved properly so that the disposal of the finished development to, for example, a financial institution is not put in jeopardy during the process of due diligence which is followed when an institution purchases a major building.

Because of the potential scale of liability should anything go wrong, it is perhaps understandable that the professionals and contractors involved will sometimes try to limit the extent and duration of their liability to a development. Wilkinson and Reed explain (2009: 208) that this is sometimes done in three ways:

1 The deeds are not signed under seal which means that the liability may last for six years and not 12.
2 The professional team and contractor will wish to limit the assignability of their deeds of collateral warranty to the first purchaser and first tenant of the completed development.
3 The professional team and contractor will try to limit their liability to remedial costs or defects and not consequential or economic loss.

Some developers have approached the problem by arranging a latent defects insurance policy for large complex schemes. This form of insurance is typically 1–2% of the building contract sum but has the advantage that the insurer is responsible for pursuing remedies with the professional team. The insurer assumes responsibility for repairing the property should a defect be discovered. The insurer usually agrees to cover a project for up to ten years from completion provided that a policy is in place before construction begins and an independent engineer's report is available on the design and cost of the building. The developer will have to pay for the fees of the independent engineer although the policy is assignable.

Handover

A short time before the date of completion and handover of a building, the architect prepares a 'snagging' list indicating all the minor defects that must be remedied before handover takes place. At that time it is useful for the development surveyor and representative of the intending occupier to accompany the architect to ensure that they are both satisfied with the snagging list prepared. At the outset of the project, the project manager will have confirmed that the building works are adequately protected by the contractor's own insurance arrangements. The contractor's insurance will no longer protect the building once it has been handed over, so one of the most important things is for the project manager to ensure that the developer had adequate insurance cover from handover until such time as the insurance cover provided by the occupier takes effect.

A building contract for a major project will normally have included a retention budget which is based upon a small percentage of the total cost which is held back by the developer until the end of the defects liability period, often six months from the date of practical completion. Special maintenance periods may be agreed for particular parts of the works such as external landscaping. The contractor is responsible for remedying any defects (other than design) which have occurred during the defects liability period provided they have not been caused by the occupier. The buildings are inspected at the end of the liability period and any obvious defects at that time which the architect could not identify are assumed to be such that the architect was prepared to accept the building subject to these defects.

The importance of the site and its environs on the handover date should not be overlooked. If during the building contract any damage is caused to adjoining property (damage to boundaries) the contractor must reinstate them. An inspection of roads, footpaths, gates, etc. is carried out to ensure that the contractor remedies any damage that has occurred. The architect should produce a building manual and maintenance schedule to assist the occupier by giving a comprehensive schedule and description of all components which might need replacing at some future date with recommendations for regular maintenance work to preserve the fabric.

10.5 Summary

The importance of effective market research at the inception of a scheme is crucial in terms of ensuring that a development will have the best chance of both reaching and appealing to potential owners and occupiers. Marketing is, as discussed above, the process responsible for identifying, anticipating and satisfying customer requirements profitably. The pricing of the property to be sold or let is obviously crucial but so are the design, location and finish.

There are numerous marketing tools available for the agent or developer to use and these include traditional brochures and advertisements as well as radio, television and the Internet. The selling process is perhaps underestimated as the agent is paramount in facilitating a transaction by finding tenants and investors and liaising with all parties through negotiations and legal formalities.

References

Barkham, R. 'Market research for office real estate', in Guy, S. and Henneberry, J. (eds), (2002) *Development and Developers: Perspectives on Property* (Oxford: Blackwell).

Cleaveley, E. S. (1984) *The Marketing of Industrial and Commercial Property* (London: Estates Gazette).

Havard, T. (2008) *Contemporary Property Development*, 2nd edition (London: RIBA Publishing).

Millington, A. F. (2000) *Property Development* (London: Estates Gazette).

Norwood, G. (2005) *21st Century Estate Agency* (London: EG Books).

Oxford Institute for Sustainable Development (2009) *Demand for Sustainable Offices in the UK*, Investment Property Forum. Available in e-format at: www.ipf.org.uk

Ratcliffe, J., Stubbs, M. and Keeping, M. (2009) *Urban Planning and Real Estate Development*, 3rd edition (London: Routledge).

RICS Economics (2009) *RICS Commercial Market Survey – Second Quarter, 2009* (London: RICS). Available in e-format at: www.rics.org.

Syms, P. (2002) *Land, Development and Design* (Oxford: Blackwell).

Wilkinson, S. and Reed, R. (2008) *Property Development*, 5th edition (London: Routledge).

Bibliography

Balchin, P., Isaac, D. and Chen, J. (2000) *Urban Economics: A Global Perspective* (London: Palgrave).

Bank of England (2009) *Trends in Lending* (London: Bank of England). Available in e-format at: www.bankofengland.co.uk/publications

Barkham, R. (2002) 'Market research for office real estate', ch. 4 in Guy, S. and Henneberry, J. (eds), *Development and Developers: Perspectives on Property* (Oxford: Blackwell Science).

Baum, A. (2008) 'Depreciation, income distribution and the UK REIT', *Journal of Property Investment and Finance*, 26(3).

Baum, A. and Crosby, N. (2008) *Property Investment Appraisal*, 3rd edition (London: Blackwell).

Bowcock, P. and Bayfield, N. (2000) *Excel for Surveyors* (London: Estates Gazette).

Bowcock, P. and Bayfield, N. (2003) *Advanced Excel for Surveyors* (London: Estates Gazette).

British Council for Offices (2009) *2009 Guide to Specification* (London: British Council for Offices).

Broomfield, R. and Drury, A. (2009) *Developing Affordable Housing: A Guide to Development and Regeneration*, 2nd edition (London: National Housing Federation).

Brown, G. R. and Matysiak, G. A. (2000) *Real Estate Investment: A Capital Market Approach* (Harlow: FT Prentice Hall).

Buckle, M. and Thompson, J. (2004) *The UK Financial System* (Manchester: Manchester University Press).

Byrne, P. (1996) *Risk, Uncertainty and Decision-Making in Property Development*, 2nd edition (Abingdon: Taylor & Francis).

Central Statistical Office (1994) *Financial Statistics* (London: CSO).

Chesters, L. (2009) 'Tesco to complete £559m property securitisation', *Property Week*, 15 September.

Cheung, E., Chan, A. P. C. and Kajewski, S. (2009) 'Reasons for implementing public private partnerships projects: perspectives from Hong Kong, Australian and British practitioners', *Journal of Property Investment and Finance*, 27(1).

Cleaveley, E. S. (1984) *The Marketing of Industrial and Commercial Property* (London: Estates Gazette).

Commission for Architecture and the Built Environment (2001) *The Value of Urban Design* (Tonbridge: Thomas Telford). Available in e-format at: www.cabe.org.uk

Commission for Architecture and the Built Environment (2003) *The Value of Housing Design and Layout* (Tonbridge: Thomas Telford). Available in e-format at: www.cabe.org.uk

Commission for Architecture and the Built Environment (2003) *Creating Excellent Buildings: A Guide for Clients* (London: CABE). Available in e-format at: www.cabe.org.uk

Commission for Architecture and the Built Environment (2006) *Design and Access Statements: How to Write, Read and Use Them* (London: CABE). Available in e-format at: www.cabe.org.uk

Commission for Architecture and the Built Environment (2007) *Housing Audit: Assessing the Design Quality of New Housing in the East Midlands, West Midlands and South West* (London: CABE). Available in e-format at: www.cabe.org.uk

Commission for Architecture and the Built Environment (2008) *Building for Life* (London: CABE). Available in e-format at: www.cabe.org.uk

Communities and Local Government (2006) *Planning Policy Statement 25: Development and Flood Risk* (London: Stationery Office). Available in e-format at: www. communities.gov.uk/planningandbuilding/planning/planningpolicyguidance/ planningpolicystatements/planningpolicystatements/pps25/

Communities and Local Government (2006) *Preparing Design Codes: A Practice Manual* (London: Department for Communities and Local Government). Available in e-format at: www.communities.gov.uk

Communities and Local Government (2006) *Code for Sustainable Homes: A Step-Change in Sustainable Home Building Practice* (London: Department for Communities and Local Government). Available in e-format at: www.planning portal.gov.uk

Communities and Local Government (2006) *Designed for Manufacture – The Challenge to Build a Quality Home for £60K: Lessons Learnt* (London: Department for Communities and Local Government). Available in e-format at: www.designfor manufacture.info

Communities and Local Government (2007) *Planning Policy Statement: Planning and Climate Change: Supplement to Planning Policy Statement 1* (London: The Stationery Office). Available in e-format at: www.communities.gov.uk/documents/ planningandbuilding/pdf/ppsclimatechange.pdf

Communities and Local Government (2008) *Planning Policy Statement 25: Development and Flood Risk-Practice Guide* (London: Stationery Office). Available in e-format at: www.communities.gov.uk/documents/planningandbuilding/pdf/pps25 practiceguide.pdf

Communities and Local Government (2008) *The Code for Sustainable Homes: Setting the Standard in Sustainability for New Homes* (London: Department for Communities and Local Government). Available in e-format at: www.communities.gov.uk

Communities and Local Government (2008) *The Killian Pretty Review Planning Applications: A Faster and More Responsive System – Final Report* (London: Department for Communities and Local Government). Available in e-format at: www.communities.gov.uk

Communities and Local Government (2009) 'Live tables on housing market and house prices – table 511 housing market: simple average house prices by dwelling type, region, United Kingdom from 1986'. Available in e-format at: www.communities.gov.uk/housing/housingresearch/housingstatistics/housing statisticsby/housingmarket/livetables/ [accessed 16.7.09]

Communities and Local Government (2009) *Code for Sustainable Homes: Technical Guide Version 2* (London: Department for Communities and Local Government). Available in e-format at: www.communities.gov.uk

Cullingworth, B. and Nadin, V. (2006) *Town and Country Planning in the UK*, 14th edition (London: Routledge).

Cyril Sweett (2005) *Putting a Price on Sustainability*, Building Research Establishment Trust.

Cyril Sweett (2009) *Costing Energy Efficiency Improvements in Existing Commercial Buildings* (London: Investment Property Forum). Available in e-format at: www.cyrilsweett.com/pdfs/IPF_low_energy_improvements_summary_report. pdf

D'Arcy, E. and Keogh, G. (2002) 'The market context of property development activity', in Guy, S. and Henneberry, J. (eds), *Development and Developers: Perspectives on Property* (Oxford: Blackwell).

Darlow, C. (1988) 'Direct project funding', in Darlow, C. (ed.), *Valuation and Development Appraisal*, 2nd edition (London: Estates Gazette).

Davidson, A. W. (2002) *Parry's Valuation and Investment Tables*, 12th edition (London: EG Books).

Day, A. L. (2007) *Mastering Financial Modelling in Microsoft Excel* (London: Prentice Hall).

Dubben, N. (2008) 'Development properties', ch. 13 in Hayward, R. (ed.) *Valuation: Principles into Practice*, 6th edition (London: EG Books).

Dubben, N. and Williams, B. (2009) *Partnerships in Property Development* (London: Wiley-Blackwell).

Dunster, B., Gilbert, G. and Simmons, C. (2008) *The Zed Book* (Abingdon: Taylor & Francis).

Eichholtz, P., Kok, N. and Quigley, J. (2009) *Doing Well by Doing Good? An Analysis of the Financial Performance of Green Buildings in the USA* (London: RICS Research Report). Available in e-format at: www.rics.org/NR/rdonlyres/44F67595-7989-45C7-B489-7E2B84F9DA76/0/DoingWellbyDoingGood.pdf

Environment Agency 'Flood Map and how to use it', web page accessed 19.08.2009 at: www.environment-agency.gov.uk/homeandleisure/floods/31656.aspx

Essex Planning Officers' Association (2005) *The Essex Design Guide*, 3rd edition (Chelmsford: Essex County Council). Available in e-format at: www.the-edi.co.uk

Evans, P. H. (1992) 'Statistical review', *Journal of Property Finance*, 3(1): 115–20.

Farrow, P. (2007) *Guide to Commercial Property Investments and REITs* (London: Sunday Telegraph and Reita).

Fawcett, S. (2003) *Designing Flexible Cashflows* (London: EG Books).

Fletcher King (2009) *Investment Bulletin* (London: Fletcher King). Available in e-format at: www.fletcherking.co.uk

Franks, J. (1998) *Building Procurement Systems: A Client's Guide*, 3rd edition (London: Longman).

Fraser, W. D. (2004) *Cash Flow Appraisal for Property Investment* (London: Palgrave Macmillan).

Garnett, G. and Perry, J. (2005) *Housing Finance* (Coventry: Chartered Institute of Housing).

Glasson, J., Therivel, R. and Chadwick, A. (2005) *Introduction to Environmental Impact Assessment*, 3rd edition (London: Routledge).

Hackett, M., Robinson, I. and Statham, G. (eds) (2007) *The Aqua Group Guide to Procurement, Tendering and Contract Administration* (Oxford: Blackwell).

Hargitay, S. E. and Yu, S. M. (1993) *Property Investment Decisions: A Quantitative Approach* (London: Spon).

Havard, T. (2008) *Contemporary Property Development*, 2nd edition (London: RIBA Publishing).

Hewitt, A. (2007) 'Realities of the Merton rule', 76 (10) *Town and Country Planning*, 332–4.

HM Government (2008) *Strategy for Sustainable Construction* (London: Department for Business, Enterprise and Regulatory Reform). Available in e-format at: www.berr.gov.uk

Hoesli, M. and MacGregor, B. D. (2000) *Property Investment: Principles and Practice of Portfolio Management* (Harlow: Longman).

Homes and Communities Agency (2009) 'Economic Appraisal Tool', web page and downloadable model at: www.homesandcommunities.co.uk/economic-appraisal-tool.htm

Homes and Communities Agency (2009) notes on Local Housing Companies can be found at: www.homesandcommunities.co.uk/local_housing_companies

Inman, P. (2007) 'Gherkin's £600m sale sets London property record', *Guardian*, 6 February.

Investment Property Databank and the University of Aberdeen (1994) *Understanding the Property Cycle* (London: RICS).

Isaac, D. (2003) *Property Finance* (Basingstoke: Palgrave Macmillan).

Isaac, D. and Steley, T. (2000) *Property Valuation Techniques* (London: Palgrave).

Isaac, D. and Woodroffe, N. (1995) *Property Companies: Share Price and Net Asset Value* (London: Greenwich University Press).

Joint Contracts Tribunal Limited (2005) *Partnering Charter (Non-binding)* (London Sweet & Maxwell Limited). Available in e-format at: www.jctltd.co.uk

Joint Contracts Tribunal Limited (2009) *Building a Sustainable Future* (London Sweet & Maxwell Limited). Available in e-format at: www.jctltd.co.uk

Joint Contracts Tribunal Limited (2009) *Deciding on the Appropriate JCT Contract* (London Sweet & Maxwell Limited). Available in e-format at: www.jctltd.co.uk

Jones, M. and O'Brien, V. (2003) *Best Practice Partnering in Social Housing Development* (London: Thomas Telford).

Keeping, M. and Shiers, D. (2002) *Sustainable Property Development* (Oxford: Blackwell Science).

Latham, M. (1994) *Constructing the Team: The Latham Report* (London: Department of the Environment).

London Borough of Camden (2006) *Unitary Development Plan* (Camden Council). Available in e-format at: www.camden.gov.uk/ccm/navigation/environment/planning-and-built-environment/our-plans-and-policies/camden-s-unitary-development-plan-udp-/

London Borough of Greenwich (2009) Decision notice on the planning application for Greenwich Market reference 09/0829/F issued on 28.8.09 (London Borough of Greenwich). Available in e-format at: www.greenwich.gov.uk

London Borough of Merton (2003) *Unitary Development Plan* (London Borough of Merton). Available in e-format at: www.merton.gov.uk/living/planning/planning-policy/udp.htm

Lumby, C. and Jones, C. (2001) *Fundamentals of Investment Appraisal* (London: Thomson Learning).

Mallinson, M. (1988) 'Equity finance', in Barter, S. L. (ed.), *Real Estate Finance* (London: Butterworths).

Marriott, O. (1962) *The Property Boom* (London: Hamish Hamilton).

Maxted, B. and Porter, T. (2007) *The UK Commercial Property Lending Market: Year End 2006 Research Findings* (Leicester: De Montfort University).

McCarthy, J. (2007) *Partnership, Collaborative Planning and Urban Regeneration* (Aldershot: Ashgate).

Medway Council (2004) 'Rochester Riverside Development Brief' (Medway Council). Available in e-format at: www.medway.gov.uk/rochester_riverside_development_brief-3.pdf

Medway Council (2004) 'Outline Planning Application MC2004/2030 regarding land at Rochester Riverside and related Section 106 agreement'. Available in e-format at: ww.medway.gov.uk/index/environment/planning/planapp/planonline.htm?cfid=12529&st=1

Millington, A. (2000) *Property Development* (London: Estates Gazette).

Millman, S. (1988) 'Property, property companies and public securities', in Barter, S. L. (ed.), *Real Estate Finance* (London: Butterworths).

Monaghan, A. (2008) 'Bluewater plunges in value as credit crisis bites', *Telegraph*, 4 August.

Montia, G. (2009) 'HSBC sells Canary Wharf headquarters', *Banking Times*, 15 November.

Morledge, R. (2008) *A Review of the Value of the Main Contractor*, Construction and Building Research Conference (London: RICS). Available in e-format at: www.rics.org

Morledge, R., Smith, A. and Kashiwagi, D. (2006) *Building Procurement* (Oxford: Blackwell).

Morley, S. (1988) 'Partnership schemes and ground rent calculations', in C. Darlow (ed.), *Valuation and Development Appraisal*, 2nd edition (London: Estates Gazette).

Morley, S. (2002) 'The financial appraisal of development projects', in Guy, S. and Henneberry, J. (eds), *Development and Developers: Perspectives on Property* (Oxford: Blackwell).

Mulhall, T. 'Sweden's showpiece', *RICS Land Journal*, November–December 2009. (London: RICS).

Murdoch, J. and Hughes, W. (2008) *Construction Contracts: Law and Management*, 4th edition (Abingdon: Taylor & Francis).

Northampton Borough Council and English Partnerships (2005) *Upton Design Code* (Northampton Borough Council). Available in e-format at: www.northampton. gov.uk

Norwood, G. (2005) *21st Century Estate Agency* (London: EG Books).

Office of the Deputy Prime Minister (2003) *Sustainable Communities: Building for the Future* (London: ODPM). Available at: www.communities.gov.uk/documents/communities/pdf/146289.pdf

Office of the Deputy Prime Minister (2005) *Planning Policy Statement 1: Delivering Sustainable Development* (London: ODPM). Available in e-format at: www.communities.gov.uk

Oxford Institute for Sustainable Development (2009) *Demand for Sustainable Offices in the UK* (London: Investment Property Forum). Available in e-format at: http://members.ipf.org.uk/membersarealive/downloads/listings1.asp?pid=292

Phillips, M. (2009) 'The rush for the exit', *Estates Gazette*, 14 March, 47–9.

Pike, R. and Neale, B. (2003) *Corporate Finance and Investment*, 4th edition (London: FT Prentice Hall).

Ramus, J., Birchall, S. and Griffiths, P. (2006) *Contract Practice for Surveyors*, 4th edition (Oxford: Butterworth-Heinemann).

Ratcliffe, J., Stubbs, M. and Keeping, M. (2009) *Urban Planning and Real Estate Development*, 3rd edition (Abingdon: Routledge).

Reita (2009) 'Understanding commercial property investment', available in e-format at: ww.reita.org

Report of the Construction Task Force, The (1998) *Rethinking Construction* (London: Department of the Environment, Transport and Regions).

RICS Economics (2009) *RICS Commercial Market Survey – Second Quarter, 2009* (London: RICS). Available in e-format at: www.rics.org

Roger Evans Associates (2007) *Delivering Quality Places: Urban Design Compendium 2* (London: English Partnerships and the Housing Corporation). Available in e-format at: www.urbandesigncompendium.co.uk

Ross, S. A., Westerfield, R. W. and Jaffe, J. F. (2007) *Corporate Finance Essentials*, 5th edition (Boston and London: McGraw-Hill Irwin).

Ross, S. A., Westerfield, R. W. and Jordan, B. D. (2008) *Corporate Finance Fundamentals*, 8th edition (New York and London: McGraw-Hill Higher Education).

Royal Institution of Chartered Surveyors (1994) *The Mallinson Report – Report of the President's Working Party on Commercial Property Valuation* (London: RICS).

Royal Institution of Chartered Surveyors (2007) *RICS Valuation Standards* ('the Red Book') 6th edition (London: RICS).

Royal Institution of Chartered Surveyors (2007) *Code of Measuring Practice*, 6th edition (London: RICS).

Royal Institution of Chartered Surveyors (2008) *Commercial Property Forecast* (London: RICS). Available in e-format at: www.rics.org/site/scripts/documents_info.aspx?documentID=548&pageNumber=2

Royal Institution of Chartered Surveyors (2008) *Valuation Information Paper No. 12: Valuation of Development Land* (London: RICS).

Royal Institution of Chartered Surveyors (2008) *Commercial Property Forecast* (London: RICS). Available in e-format at: www.rics.org/NR/rdonlyres/631D9200-FADC-48D4-958D-B0C8F5B8773B/0/commercial_forecast_1208.pdf

Royal Institution of Chartered Surveyors (2009) *RICS Guidance Note: Development Management* (London: RICS).

Royal Institution of Chartered Surveyors (2009) *RICS Information Paper: Flooding: Issues of Concern to Chartered Surveyors* (London: RICS).

Royal Institution of Chartered Surveyors (2009) *RICS Information Paper: Planning Act 2008: Delivering Infrastructure* (London: RICS).

Russell, J. (2009) 'Work to start on £2bn shard of glass', *Telegraph*, 24 February.

Savills (2009) *Commercial Development Activity* (London: Savills). Available in e-format at: www.savills.co.uk

Sayce, S., Smith, J., Cooper, R. and Venmore-Rowland, P. (2006) *Real Estate Appraisal: From Value to Worth* (Oxford: Blackwell).

Scarrett, D. (2008) *Property Valuation. The Five Methods*, 2nd edition (London: Routledge).

Scott, M. (2008) 'The heat is on', *RICS Business*, April, 14–17.

Segro plc (2009) *Half Yearly Results to August 2009*. Available in e-format at: www.segro.com

S. G. Warburg Research (1993) *UK Property: Monthly (November) Review* (London: S. G. Warburg).

Shapiro, E., Davies, K. and Mackmin, D. (2009) *Modern Methods of Valuation*, 10th edition (London: EG Books).

Smith, R. E. (2006) *Planning Control – Development Permission and Enforcement* (London: RICS Books).

Stern Review, The (2006) *The Economics of Climate Change* (London: HM Treasury). Available in e-format at: www.hm-treasury.gov.uk/sternreview_index.htm

Syms, P. (2002) *Land, Development and Design* (Oxford: Blackwell).

Syms, P. (2004) *Previously Developed Land: Industrial Activities and Contamination*, 2nd edition (Oxford: Blackwell Science).

Towers, G. (2005) *At Home in the City: An Introduction to Urban Housing Design* (London: Architectural Press).

Walker, A. (2007) *Project Management in Construction*, 5th edition (Oxford: Blackwell).

Westminster City Council (2007) *Unitary Development Plan* (London: Westminster City Council). Available in e-format at: www.westminster.gov.uk/services/environment/planning/unitarydevelopmentplan/

Westminster City Council (2008) *Supplementary Planning Guidance on Planning Obligations* (London: Westminster City Council). Available in e-format at: www.westminster.gov.uk

Whitaker, A. (2007) 'Wanted – a national framework', 76 (10) *Town and County Planning*, 335.

Wilkinson, S. and Reed, R. (2008) *Property Development*, 5th edition (Abingdon: Routledge).

World Commission on Environment and Development (Brundtland Report) (1987) *Our Common Future* (Oxford: Oxford University Press).

Wyatt, P. (2007) *Property Valuation in an Economic Context* (Oxford: Blackwell).

Index